RESTITUTION FOR A FAILURE OF CONDITION

This book examines the justification for restitutionary awards for a failure of condition and considers when, in the light of this justification, such awards should be made. It argues that such awards give effect to, but do not enforce, an agreement between the parties. Innovative and thought-provoking, this book presents a significant new way of understanding restitution for failure of condition.

Volume 64 in the series Hart Studies in Private Law

HART STUDIES IN PRIVATE LAW

This monograph series brings together in one place two types of book: works which examine in-depth the fundamental doctrines and principles of private law, and works which engage with the theoretical underpinnings of private law. The series thus aims to contribute to ever-evolving debates about the nature of private law such as problems of classification and taxonomy, remedies, the relationship with public law and the boundaries of private law generally.

The series includes, but is not confined to, works on contract, tort, unjust enrichment, equity, property and the conflict of laws, welcoming work which intersects with other fields of study to enable a deeper understanding of private law theory and practice.

Restitution for a Failure of Condition

Timothy Pilkington

•HART•
OXFORD • LONDON • NEW YORK • NEW DELHI • SYDNEY

HART PUBLISHING
Bloomsbury Publishing Plc
Kemp House, Chawley Park, Cumnor Hill, Oxford, OX2 9PH, UK
1385 Broadway, New York, NY 10018, USA
Bloomsbury Publishing Ireland Limited, 29 Earlsfort Terrace, Dublin 2, D02 AY28, Ireland

First published in Great Britain 2026

1

A catalogue record for this book is available from the British Library.

A catalogue record for this book is available from the Library of Congress.

ISBN: HB: 978-1-50998-991-1
ePDF: 978-1-50998-993-5
ePub: 978-1-50998-992-8

Typeset by Amnet

DEDICATION

For my parents

CONTENTS

FOREWORD

Few areas of the law have generated as much academic controversy and for so long as the law of restitution. Dr Pilkington is to be congratulated on an outstanding and original contribution to that debate in this deeply thoughtful and insightful work.

Dr Pilkington advances the thesis that there is a category of case where the ground for restitution is a failure of condition. That ground is not to be confused with (total) failure of consideration. The claimant and the defendant may have agreed that the defendant's entitlement against the claimant to a payment, or to the performance of a service, or to a transfer of a right, remains subject to a condition that has now failed. Restitution is justified to ensure that the defendant is not entitled against the claimant to the payment, the performance of the service or the transfer of the right in circumstances where it was agreed that the defendant was not so entitled. Where, however, restitution is awarded for payments made under void contracts, the ground for restitution should be seen as 'no consideration', rather than failure of condition, consistently with nineteenth century usage.

The relevant principles are thus seen as pertaining to the law concerning agreements, rather than to some body of principles (whether conceived of as 'unjust enrichment at the plaintiff's expense' or otherwise) which operate independently of agreement. Dr Pilkington treats agreements rightly as a much larger category of legal thought than contracts, in that contracts are a specific kind of agreement identified by reference to their legally binding and enforceable nature. Agreements, however, extend to informal agreements and to what might be regarded as shared understandings, objectively manifested, which are unenforceable but which still confer legally recognised entitlements and duties on the parties. The law can give effect to what the parties have agreed in ways which do not compel compliance with the agreement. Entitlements can reflect what parties deserve (or do not deserve) without being cast in the mould of a contractual claim-right and correlative obligation.

The recognition of 'failure of condition' as a distinct category of case, separate from (total) failure of consideration, opens the door to some intriguing reflections on past decisions. Those concerned with the obvious injustice of *Baltic Shipping Co v Dillon* (1993) 176 CLR 344, where the High Court reversed the New South Wales Court of Appeal and found that a passenger was not entitled to a full refund of her fare despite the ship having sunk 10 days into a 14-day pleasure cruise, will be heartened by Dr Pilkington's thesis. Those troubled by the implications of *Roxborough v Rothmans of Pall Mall Australia Ltd* (2001) 208 CLR 516 and *Mann v Paterson Constructions Pty Ltd* (2019) 267 CLR 560 for the subsidiarity of restitutionary claims to the law of contract may find some intellectual comfort in Dr Pilkington's analysis of those cases.

The thesis advanced in the book also has important implications for the wider debate concerning the underpinnings of the law of restitution. On Dr Pilkington's analysis, there is no need to find (or invent by fictions) an enrichment to the defendant, or to establish that any such enrichment is at the plaintiff's expense. There is thus no need to try to force cases such as *Planché v Colburn* (1831) 8 Bing 14; 131 ER 305 and *Brewer Street Investments Ltd v Barclays Woollen Co Ltd* [1954] 1 QB 428 into an 'unjust enrichment' framework, when the defendant in those cases was plainly not enriched. The author notes that *Planché v Colburn* was regarded as uncontroversial until the development of unjust enrichment theory. The obvious justice of the case must raise doubts in the mind of even the most ardent unjust enrichment theorist.

There are many aspects of Dr Pilkington's methodology and general approach which are refreshing. He recognises that questions as to what the law is, and what the law ought to be, do not exhaust the relevant inquiries. Questions as to why the law is as it is, which Dr Pilkington refers to as explanatory (rather than descriptive or prescriptive) claims about the law, are at the heart of the interpretive task of ascertaining legal principles. Dr Pilkington also emphasises the importance of the proper use of legal language; that is, as generally reflecting conventional usage as far as possible. That is of particular relevance in the law of restitution, where academic writers often strain to find novel and idiosyncratic meanings of everyday words, such as 'enrichment' and 'expense'. Dr Pilkington is well justified in deprecating what he calls 'unjust enrichment jargon'. In addition, the judicious use of examples to illustrate propositions, whether drawn from the facts of decided cases or constructed by the author himself, brings to life the arguments being advanced and provides a useful test for the cogency of those arguments.

Dr Pilkington commendably gives credit where due to his intellectual adversaries. For example, he acknowledges a role to play for Birks' 'subsequent absence of basis' justification for restitution, albeit a very limited one, namely in cases where the juristic reason for a performance (such as a contractual obligation) has been rescinded ab initio by reason of matters occurring after the performance has taken place. And like all first-rate scholars, the author does not merely falsify the various tenets of received wisdom, but positively constructs an alternative approach. That is particularly timely now that scholars and judges are looking for ways to retreat from the unjust enrichment framework, without wanting to return to the past. While much of Dr Pilkington's thesis as to restitutionary claims in the context of agreements is consonant with the nineteenth century concern with requests by defendants which are acted upon by claimants, that particular terminology has not been adopted.

No book on the law of restitution is ever likely to command universal agreement. However, one need not agree with all of Dr Pilkington's arguments and conclusions to admire the quality of his scholarship and erudition, and the felicity with which they are expressed.

Hon Justice Ian Jackman
Judge, Federal Court of Australia
15 September 2025

PREFACE

This book is an expanded and revised version of a DPhil thesis that I completed at St John's College, Oxford in 2023.

I was first introduced to conditions in Denis Harley's contract seminars at the University of New South Wales. One of the ideas that Denis articulated in those seminars was that important parts of the law of contract could be understood through the lens of conditions. For example, if A promises to pay B £1,000 following B's substantial performance of an entire service obligation, A's obligation to pay £1,000 will generally be conditional upon B substantially performing its service obligation at or by a certain time. Until that condition is fulfilled, A will not come under an obligation to pay £1,000 to B. If it becomes impossible for the condition to be fulfilled, a condition that A's payment obligation was subject to will have failed, and A may permanently withhold paying £1,000 to B. The preferable view is that the conditions that A's payment obligation was subject to formed part of the parties' agreement.[1]

But what happens if this example is flipped around? So, this time A pays £1,000 to B in advance in exchange for B providing it with a service. In this variation, it has always seemed obvious to me that if B does not substantially perform its service obligation, A should be entitled to recover its £1,000 payment: that is, there should be 'symmetry' between the result that is brought about in the two examples. The only difference is in how this is achieved: in the case where B was obliged to perform the services in advance of payment, it is by recognising that A does not come under a £1,000 payment obligation if B does not substantially perform; in the case where A pays £1,000 in advance, it is by requiring B to make restitution of the payment if B does not substantially perform.

However, it is controversial whether the law generally does this, and when it does, why. In the case where A pays £1,000 in advance, there is a rule – known as the 'total failure of consideration' rule – which says that A can only recover the payment if B performs no part of its service obligation. Further, some believe that in the advance payment case, A can only recover its £1,000 payment if the parties' contract is terminated. This is based upon a misunderstanding of termination, which only discharges obligations that have not unconditionally accrued for performance and does not 'invalidate' obligations that have been performed. To make matters worse, the leading account of why restitution is awarded in

[1] See J English, *Discharge of Contractual Obligations* (Oxford, Oxford University Press, 2025). cf A Burrows, 'Discharge of Contractual Obligations by Jordan English' (Speech delivered at Middle Temple London, 25 November 2025).

the advance payment example claims that, unlike where B performs services in advance of payment, the condition is not found in the parties' agreement but exists due to A having subjectively intended the condition.

This book argues that where A undertakes a performance in exchange for a counter-performance that B does not provide, it is the parties' agreement that makes B's entitlement to the performance A has rendered conditional upon B's counter-performance, and which may justify restitution if that counter-performance is not substantially provided. Underpinning this argument is a belief that 'unjust enrichment theory' is fatally flawed. As explained in chapter 1, this is the theory that most restitutionary awards involve the restoration of a 'benefit' conferred by A upon B in circumstances where A did not intend to benefit B. If we are to rid ourselves of unjust enrichment theory, it is not enough to point to the errors in its ways; plausible alternative explanations of the grounds upon which restitution may be awarded need to be developed. This book attempts to do that in respect of one category of restitutionary claims: claims for restitution for a failure of condition.

Although this book focuses principally on English law, I hope that it will be of interest in Australia, where I received the first part of my legal education – and in New Zealand, where I now practise.

Royalties from this book will be donated to Kidney Health New Zealand | Tākihi Hauora Aotearoa.

ACKNOWLEDGEMENTS

This book was completed in my first two years of practice at the bar. As others who have taken that path know, the demands of a busy practice are not conducive to writing a book on restitution. Without the encouragement of my DPhil supervisor, Ben McFarlane, and my examiners, James Edelman and Robert Stevens, to publish the doctorate, I might not have finished.

My work on failure of condition has benefitted from comments and discussions with many brilliant lawyers over the years. They include: Jonas Atmaz Al-Sibaie, Kit Barker, Penelope Bristow, Mitchell Cleaver, Henry Cooney, Steven Elliott, James Edelman, John Eldridge, Eleanor Eldridge, Jordan English, Matthew Frey, Alexander Georgiou, Rory Gregson, Mohammud Jaamae Hafeez-Baig, KV Krishnaprasad, Ben McFarlane, Edwin Peel, Robert Stevens, Andreas Televantos, Marcus Teo, Frederick Wilmot-Smith and David Winterton.

I am grateful to Ian Jackman for generously agreeing to write the foreword. His book on restitution was one of the first books that I read on the subject – its influence will be apparent.

I also thank the following colleagues at the New Zealand bar: Sebastian Bisley, Andrew Butler, Simon Foote, Jason Goodall and Robert Kirkness. My work with them has improved this book.

Finally, thank you to Nina, Mum, Dad and Ella for your unconditional love. I could not have done it without you.

TABLE OF CASES

United Kingdom

Australia

Canada

New Zealand

Singapore

United States

TABLE OF STATUTES

United Kingdom

1

Introduction

I. The Book

A. Subject and Context

In English law, one of the grounds upon which restitution may be awarded is 'failure of consideration',[1] which this book will refer to as 'failure of condition'.[2] As discussed in chapter 3, the reason for preferring this terminology is that failure of condition is the language that most accurately reflects the underlying justification for these restitutionary awards. Any definition of failure of condition, and, relatedly, the requirements that must be satisfied before it may justify restitution, is controversial in virtually every respect. To get a flavour of failure of condition as a ground for restitution, the most helpful course is therefore to begin with some examples where it is generally accepted that failure of condition is the ground for restitution:

(1) C and D enter into a contract whereby C agrees to pay £1,000 to D in advance in exchange for D cleaning C's windows. After the payment is made, but before D has started the work, the contract is terminated for D's repudiation.[3]

(2) C and D enter into an unenforceable contract whereby C undertakes to construct a barn on D's land in exchange for payment following substantial completion. After the work is substantially complete, D refuses to pay the agreed sum.[4]

(3) C and D enter into a contract whereby C undertakes an entire obligation to construct a barn on D's land in exchange for payment following substantial completion. After the work is half complete, the contract is terminated for D's repudiation.[5]

[1] *Fibrosa Spolka Akcyjna v Fairbairn Lawson Combe Barbour Ltd* [1943] AC 32. 'Failure of consideration' is also sometimes referred to as 'failure of basis': see, eg, *Dargamo Holdings Ltd v Avonwick Holdings Ltd* [2022] 1 All ER 1244, [79] (Carr LJ); *Barton v Morris* [2023] AC 684, [78] (Lady Rose), [231]–[232] (Lord Burrows).

[2] An early example of the recognition of failure of condition as a ground for restitution is *Baltic Shipping Co v Dillon* (1993) 176 CLR 344, 351–53, 359 (Mason CJ), 385 (Gaudron J), 389–93 (McHugh J).

[3] See, eg, *Giles v Edwards* (1797) 7 TR 181; 101 ER 920; *Wilkinson v Lloyd* (1845) 7 QB 27; 115 ER 398; *Prinwalla Holdings Pty Limited v Stanton (WA) Pty Limited* [2016] NSWSC 963.

[4] *Scarisbrick v Parkinson* (1869) 20 LT 175; *Pavey & Matthews Pty Ltd v Paul* (1987) 162 CLR 221.

[5] *Mann v Paterson Constructions Pty Ltd* (2019) 267 CLR 560.

In each of these scenarios, C will generally be entitled to restitution against D. Why? The orthodox view, which is discussed in chapter 2, is that C's intention to enrich D at its expense was subject to a condition that has now failed.[6] Restitution, this theory claims, should be awarded to ensure that D is not enriched in circumstances where C did not intend for D to be enriched at its expense.[7] Call this the qualified intention theory of failure of condition.

According to the qualified intention theory, restitutionary awards for a failure of condition form part of a law of unjust enrichment.[8] The prevailing interpretation is that the law of unjust enrichment comprises the category of events justifying a restitutionary response analogous to the event justifying restitution of a mistaken payment of a non-existent debt.[9] In the perceived core case of a mistaken payment of a non-existent debt, it is claimed that the reason D must make restitution is that D was enriched at C's expense in circumstances where C's intention to enrich D was defective.[10] The analogy drawn between mistake and failure of condition is that, as in cases involving the mistaken payment of a non-existent debt, C did not intend for D to be enriched at its expense in the circumstances.[11]

B. Objectives and Claims

The objective of this book is to examine the justification for restitutionary awards for a failure of condition and the implications of this justification for when restitution for a failure of condition should be awarded. Consideration is also given, in chapter 7, to the content of the restitutionary duty that D comes under following a failure of condition: that is, to when D's restitutionary duty should take the form of a duty to pay a monetary sum and when this restitutionary duty should instead take the form of a duty to transfer a specific right, or a duty to transfer a right of a certain kind.

Although a significant number of cases and examples are discussed, the book does not aim to exhaustively state the positive law. Its objective is to consider what justifies restitutionary awards for a failure of condition and when, in the light of this justification, such awards should be made. The intended audience of the work

[6] A Burrows, 'Conditional Intention as an Unjust Factor' in E Bant, K Barker and S Degeling (eds), *Research Handbook on Unjust Enrichment and Restitution* (UK, Edward Elgar Publishing, 2020) 346–47.

[7] ibid.

[8] ibid 346–47; J Edelman and E Bant, *The Law of Unjust Enrichment*, 2nd edn (Sydney, Hart Publishing, 2016) ch 11; C Mitchell, P Mitchell and S Watterson, *Goff & Jones on Unjust Enrichment*, 10th edn (UK, Sweet & Maxwell, 2022) chs 12–16.

[9] P Birks, *Unjust Enrichment*, 2nd edn (Oxford, Oxford University Press, 2005) ch 1; A Burrows, 'In Defence of Unjust Enrichment' (2019) *CLJ* 521, 541–44.

[10] Burrows, 'In Defence of Unjust Enrichment' (n 9) 541–42. For criticism, see F Wilmot-Smith, 'Should the Payee Pay?' (2017) *OJLS* 844; R Stevens, *The Laws of Restitution* (Oxford, Oxford University Press, 2023) ch 3.

[11] Burrows, 'In Defence of Unjust Enrichment' (n 9) 542.

is therefore principally academics, and practitioners and judges confronted with questions of principle on the subject. While the primary focus is on English law, most of the arguments made are relevant to other common law jurisdictions.

Almost all the major claims made by this book are at odds with the orthodox view. As to the justification for restitution for a failure of condition, it is argued that these awards give effect to an agreement between C and D that D's entitlement against C to a performance C rendered (eg, a payment or transfer of a right), or an act performed by C for D (eg, a performance of a service), remained subject to a condition that has now failed. The justification for restitution for a failure of condition is, on this view, to ensure that D is not entitled against C to a performance rendered or an act performed in circumstances where these parties agreed that D was not so entitled.

Although a justification for restitution for a failure of condition resembling this one has recently been put forward,[12] the exact contours and implications of this agreement theory of failure of condition are yet to be worked out. This work attempts to fill those gaps. In particular, the book focuses on the practical doctrinal implications of this theory of restitution for a failure of condition; limited attention is given to issues that do not bear upon how cases should be decided. There are also certain differences between the agreement theory of failure of condition advanced and this existing agreement theory, with one example being that it is argued that the provision of a service should not necessarily be classified as a 'performance'.

As to when restitution for a failure of condition should be awarded, the book claims that where C and D agreed that D's entitlement against C to a performance rendered, or an act performed by C for D, remained subject to a condition and that condition has failed, this is sufficient to justify restitution. On this view, D does not need to have been enriched at C's expense, nor must there have been a total failure of consideration, before restitution for a failure of condition may be awarded.

In terms of the form of the restitutionary duty that D comes under following a failure of condition, it is argued that although D's restitutionary duty will generally take the form of a duty to pay a monetary sum to C, there are cases where D should come under a restitutionary duty, which a court should sometimes specifically enforce, to transfer a right to C. It is further argued that if D comes under a specifically enforceable restitutionary duty to transfer a specific right to C following a failure of condition, a trust should arise.

C. Implications

The justification for restitution for a failure of condition defended by this book is both practically and theoretically significant. First, under the account put forward,

[12] R Stevens, 'The Unjust Enrichment Disaster' (2018) 134 *LQR* 574, 585; Stevens, *The Laws of Restitution* (n 10) ch 7.

the subject matter of the claim (ie, what is reversed via an award of restitution) is a payment made by C to D, a service performed by C for D, or a transfer of a right from C to D, as opposed to D's enrichment at C's expense. A consequence of this interpretation is that restitution may be justified in cases such as *Planché v Colburn*[13] and *Brewer Street Investments Ltd v Barclays Woollen Co Ltd*[14] where the defendant was not enriched.

Secondly, if restitution for a failure of condition gives effect to an agreement, there should never be a change of position defence to such claims, because such a defence would undermine the parties' agreement. For the same reason, counter-restitution should often not be required.

Thirdly, under the agreement theory, failure of condition is the ground for restitution in a narrower range of cases than is conventionally believed. In chapter 3, it is explained that the reason for awarding restitution of a payment made under a void contract is not invariably failure of condition, but sometimes the absence of a juristic reason for the payment, a consequence of which is that a change of position defence should potentially be available in such cases.

Fourthly, under the agreement theory, there is no convincing justification for there having to be a 'total failure of consideration' before restitution for a failure of condition may be awarded. On this view, cases such as *Whincup v Hughes*[15] and *Giedo van der Garde BV v Force India Formula One Team Ltd*[16] would be decided differently.

Fifthly, under the agreement theory, where C transfers a right to D on a condition that has now failed, D may come under a restitutionary duty to transfer a right to C. In some circumstances, D's restitutionary duty will be to transfer the specific right that it received back to C. In others, D's restitutionary duty will be to transfer a right to C of the same kind as the right that it received. Where D comes under a specifically enforceable duty to transfer a specific right to C following a failure of condition, D should be regarded as holding that right on trust.

Finally, under the agreement theory, failure of condition is not a ground for restitution within a law of unjust enrichment. Rather, failure of condition forms part of the law of agreements of which the law of contract is one significant part.

D. Failure of the Condition of an Obligation

There is a category of restitutionary claims that this book is not about, but which might appear similar. This category comprises the failure of a condition that an obligation was subject to. For example, imagine that C owes an obligation to pay D

[13] *Planché v Colburn* (1831) 5 Car & P 58; 172 ER 87.
[14] *Brewer Street Investments Ltd v Barclays Woollen Co Ltd* [1954] 1 QB 428.
[15] *Whincup v Hughes* (1871) LR 6 CP 78.
[16] *Giedo van der Garde BV v Force India Formula One Team Ltd* [2010] EWHC 2373 (QB).

£10,000 within 10 days of D obtaining a certain licence. D obtains the licence and C makes the £10,000 payment. However, before C made the payment, unknown to C, D's licence was cancelled. Here, C should generally be entitled to restitution of its £10,000 payment because C's payment obligation will have remained conditional, even after it had fallen due, upon D having the licence at the time the payment was made. When D's licence was cancelled, a condition that C's payment obligation remained subject to failed, with the consequence that the juristic reason for the £10,000 payment failed.

This category of cases was recently described by the High Court of Australia in *Gray v Lavan*[17] as involving an 'initial' as opposed to 'subsequent' failure of condition. An example given by the Court was *Roxborough v Rothmans of Pall Mall Australia Ltd.*[18] In that case, the claimants made payments representing licence fees under 'valid' contracts, albeit pursuant to an obligation that (under the parties' contract) was conditional upon a statutory obligation owed to the Commonwealth of Australia to pay a licence fee. The statutory obligation owed to the Commonwealth was unconstitutional, which meant that an agreed condition that the claimants' contractual payment obligation was subject to was absent.[19]

There is sometimes a failure to appreciate that although an obligation may have accrued or fallen due, in the sense that there are no (substantive or temporal) conditions precedent to the obligation, the obligation may remain conditional until it has been performed. Such a condition is sometimes referred to as a 'condition subsequent' to the obligation. Where an obligation has accrued and is not subject to any conditions subsequent, the obligation can be described as having 'unconditionally accrued'. In most cases, obligations that have unconditionally accrued will continue to exist (and be enforceable) following contractual termination. Obligations that have conditionally accrued will, on the other hand, usually not survive termination.

The category of cases involving the failure of a condition that an obligation was subject to does not, however, swallow up those cases examined in this book, as the High Court at one point seemed to suggest in *Gray v Lavan.*[20] This is because, as discussed in chapter 2, it is an error to think that an obligation that has been performed (and which existed at the time of the performance) can remain conditional after the obligation has been performed. Thus, if at the time C pays £1,000 to D, C was obliged to make the payment, C's payment obligation cannot remain conditional following the £1,000 payment. This is because an obligation, once performed, no longer exists. If an obligation no longer exists, it cannot remain conditional.

[17] *Gray v Lavan* [2025] HCA 42, [37]–[38].
[18] *Roxborough v Rothmans of Pall Mall Australia Ltd* (2001) 208 CLR 516.
[19] ibid [27].
[20] *Gray v Lavan* (n 17) [37]–[39].

II. Restitution for a Failure of Condition: an Overview

It is difficult to understand legal concepts without some appreciation of their history.[21] This section provides an overview of the historical development of failure of condition as a ground for restitution in English law. The section then sets out in more detail the kinds of cases where failure of condition is now regarded as justifying an award of restitution.

A. Historical Development

i. Eighteenth and Early-Nineteenth Century: Failure of Juristic Reason

The historical antecedent to a claim for restitution for a failure of condition was the action for money had and received upon a consideration that failed. The consideration for something is the reason for that thing.[22] A failure of the consideration for a payment is therefore a failure of the reason for the payment. The concept of the reason for a payment is, however, ambiguous and may be understood as referring to (among other things) the agreed purpose for which a payment was made; the payor's purpose for making a payment; what caused a payment to be made; or the juristic reason[23] for a payment.

When the action for money had and received upon a consideration that failed came to prominence in the eighteenth century, the most notable situation where the action succeeded was where C made a payment to D in the performance of a contractual payment obligation, but D, in breach of contract, failed to perform its side of the contract.[24] In this circumstance, C could elect to affirm the contract and claim damages or accept D's repudiation, thereby rescinding the contract ab initio.[25] If C accepted the repudiation, there was a failure of consideration justifying an action for money had and received.

In *Dutch v Warren*,[26] Pratt CJ said that for there to be an action for money had and received upon a consideration that failed:

[21] J Wigmore, 'Responsibility for Tortious Acts: Its History' in Association of American Law Schools (ed), *Select Essays in Anglo-American Legal History*, vol 3 (Boston, Little, Brown, and Company, 1909) 474.

[22] *Barnes v Eastenders Cash & Carry Plc* [2015] AC 1, [106]–[107] (Lord Toulson). See also AWB Simpson, *A History of the Common Law of Contract* (Oxford, Clarendon Press, 1975) 321; P Birks, *An Introduction to the Law of Restitution*, rev edn (Oxford, Oxford University Press, 1989) 223.

[23] The concept of a juristic reason is discussed below.

[24] *Giles v Edwards* (n 3).

[25] See ibid. Under the modern law, a contractual breach or repudiation does not justify rescission ab initio: see, eg, *McDonald v Dennys Lascelles Ltd* (1933) 48 CLR 457; *Johnson v Agnew* [1980] AC 367.

[26] *Dutch v Warren* (1721) 1 Str 406; 93 ER 598.

> the contract must be totally rescinded, and appear unexecuted in every part at the time of bringing the action; since otherwise, the contract is affirmed by the plaintiff's having received part of that equivalent for which he paid his consideration and it is then reduced to a mere question of damages.[27]

In *Moses v Macferlan*,[28] Lord Mansfield similarly stated:

> If one man takes another's money to do a thing and refuses to do it; it is a fraud: and it is at the election of the party injured, either to affirm the agreement, by bringing an action for the non-performance of it; or to disaffirm the agreement ab initio, by reason of the fraud, and bring an action for money had and received to his use.[29]

The most convincing explanation for why the availability of an action for money had and received upon a consideration that failed depended on rescission ab initio is that the consideration for the payment was, in this period, generally understood as the payment obligation that C had performed.[30] The reason that there may be a failure of the consideration for C's payment where there was a failure of counter-performance by D was that the payment obligation C performed was, due to the rescission of the contract ab initio, deemed to have never existed.[31] The sense in which C's payment obligation (ie, the consideration for the payment) failed is that, although at the time the payment was made there was a consideration for the payment, that consideration ceased to exist because of the rescission of the contract.

To the extent that a failure of consideration involved a failure of the payment obligation performed, for reasons that will become apparent below, in the eighteenth and early-nineteenth centuries a failure of consideration can be understood as referring to a failure of the juristic reason for a payment. It is also worth observing that in these earlier cases there is no mention of failure of consideration justifying an award of restitution. Rather, the action was generally understood as one to enforce an implied promise to reverse a payment.[32]

A failure of the juristic reason for a payment was, however, not the only way that failure of consideration was used in the eighteenth and early-nineteenth centuries. The concept is also apparent in actions for the agreed sum.[33] The classic example where failure of consideration appeared in this context was where a seller supplied

[27] ibid 406; 599.

[28] *Moses v Macferlan* (1760) 2 Bur 1005; 97 ER 676. See further *Towers v Barrett* (1786) 1 Term Rep 133, 136; 99 ER 1014, 1016 (Buller J); W Evans, 'An Essay on the Action for Money Had and Received' (1998) 6 *Restitution Law Review* 1, 11.

[29] *Moses v Macferlan* (n 28) 1011; 680.

[30] *Bostock v Jardine* (1865) 3 H & C 700, 705–06; 159 ER 707, 709 (Martin B); Evans, 'An Essay on the Action for Money Had and Received' (n 28) 11 ('the contract'; 'the contracting relation')

[31] *Mackender v Feldia AG* [1967] 2 QB 590, 603 (Diplock LJ); *Johnson v Agnew* (n 25), 393 (Lord Wilberforce); *Islington London Borough Council v Uckac* [2006] 1 WLR 1303, [26] (Dyson LJ). cf A Burrows, *The Law of Restitution*, 3rd edn (Oxford, Oxford University Press, 2011) 172.

[32] T Gallanis (ed), *The Oxford Edition of Blackstone's Commentaries on the Laws of England: Book III* (Oxford, Oxford University Press, 2016) 159–63; IM Jackman, *The Varieties of Restitution*, 2nd edn (Annandale, The Federation Press, 2017) ch 2.

[33] F Wilmot-Smith, 'Reconsidering "Total" Failure' (2013) 72 *CLJ* 414, 424–25.

goods in exchange for payment following delivery.[34] If the goods delivered were defective, the buyer generally had to pay the price and then claim damages.[35] An exception was where there was a 'failure of consideration', in which case the buyer could refuse to pay the price. Here, a failure of consideration referred to a substantial failure by the seller to perform its obligation to supply certain goods, which prevented the buyer's obligation to pay the price from accruing.[36]

ii. Nineteenth Century: Failure of a Non-Juristic Reason

From about the mid-nineteenth century, courts began using failure of consideration to refer to a substantial failure of counter-performance in the context of actions for money had and received.[37] One explanation for this shift in usage may have been a growing appreciation that a serious contractual breach or repudiation did not justify rescission of the contract ab initio.[38] If a breach or repudiation did not justify rescission, it was difficult to maintain that where D wrongly failed to counter-perform this may result in a failure of the payment obligation that C had performed. Another factor that likely contributed to this change in how failure of consideration was understood is that, as observed above, in cases involving actions for the agreed sum, failure of consideration was used to refer to a substantial failure of performance.[39] It is not difficult to see how this usage could be transplanted into the different context of an action for money had and received.

In the nineteenth century, failure of consideration was a ground for an action for money had and received distinct from 'no consideration' or 'without consideration'. This is evident from *Bostock v Jardine*,[40] where Martin B said that for the action for money had and received brought in that case to succeed it had to be established 'either that there was no consideration whatever for the payment, or that the consideration has wholly failed'.[41] 'No consideration' gave rise to an action for money had and received where there was no consideration for a payment when the payment was made.[42] Failure of consideration, on the other hand, gave rise to an action for money had and received where there was a consideration for a payment when the payment was made but that consideration subsequently ceased to exist.[43]

[34] *Boone v Eyre* (1777) 1 H BL 273n; 126 ER 160n; *Tye v Gwynne* (1810) 2 Campbell 346, 347; 170 ER 1179.

[35] *Obbard, assignees of Blofeld (a bankrupt) v Bentham* (1830) M & M 483, 486; 173 ER 1232, 1233 (Lord Tenterden CJ). See also *Behn v Burness* (1863) 3 B & S 751; 122 ER 281; J Chitty and T Chitty, *A Practical Treatise on the Law of Contracts*, 3rd edn (London, Saunders and Benning, 1841) 773–74.

[36] Wilmot-Smith, 'Reconsidering "Total" Failure' (n 33) 424–25.

[37] *Whincup v Hughes* (1871) LR 6 CP 78, 86 (Brett J); *Wilson v Church* (1879) 13 Ch D 1, 49–50 (Brett LJ); *Biggerstaff v Rowatt's Wharf Ltd* [1896] 2 Ch 93, 100–01 (Lindley LJ).

[38] T Baloch, *Unjust Enrichment and Contract* (Oxford, Hart Publishing, 2009) 124–28.

[39] It is also likely that the way the rule was stated by certain treatise writers influenced this shift: see, eg, J Chitty and J Russell, *A Practical Treatise on the Law of Contracts*, 5th edn (London, S Sweet, 1853) 543–44.

[40] *Bostock v Jardine* (n 30).

[41] ibid 705; 709.

[42] See the cases discussed at nn 47–55 below.

[43] See, eg, *Giles v Edwards* (n 3).

The idea that failure of consideration and no consideration were distinct is reflected in Sir William Evans' celebrated *Essay On the Action for Money Had and Received*,[44] first published in 1803. Evans begins chapter 2, 'Money Paid on a Consideration which has Failed', with the following: 'Money paid under a condition which happens to fail, is, in the civil law, the subject of distinct title, *De condictione causa data causa non secuta*. This may happen through the misconduct of the defendant, through a change of inclination in the plaintiff, or from accidental circumstances.'[45] In a separate chapter, 'Of Money Paid on Illegal Contracts', Evans deals with cases involving payments made under void contracts. According to Evans, an action for money had and received lay here as the payment was 'without consideration'.[46]

Consistent with Evans' taxonomy, there are numerous eighteenth and nineteenth-century cases where no consideration was treated as justifying an action for money had and received in respect of a payment made under a void contract. In *Jaques v Golightly*,[47] the claimant recovered a payment made to insure lottery tickets. Blackstone J held that 'the contract on which [the claimant] has paid his money is not criminal, but merely void; and therefore, having advanced his premium without any consideration, he is entitled to recover it back.'[48]

In *Walker v Liscarray*,[49] the claimant sought to recover a payment made for the grant of an annuity that was void. Although the action failed, Lord Ellenborough said that where a payment is made for a void annuity there is 'no consideration for the money paid'.[50]

In *Strickland v Turner*,[51] the claimant purchased a life annuity from the defendant. Before the formation of the contract, and unknown to both parties, the annuitant had died. It was held that the contract was void for common mistake and that the claimant could recover the payment as it was 'wholly without consideration'.[52]

In *Re Phoenix Life Assurance Co*,[53] premiums were paid under void insurance contracts. The premiums were held to be recoverable because there was 'no consideration for the premiums [the insured] paid'.[54] Similar is *Flood v Irish Provident Assurance Co Ltd*,[55] where premiums paid under void insurance contracts were recoverable as the premiums were 'without consideration'.[56]

[44] Evans, 'An Essay on the Action for Money Had and Received' (n 28).
[45] ibid 9.
[46] ibid 15, 16, 17, 19, 20.
[47] *Jaques v Golightly* (1746) 2 Black W 1073; 96 ER 632.
[48] ibid 1075; 632.
[49] *Walker v Liscarray* (1807) 6 ESP 98; 170 ER 842.
[50] ibid 99; 842.
[51] *Strickland v Turner* (1852) 7 Exch 208; 155 ER 919.
[52] ibid 219; 924.
[53] *Re Phoenix Life Assurance Co* (1862) 2 J & H 441; 70 ER 1131.
[54] ibid 448; 1134 (Sir Page Wood VC).
[55] *Flood v Irish Provident Assurance Co Ltd* [1912] 2 Ch 597.
[56] ibid 600 (Walker LC). See also *Hudson v Robinson* (1816) 4 M & S 475, 478; 105 ER 910, 911 (Lord Ellenborough CJ).

iii. Twentieth Century: Restitution for a Failure of Consideration

The most significant decision at the beginning of the twentieth century involving an action for money had and received upon a consideration that failed was *Chandler v Webster*.[57] That case involved a claim to recover an advance payment made before the frustration of the contract's obligations. The claim was rejected on the basis that frustration does not rescind a contract's obligations ab initio, which the court regarded as having the consequence that the consideration for the payment did not fail.[58] *Chandler v Webster* is explicable on the basis that, consistently with earlier authority mentioned above,[59] the court treated a failure of consideration as denoting a failure of the juristic reason for a payment and considered that rescission of the contract ab initio was necessary to remove the juristic reason for a payment made in the contract's performance.[60]

Chandler v Webster was overruled in *Fibrosa Spolka Akcyjna v Fairbairn Lawson Combe Barbour Ltd*.[61] For present purposes, *Fibrosa* is significant for two reasons. The first is that the House of Lords rejected the proposition that the contract had to be rescinded ab initio for there to be a failure of consideration in respect of a payment made in the performance of a contract.[62] The second is that failure of consideration was treated as justifying an award of restitution independently of an (actual or fictional) implied promise to make restitution.[63] This latter holding is significant because, as observed, the action for money had and received upon a consideration that failed was previously understood as an action to enforce an implied promise to reverse a payment.

iv. Twenty-First Century: Unjust Enrichment

A failure of consideration did not historically justify a claim for restitution of a performance of services. Where, for example, services were performed under an unenforceable contract in exchange for a counter-performance that was not provided,[64] or where a service provider was wrongly deprived by the party who requested the services of an opportunity to earn the agreed counter-performance,[65]

[57] *Chandler v Webster* [1904] 1 KB 493.
[58] ibid 499 (Collins MR). See also 501 (Romer LJ).
[59] See nn 26–29. See also *Blakeley v Muller* [1903] 2 KB 760, 761–62 (Wills J).
[60] *Chandler v Webster* (n 57) 499–500 (Collins MR), 501 (Romer LJ).
[61] *Fibrosa Spolka Akcyjna v Fairbairn Lawson Combe Barbour Ltd* (n 1). See also *Cantiare San Rocco SA v Clyde Shipbuilding and Engineering Co* [1924] AC 226.
[62] *Fibrosa Spolka Akcyjna v Fairbairn Lawson Combe Barbour Ltd* (n 1) 47–49 (Viscount Simon LC), 52–53 (Lord Atkin), 56–57 (Lord Russell), 60 (Lord Macmillan), 69, 72 (Lord Wright), 81–82 (Lord Porter).
[63] ibid 61 (Lord Wright), 74 (Lord Roche), 77 (Lord Porter).
[64] *Scarisbrick v Parkinson* (n 4).
[65] *Planché v Colburn* (1831) 8 Bing 14; 131 ER 305.

the action was for non-contractual quantum meruit.[66] An action for non-contractual quantum meruit was generally understood as an action to enforce a fictional implied promise to pay the reasonable value of the services performed.[67]

In *An Introduction to the Law of Restitution*,[68] Professor Birks argued that failure of consideration should be regarded as a ground for restitution of a 'transfer of value' in the form of services.[69] According to Birks, the event triggering an entitlement to certain non-contractual quantum meruit awards was materially identical to the event justifying an action for money had and received upon a consideration that failed, with this event being a transfer of value on a 'basis' that failed.[70] 'Basis', Birks explained, referred to the purpose of, the reason for, or the condition of a transfer of value.[71]

In *Cobbe v Yeoman's Row Management Ltd*,[72] judicial recognition was given to the idea that failure of consideration provided a ground for restitution of a performance of services. Lord Scott said:

> Where an agreement is reached under which an individual provides money and services in return for a legal but unenforceable promise which the promisor, after the money has been paid and the services provided, refuses to carry out, the individual would be entitled, in my opinion, to a restitutionary remedy. The consideration in return for which the money was paid and the services were provided would have wholly failed. In such a case the money paid, with interest thereon, could be recovered, together, in my opinion, with a fee for the services.[73]

The idea that a failure of consideration may justify restitution of a performance of services has subsequently been endorsed by the Supreme Court on several occasions.[74] For example, in *Barnes v Eastenders Cash & Carry Plc*,[75] Lord Toulson stated that 'Birks' reference to failure of the consideration for "a payment" would apply equally to failure of the consideration for the provision of services'.[76]

[66] For further discussion of the circumstances in which courts have awarded quantum meruit, see R Havelock, 'A Taxonomic Approach to Quantum Meruit' (2016) 132 *LQR* 470.

[67] See Gallanis, *Blackstone's Commentaries* (n 32) 159–63; D Ibbetson, *A Historical Introduction to the Law of Obligations* (Oxford, Oxford University Press, 2001) 276–81.

[68] Birks, *An Introduction to the Law of Restitution* (n 22).

[69] ibid 223–25. See also P Birks, 'No Consideration: Restitution after Void Contracts' (1993) 23 *University of Western Australia Law Review* 195, 208–14.

[70] Birks, *An Introduction to the Law of Restitution* (n 22) 226–27.

[71] ibid 223–26.

[72] *Cobbe v Yeoman's Row Management Ltd* [2008] 1 WLR 1752.

[73] ibid [43].

[74] *Benedetti v Sawiris* [2014] AC 938, [86] (Lord Reed), [175] (Lord Neuberger); *Barnes v Eastenders Cash & Carry Plc* (n 22) [108] (Lord Toulson); *Barton v Morris* (n 1) [77]–[87] (Lady Rose), [227]–[233] (Lord Burrows). For Australian support, see *Mann v Paterson Constructions Pty Ltd* (n 5) [30] (Kiefel CJ, Bell and Keane JJ), [168] (Nettle, Gordon, and Edelman JJ). cf *Mann v Paterson Constructions Pty Ltd* (n 5) [77]–[79] (Gageler J); Jackman, *The Varieties of Restitution* (n 32) ch 6.

[75] *Barnes v Eastenders Cash & Carry Plc* (n 22).

[76] ibid [108] (Lord Toulson).

The most recent step has been for courts to suggest that claims for restitution for a failure of condition form part of a law of unjust enrichment.[77] In *Dargamo Holdings Ltd v Avonwick Holdings Ltd*,[78] Carr LJ said:

> The core concept of 'failure of basis' is that a benefit has been conferred on a joint understanding that the recipient's right to retain it is conditional. If the condition is not fulfilled, the recipient must return the benefit. Whilst failure of [condition] ranks alongside the unjust factors of mistake, duress and undue influence as a factor negativing consent, it differs in that it is concerned with qualification of consent, as opposed to impaired or vitiated consent.[79]

A perceived consequence of failure of condition forming part of a law of unjust enrichment has been that for C to be entitled to restitution for a failure of condition, D must have been enriched at C's expense.[80] There is also now authority for the proposition that a change of position may provide a defence to a claim for restitution for a failure of condition.[81] It is argued in chapters 3 and 4 respectively that these propositions are incorrect.

B. Cases where Restitution for a Failure of Condition has been Awarded

The focus of this section now turns to cases where failure of condition provides the ground for restitution. The objective is not to examine these cases or to exhaustively set out when a failure of condition may justify an award of restitution, but to provide some examples where it is now generally accepted that a party may be entitled to restitution for a failure of condition.

i. Failure of Counter-Performance

The classic case where a failure of condition justifies an award of restitution is where an advance payment is made by C in the performance of a contractual obligation in exchange for D's performance of a dependent obligation,[82] which D fails to perform. In *Giles v Edwards*,[83] the claimants entered into a contract with

[77] ibid [99]–[109] (Lord Toulson); *Barton v Morris* (n 1) [77] (Lady Rose), [226]–[233] (Lord Burrows).

[78] *Dargamo Holdings Ltd v Avonwick Holdings Ltd* (n 1).

[79] ibid [79].

[80] *Barton v Morris* (n 1) [77] (Lady Rose), [227]–[232] (Lord Burrows).

[81] *Banca Intesa Sanpaolo SpA v Comune di Venezia* [2022] EWHC 2586 (Comm), [394]–[397] (Foxton J).

[82] A dependent obligation is an obligation owed by D that is conditional upon a prior performance by C. If, for example, D's obligation to perform a service is conditional upon C's prior performance of a payment obligation, then D's obligation will be a dependent obligation. It is D's obligation and not D's promise that is conditional.

[83] *Giles v Edwards* (n 3). See also *Holmes v Hall* (1704) 6 Mod 161; 87 ER 918; *Dutch v Warren* (1721) 1 Str 406; 93 ER 598.

the defendant to purchase the defendant's cordwood growing at Tredgodoer in Shropshire. It was customary for the seller to cut and cord the wood, and then for the buyer to re-cord the wood at which point a title to the wood would pass. The claimants made an advance payment of 20 guineas. The defendant corded one-sixth of the wood, only some of which the claimants re-corded, before the contract was rescinded[84] for the defendant's repudiation. The claimants successfully brought an action for money had and received upon a consideration that failed in respect of their advance payment.

There are also cases where restitution for a failure of condition has been awarded where services were performed in exchange for an agreed sum that was not paid. In *Pavey & Matthews Pty Ltd v Paul*,[85] the claimant builder entered into an unenforceable contract for the provision of building work on the defendant's land in exchange for payment according to prevailing rates following substantial performance. After the work was substantially complete, the defendant paid the claimant $36,000 but the claimant successfully argued that the defendant was required to pay $62,945.50 for the work, this being the prevailing rate. Due to the defendant having failed to pay the agreed sum, it was held that the claimant was entitled to an award of non-contractual quantum meruit, which is now widely regarded as having been an award of restitution for a failure of condition.[86]

ii. *Wrongful Deprivation of an Opportunity to Earn the Agreed Counter-Performance*

Another situation where restitution for a failure of condition has been awarded is where D wrongly deprives C of an opportunity to earn the agreed counter-performance. In *Mann v Paterson Constructions Pty Ltd*,[87] the claimants, the Manns, entered into a contract with the defendant builder for the construction of two townhouses on land that the Manns owned. The contract was 'divisible into several entire stages',[88] meaning it was agreed that the builder was unconditionally entitled to part of the price following substantial completion of certain stages of the work. The parties fell into dispute when the work was at an advanced stage of completion and the builder terminated the contract. When the contract was terminated, the builder had only partly (ie, not substantially) completed certain stages of the work and sought restitution of its performance of the work on these stages. It was held that the builder could bring a claim for restitution of its performance of these parts of the work for a failure of condition.

[84] The language used in the judgments tends to suggest that the court regarded the contract as having been rescinded ab initio.

[85] *Pavey & Matthews Pty Ltd v Paul* (n 4).

[86] Burrows, *The Law of Restitution* (n 31) 382–83; Stevens, *The Laws of Restitution* (n 10) 132, 144.

[87] *Mann v Paterson Constructions Pty Ltd* (n 5). See also *Renard Constructions (ME) Pty Ltd v Minister for Public Works* (1992) 26 NSWLR 234.

[88] ibid [174] (Nettle, Gordon, and Edelman JJ).

iii. Failure to Earn the Agreed Counter-Performance for a Payment

Where a contract is terminated following C's part performance of a payment obligation, unless the payment is a deposit, C is generally entitled to restitution for a failure of condition against D.[89] This is true even if the contract has been terminated for C's breach or repudiation. In *Mayson v Clouet*,[90] a contract for the sale of a fee simple title to land provided that the price was to be paid by a deposit, two instalments, and the balance within 10 days of a certificate being produced showing certain buildings on the land had been completed. The purchaser's obligation to pay the price was entire. The purchaser paid the deposit and two instalments but failed to pay the balance. The vendor terminated the contract. It was held that although the contract had been terminated for the purchaser's repudiation, the purchaser could recover the instalments that it had paid.

iv. Anticipated Contracts that do not Materialise

A failure of condition may also justify restitution of a performance of services undertaken in anticipation of forming a contract.[91] In *William Lacey (Hounslow) Ltd v Davis*,[92] the claimant builders submitted a tender for building work on land that had been damaged. The defendant, who had a title to the land and invited the tender, led the builders to reasonably believe that a contract for the building work would be formed between them. Later, at the defendant's request, the claimants submitted detailed and revised estimates of the work. The contract, which it was anticipated would have imposed an obligation on the defendant to reimburse the claimants for the work, was never formed and the defendant sold its title to the land. Barry J held that the claimants were entitled to an award of non-contractual quantum meruit for the work they had performed at the defendant's request. This quantum meruit award is again now widely regarded as an award of restitution for a failure of condition.[93]

III. Concepts

This section clarifies the content of certain concepts that are important to the arguments made by this book. These are conditions; restitution; contracts; unenforceable contracts; void contracts; and juristic reasons.

[89] *Fibrosa Spolka Akcyjna v Fairbairn Lawson Combe Barbour Ltd* (n 1).

[90] *Mayson v Clouet* [1924] AC 980.

[91] Burrows, *The Law of Restitution* (n 31) 371–80; Mitchell, Mitchell and Watterson, *Goff & Jones* (n 8) ch 16.

[92] *William Lacey (Hounslow) Ltd v Davis* [1957] 1 WLR 932.

[93] Burrows, *The Law of Restitution* (n 31) 373–74; Mitchell, Mitchell and Watterson, *Goff & Jones* (n 8) 551–52, [16-01]–[16-02].

A. Conditions

The common law sometimes uses the same word in multiple ways. An example of this is the word 'condition'. Just in the contractual context, condition has been used to refer to the state or quality of a thing;[94] an obligation any breach of which confers a power to terminate;[95] and an event or state of affairs the occurrence or existence of which qualifies the existence of an obligation or the formation of a contract.[96]

In English, condition has two principal meanings. The first is the state or quality of something. For example, a building might be in a bad condition. This usage of condition is irrelevant to this book. The second meaning of condition is something that must exist, be the case, or happen for something else to exist, be the case, or happen. For example, a condition of a liquid being water is that it consists of two hydrogen atoms attached to an oxygen atom at an angle of 104.5°.[97] It is this latter usage of condition that is relevant here.

A distinction is commonly drawn between necessary and sufficient conditions. If X is always accompanied by Y, but Y is not always accompanied by X, then X is a sufficient but not necessary condition for Y. So, a contract is a sufficient but not necessary condition for an agreement: if there is a contract there is an agreement, but there can be an agreement without there being a contract. By contrast, if Y is always accompanied by X, but X is not always accompanied by Y, X is a necessary but not sufficient condition of Y. Thus, an agreement is a necessary but not sufficient condition for a contract: there can be an agreement without there being a contract, but there cannot be a contract without there being an agreement.

For something to be a condition, there must be something conditional upon it. If, for example, a condition precedent to D's obligation to perform certain services falling due is that a payment is made by C, what is conditional upon the payment being made is D's obligation to perform the services. One of the arguments made in chapter 3 is that D's entitlement to a performance may *remain* conditional after the performance has been rendered. As it is used here, entitlement does not refer to a (claim-)right but to the deservingness (of one party against another) of the performance rendered or the act performed, which is the other way entitlement is used.

The occurrence of an event or the existence of a state of affairs may be a condition precedent or subsequent to X. Suppose that parties enter into a contract whereby C is obliged to pay £10,000 to D in advance in exchange for D repainting C's house. In this example, on the contract's proper construction, it will generally be a condition precedent to D's obligation to repaint C's house that C has made the £10,000 advance payment to D at or by a certain time. It will also generally

[94] Sale of Goods Act 1979, s 14.
[95] A Burrows, *A Restatement of the English Law of Contract*, 2nd edn (Oxford, Oxford University Press, 2020) 118.
[96] American Law Institute, *Restatement of the Law Second: Contracts 2d* (1981) 160 §224, comment (a).
[97] Although see H Putnam, 'Meaning and Reference' (1973) 70 *Journal of Philosophy* 699, 700–02.

be a condition subsequent to D's obligation to repaint the house that D does not die before the work is complete. In other words, after D's obligation to repaint the house has fallen due, the obligation will remain conditional upon D not dying before the work is complete.

Conditions may be obligational or non-obligational, with the former often being referred to as 'promissory' conditions and the latter 'contingent' conditions. Suppose, again, that C and D enter into a contract whereby it is a condition precedent to D's duty to repaint C's house falling due that C makes a £10,000 payment to D in advance. In this example, C's £10,000 payment obligation is a 'promissory' (or obligational) condition. The condition is 'promissory' in the sense that C owes a promissory obligation to ensure the state of affairs that D's obligation to repaint C's house is conditional upon materialises (ie, that the £10,000 payment is made). By contrast, a 'contingent' (or non-obligational) condition exists where there is no obligation to ensure the state of affairs that something is conditional upon materialises or sustains itself. For example, C and D may enter into a unilateral contract whereby it is a condition precedent to D's obligation to pay a certain sum that C provides a service even though C is not obliged to provide the service.[98]

B. Restitution

'Restitution' refers to the restoration of something to a previous state or the reversal of something that has occurred. An order requiring D to make restitution to C is therefore an order that aims to restore C and D to a previous state or to reverse something that has happened between them. On this interpretation, an order that does not restore both C and D to a previous state, or which does not reverse something that has happened between them, is not an order for D to make restitution to C.

One issue that arises regarding restitutionary awards concerns what these awards reverse. In chapter 4, it is argued that restitutionary awards for a failure of condition reverse a payment made by C to D, a performance of a service by C for D, or a transfer of a right from C to D. It is further suggested that, at a more general level, payments and transfers of rights can be classified as a 'performance' and services as an 'act performed'. This division is based on the fact that payments and transfers of rights are juristic events that generally only occur following a tender and acceptance, whereas a performance of services is not necessarily a juristic event (although it sometimes will be) that can occur without a tender and acceptance. However, this added conceptual layer is capable of causing confusion. It is therefore generally preferable to refer to restitutionary awards simply as reversing a payment, performance of a service or transfer of a right. Despite this, this book does refer at points to a 'performance' or an 'act performed' as the thing that restitution reverses. This is principally to avoid excessive verbiage.

[98] *Steele v Tardiani* (1946) 72 CLR 386.

C. Contracts

An agreement is not synonymous with a contract. Suppose that I agree with my parents to take their dogs for a walk this afternoon. Here, we have made an agreement but not a contract.[99] An agreement is, however, necessary for the existence of a contract. This is evident from the requirements of offer and acceptance, which are the (arguably imperfect)[100] tools by which the law generally determines whether an agreement has been made. The difficult question is what kind of agreement a contract is.

One view is that a contract is an agreement that has legal effects. This is incorrect. Suppose that a father, C, and his son, D, agree that if D helps repaint the family home over the summer, C will pay D the money he needs to buy a certain car. D helps repaint the home, and C pays D the sum he needs to buy the car. Before D has purchased the car, C asks for the money back but D refuses. In this example, the agreement would not be enforceable because, objectively considered, it was not intended to create legal relations.[101] Further, the payment was not gratuitous as D has provided consideration. But the payment will not be recoverable because there is a juristic reason for the payment, with this juristic reason being C's 'natural obligation' to make the payment.[102] The agreement, therefore, has certain legal effects. It would, however, be a strange use of language to refer to an informal agreement between family members as a contract. Relatedly, to form a contract there must have been an intention to create legal relations, which is absent in the example.

Another interpretation is that a contract is an agreement that is, objectively considered, intended to create legal relations. But where there is a void contract, the parties intend for their agreement to create legal relations, and yet a void contract is not a contract.[103]

A further interpretation is that a contract is an agreement that is, objectively considered, intended to create legal relations and which does create valid legal relations. On this view, an agreement does not have to be enforceable for the agreement to be a contract because an unenforceable agreement may create valid legal relations.[104] The difficulty with this definition is that it suggests requirements such as consideration and certainty are not necessary to form a contract. Although no case has directly considered the point, there are statements in leading cases to the effect that consideration and certainty are relevant to the enforceability of the obligations an agreement creates.[105] To the extent that consideration and certainty

[99] *Balfour v Balfour* [1919] 2 KB 571, 578 (Atkin LJ).

[100] *New Zealand Shipping Co Ltd v AM Satterthwaite (The Eurymedon)* [1975] AC 154, 167 (Lord Wilberforce).

[101] *Balfour v Balfour* (n 99).

[102] *Farmer v Arundel* (1722) 2 Wm Bl 824, 825–26; 96 ER 485, 486 (De Grey CJ); *Re Magarey Farlam Lawyers Trust Accounts (No 3)* (2007) 96 SASR 337, [166] (Debelle J).

[103] *Fawcett v Star Car Sales Ltd* [1960] NZLR 406, 412 (Gresson P); *Ingram v Little* [1961] 1 QB 31, 55 (Pearce LJ).

[104] *Moses v Macferlan* (n 28) 1012; 680–81 (Lord Mansfield).

[105] As to consideration, see *Dunlop Pneumatic Tyre Co Ltd v Selfridge & Co Ltd* [1915] AC 847, 853 (Viscount Haldane LC), 855 (Lord Dunedin). As to uncertainty, see *Scammell & Nephew Ltd v Ouston* [1941] AC 251, 261 (Lord Russell); *Blue v Ashley* [2017] EWHC 1928 (Comm), [61] (Leggatt J).

are relevant to enforceability and not validity, and necessary to form a contract, this suggests that an agreement that creates valid but unenforceable legal relations is not a contract.

The preferable view is that a contract is an agreement that gives rise to a legally enforceable promissory obligation or warranty.[106] Both promises and warranties are forms of undertakings. A promise is an undertaking to do or not do something. A warranty is an undertaking that a certain state of affairs does, does not, will or will not exist. Given that promises and warranties are both forms of undertakings, it can also be said that a contract is an agreement containing an undertaking that creates enforceable rights to what has been undertaken.

D. Unenforceable Contracts

An unenforceable agreement is an agreement that does not give the parties to the agreement an enforceable right to the performance of any of the promises or warranties contained in the agreement. An unenforceable agreement may, however, confer legally recognised rights, duties, powers, etc, upon the parties.[107] If an unenforceable agreement could not create legally recognised obligations, contrary to what the authorities suggest,[108] a payment made in the performance of an unenforceable agreement should be prima facie recoverable because there would be no juristic reason for the payment. The authorities also support the proposition that the tort of inducing a breach of 'contract' applies to certain unenforceable agreements.[109] If unenforceable agreements could not create legally recognised obligations, it would not be meaningful to speak of inducing a breach of an unenforceable agreement because there would be no obligations to induce the breach of.

Where an unenforceable agreement creates valid but unenforceable legal obligations, it is difficult to identify a more suitable label than 'unenforceable contract' to signify this and differentiate such an agreement from an agreement that does not create valid obligations.[110]

E. Void Contracts

There are two ways of understanding the concept of a void contract. One is that a void contract is an agreement that, although intended to create legal relations,

[106] See, to similar effect, R Stevens, 'Before We Begin: Defining Contract' (draft manuscript) 1.
[107] *Moses v Macferlan* (n 28) 1012; 680–81 (Lord Mansfield).
[108] *Thomas v Brown* (1876) 1 QBD 714.
[109] *Smith v Morrison* [1974] 1 WLR 659.
[110] See, eg, *Steadman v Steadman* [1976] AC 536, 548 (Lord Morris), 558 (Lord Simon); *International Energy Group Ltd v Zurich Insurance Plc* [2016] AC 509, [69] (Lord Mance); *Patel v Mirza* [2017] AC 467, [6], [46], [102] (Lord Toulson).

is (at least on its own)[111] a legal nullity.[112] That is, the agreement does not create or affect legal relations at all. Another interpretation is that a void contract is an agreement that was intended to create certain legal relations, such as a duty to pay a sum of money, but which does not create any legally recognised obligations.

Some statements support the proposition that a void contract is a complete legal nullity. In *Ingram v Little*,[113] for example, it was said that a void contract is 'a contract that is perfect in form but void of substance'. Similarly, in *Credit Suisse v Allerdale Borough Council*,[114] Hobhouse LJ said that where a company enters into a contract that is void as ultra vires, then 'the document and the agreement it contains do not have effect as a legal contract. It exists in fact but not in law. It is a legal nullity.'[115]

There are, however, cases where the parties' agreement has not been treated as a legal nullity despite their contract being void. An example is *School Facility Management Ltd v Governing Body of Christ the King College*,[116] where regard was had to the terms of a void contract in determining whether there had been a failure of condition in respect of various payments.[117]

Which of these interpretations of void is correct should depend upon the interpretation of the statute or the general law rule rendering the contract void.[118] There is no logical reason why, in every case of a void contract, the parties' agreement should be regarded as a complete nullity. In some cases, only the promissory obligations created by the agreement should be. On this interpretation, just as legal consequences can flow from the fact of ultra vires and invalid administrative actions,[119] so too can the fact of a now failed agreed condition potentially justify restitution despite the promissory obligations in the agreement being a nullity.[120] However, there is also no logical reason why a void contract cannot be a complete nullity. Given that a contract comprises both an agreement and the enforceable undertakings that the agreement gives rise to, there will plausibly be cases where the proper interpretation of 'void' is that both the agreement and the obligations that the agreement was intended to create are a complete nullity.

[111] Arguably, where a contract is void the agreement can still be relevant for the purposes of estoppel: see B McFarlane, 'Proprietary Estoppel and Failed Contractual Negotiations' (2005) *Conveyancer and Property Lawyer* 501, 509–14.

[112] This does not mean that, factually speaking, the agreement is treated as never having existed: *Credit Suisse v Allerdale Borough Council* [1997] QB 306, 350 (Hobhouse LJ); *Guinness Mahon & Co Ltd v Kensington and Chelsea Royal London Borough Council* [1999] QB 215, 240 (Robert Walker LJ).

[113] *Ingram v Little* [1961] 1 QB 31, 63–64.

[114] *Credit Suisse v Allerdale Borough Council* (n 112).

[115] ibid 350.

[116] *School Facility Management Ltd v Governing Body of Christ the King College* [2021] 1 WLR 6129.

[117] ibid [86]–[94].

[118] cf J Edelman, 'The Laws of Restitution by Robert Stevens' (2024) 140 *LQR* 321, 325.

[119] *Boddington v British Transport Police* [1999] 2 AC 143, 172.

[120] Edelman, 'The Laws of Restitution by Robert Stevens' (n 118) 321, 325.

F. Juristic Reasons

In the Canadian case of *Rathwell v Rathwell*,[121] Dickson J stated that in a claim for restitution for 'unjustified enrichment', it is necessary to demonstrate 'the absence of any juristic reason – such as a contract or disposition of law – for the enrichment'.[122] This was endorsed by the Supreme Court of Canada in *Garland v Consumers' Gas Co*,[123] where Iacobucci J famously said:

> the proper approach to the juristic reason analysis is in two parts. First, the plaintiff must show that no juristic reason from an established category exists to deny recovery. By closing the list of categories that the plaintiff must canvass in order to show an absence of juristic reason, [Professor Lionel] Smith's objection[124] to the Canadian formulation of the test that it required proof of a negative is answered. The established categories that can constitute juristic reasons include a contract, a disposition of law, a donative intent, and other valid common law, equitable or statutory obligations. If there is no juristic reason from an established category, then the plaintiff has made out a prima facie case under the juristic reason component of the analysis.

Different labels have been adopted for the concept of a juristic reason. In English law, 'consideration' has generally been used.[125] Other legal systems and commentators have used legal ground,[126] legal cause,[127] legal justification,[128] good reason,[129] or legal basis.[130] The terminology of juristic reason is used by this book principally due to the pedigree it has in Canadian law.

Juristic reasons are reasons that the law regards as providing a good reason for the occurrence of a certain kind of legal event – namely, the rendering of a performance. As noted, examples of a performance are a payment and a transfer of a right. Where there was a juristic reason for a performance, the law regards the recipient of the performance as prima facie deserving of (ie, entitled to) the performance rendered. Examples of juristic reasons are obligations imposed via an agreement, statute, judgment, arbitration award, declaration of trust, or deed; natural obligations; secondary obligations arising following a breach of duty; and gifts. There is, however, ambiguity as to the scope of the concept of a juristic reason. For example,

[121] *Rathwell v Rathwell* [1978] 2 SCR 436.
[122] ibid 455.
[123] *Garland v Consumers' Gas Co* (2004) 237 DLR (4th) 385, [44].
[124] L Smith, 'The Mystery of "Juristic Reasons"' (2000) 12 *Supreme Court Law Review* (2d) 211, 212–13.
[125] *Westdeutsche Landesbank Girozentrale v Islington London Borough Council* [1994] 1 WLR 938, 953 (Leggatt LJ).
[126] German law.
[127] Roman, Scots and French law.
[128] Quebec law. See also *Westdeutsche Landesbank Girozentrale v Islington London Borough Council* (n 125) 953 (Leggatt LJ).
[129] Stevens, *The Laws of Restitution* (n 10) 78–80.
[130] Birks, *Unjust Enrichment* (n 9) ch 5.

it is sometimes suggested that D's provision of a counter-performance can provide a juristic reason (ie, 'good consideration') for a performance by C.[131]

IV. Method

A. Kinds of Claims

There are, at a general level, three principal kinds of claims that can be made about the law. These are: (1) descriptive claims; (2) explanatory claims; and (3) prescriptive claims. Claims falling into the former two categories are 'is' claims. Claims falling into the latter category are 'ought' claims.

A descriptive claim is a claim about the facts that exist at a certain point in time. A claim regarding what the law is at a particular time is a descriptive claim: it is a claim about a particular fact, namely legal rules that exist in a jurisdiction at a given time. Explanatory claims about the law are 'why' claims. For example, an argument that a historic event caused a change in the law is an explanatory claim. Prescriptive claims are 'ought' claims. For example, a claim that estoppel should not be a cause of action but merely stop a party from proving a fact (evidential estoppel) or from asserting a right, power,[132] or immunity[133] (equitable estoppel) is a prescriptive claim.

A claim may simultaneously be descriptive and explanatory. So, when it is said that the justification for a rule is X, this can be understood as both a descriptive and explanatory claim. The sense in which it is descriptive is that it is a claim about a certain kind of fact: the justification for a rule. But it also has an explanatory component because it purports to explain why, from a normative perspective, there is such a rule. It is possible to concurrently maintain that X is the justification for a rule that has the best 'fit' with the positive law and that X is not a good reason for the rule. One might, for example, claim that deterrence is the justification for a private law rule that has the best fit with the law while also maintaining that deterrence should be irrelevant in judge-made private law.

As observed above, the objective of this book is to examine the justification for restitutionary awards for a failure of condition and to consider when, in the light of this justification, such awards should be made. An argument as to what the positive law should be given the justification for restitution for a failure of condition put forward is a prescriptive claim.[134] An argument as to what justifies restitution for a failure of condition is an explanatory claim: it is a claim about why, normatively, the law makes these restitutionary awards. To answer this question, it is necessary to 'interpret' the positive law. In other words, what needs to

[131] *Redlands City Council v Kozik* (2024) 418 ALR 1, [85], [87], [199].

[132] *Hughes v Metropolitan Railway Co* [1877] 2 App Cas 439.

[133] *Commonwealth of Australia v Verwayen* (1990) 170 CLR 394.

[134] The positive law pertaining to when a claim is available does not necessarily correspond with when the claim should be available according to the best justification for the claim.

be considered is the justification that has the best 'fit' with the law.[135] To say that a justification 'fits' the law means the justification can account for a significant part of the relevant positive law's content.[136] The fact that a justification does not explain every aspect of the law or case on a subject does not necessarily mean that it must be rejected: what one is looking for is the best available justification.

In considering whether a justification has a good fit with the law, a useful cross-check is to consider whether the positive law rule is the rule that would be adopted if one started with the posited justification and reasoned downwards to what the law should be. If applying this approach the rule that would follow from the suggested justification is not the positive law rule, this is a strong indication that the suggested justification has a poor fit with the law.

B. Language

One of the principal commitments of this book is to the idea that the language the law uses, and the language used to justify the law, should generally reflect conventional usage as far as possible. The law's use of language in ways that do not reflect conventional usage obscures its content and justification, making confusion and error more likely. Moreover, it is beyond the competence of lawyers, including judges, to change the meaning of words. If a judge implausibly defines 'motorcar' as a vehicle with wheels, this does not mean that 'motorcar' now means a vehicle with wheels. The same is true of enrichment, loss, gain, cause, and so on. The meaning of a word is a question of social fact that a judge, on their own, cannot change.

The best (and perhaps only) way of determining the meaning of a word is through examples of its use. Although judges (probably of necessity) often attempt to identify the necessary and sufficient conditions of something being X, most language does not work in this way. Thus, it would be surprising if the usage of the word 'chair' corresponded to some neatly identifiable set of necessary and sufficient conditions. Language is messy, and there are likely peripheral cases where there is, as a matter of social fact, no true answer to whether or not something is a 'chair' – some competent uses of English would regard the thing as a chair while others would not.

C. Examples

Numerous examples are used throughout this book. Occasionally, due to there being no case where the fact pattern in the example has arisen, the examples are constructions. More often, the examples are simplified versions of the facts

[135] R Dworkin, *Law's Empire* (Massachusetts, Harvard University Press, 1986) ch 7.
[136] ibid 238–50.

of real cases. It is extremely difficult to understand and explain the law without examples. One reason for this is that the concepts that the law uses often mean different things to different people. It is just as difficult to evaluate the justice of a rule without considering how the rule would apply to various fact patterns. The consideration of examples enables us to see the results that a rule would produce, thereby helping us test the justice of the rule.[137] Further, as demonstrated by the discussion above of what a contract is, examples also enable us to evaluate the plausibility of a definition of a concept.

V. Structure

The remainder of this book is divided into six chapters and a conclusion. Chapter 2 examines the leading alternative theories of restitution for a failure of condition to the agreement theory defended by the book. These are the implied promise theory; the absence of basis theory; and the qualified intention theory. It is shown that none of these theories is convincing.

Chapter 3 sets out the content of the agreement theory of failure of condition. The chapter begins by explaining that, in the view of this theory, restitutionary awards for a failure of condition give effect to, but do not enforce, an agreement between C and D that D's entitlement against C to a performance rendered by C, or an act performed by C for D, remained subject to a condition that has now failed. The chapter then examines the kind of agreement that is required before D's entitlement against C to a performance rendered, or an act performed, may remain subject to a condition that may justify restitution if the condition fails. Next, the scope of failure of condition as a ground for restitution is discussed. Finally, the chapter considers several implications of preferring the agreement theory to other theories of failure of condition.

Chapter 4 argues that enrichment and at the expense of should not be elements of restitutionary claims for a failure of condition. The approach taken to establishing this is to consider the justifications for enrichment and at the expense of, and then whether these justifications provide a good reason for their recognition in the failure of condition context. Having rejected the proposition that D should need to be enriched at C's expense before restitution for a failure of condition may be awarded, consideration is given to what should replace enrichment at the expense of. It is argued that what is required is a performance between C and D or an act performed by C for D. Finally, the chapter discusses certain consequences of rejecting enrichment as an element of the claim.

Chapter 5 considers whether it should be necessary for there to have been a 'total failure of consideration' before restitution for a failure of condition may be awarded. The chapter commences by examining the historical basis for the total

[137] Although, see J Gardner, *From Personal Life to Private Law* (Oxford, Oxford University Press, 2018) 10–11.

failure rule. Next, the content of the total failure rule is considered. The chapter then discusses the justifications that have been provided for the total failure rule and argues that none of these justifications is convincing. Finally, the chapter examines the approach to be taken to determining the availability of restitution for a failure of condition in cases where the total failure rule presently precludes a claim for restitution and demonstrates that certain cases would be decided differently if the rule was abolished.

Chapter 6's objective is to consider the relationship between contract and restitution for failure of condition, and the availability of restitution of a performance of a contractual obligation for a failure of condition. The chapter begins by explaining that, in the context of contractual performances, it is the content of the contract performed that justifies restitution for a failure of condition. On this view, restitutionary awards for a failure of condition are not 'subsidiary' or 'complementary' to the law of contract. The chapter then considers when, in the light of the interpretation of the relationship between failure of condition and contract put forward, restitution of a contractual performance for a failure of condition should be available and how the agreed price should, if at all, affect the sum awarded.

Chapter 7 examines whether, and if so when, D should come under a restitutionary duty to transfer a right to C following a failure of condition and when a trust should arise. The principal claims advanced are as follows. First, where C and D agreed that D's entitlement against C to a transfer of a right remained subject to a condition that has now failed, D may come under a restitutionary duty to transfer a specific right or a right of a certain kind to C. Secondly, the considerations that justify refusing to order D to specifically perform a contractual duty to transfer a right apply in the failure of condition context. Finally, where D comes under a specifically enforceable restitutionary duty to transfer a specific right to C, a trust should arise.

Chapter 8 provides a conclusion.

2

Alternative Theories of Failure of Condition

I. Introduction

In attempting to understand the justification for a particular claim, it is helpful to start by explaining why certain justifications for the claim are unconvincing. The purpose of this chapter is to demonstrate that the most notable alternative theories of restitution for a failure of condition to the agreement theory defended by this book are wrong. These theories are the implied promise theory; the absence of basis theory; and the qualified intention theory. By far the most prominent of these theories is the qualified intention theory.[1] The bulk of this chapter is therefore focused on demonstrating that the qualified intention theory is incorrect.

II. The Implied Promise Theory

According to the implied promise theory, restitutionary awards for a failure of condition enforce a promissory obligation owed by D to make restitution to C.[2] So, suppose that C makes an advance payment of £1,000 to D in exchange for D's performance of a dependent service obligation that D wrongly performs no part of.[3] The implied promise theory maintains that the reason C will generally be entitled to restitution of its £1,000 advance payment is that D impliedly promised to make restitution to C in the circumstances. On this view, claims for restitution for a failure of condition are indistinguishable from (or extremely similar to) actions for the agreed sum.

[1] In Australia, there are signs that the absence of basis theory may now be the prevailing view: see *Gray v Lavan* [2025] HCA 42, [37]–[40].

[2] For sympathy towards the implied promise theory, see SJ Stoljar, *The Law of Quasi-Contract* (Sydney, Law Book Co, 1964) 5–6, ch 8, see especially 209–11; P Jaffey, *The Nature and Scope of Restitution: Vitiated Transfers, Imputed Contracts and Disgorgement* (Oxford, Hart Publishing, 2000) chs 2 and 3; A Georgiou, 'Mistaken Payments, Quasi-Contracts, and the "Justice" of Unjust Enrichment' (2022) 42 *OJLS* 606.

[3] A wrong is a breach of duty: P Birks, 'The Concept of a Civil Wrong' in D Owen (ed), *Philosophical Foundations of Tort Law* (Oxford, Oxford University Press, 1997).

The content of the implied promise theory is not completely clear. In particular, it is uncertain whether D's implied promise to make restitution must satisfy the requirements for the implication of a term in fact into a contract. But it would be unusual if the law were prepared to recognise and enforce an implied promissory obligation to make restitution if that promise did not meet the requirements for a term implied in fact. This is because it would mean that implied promissory obligations to make restitution were more readily recognised and enforced than other implied promissory obligations.

There are cases where C has a claim for restitution for a failure of condition where it is plausible, as the implied promise theory maintains, to regard D as having impliedly promised to make restitution. This is particularly true where the performance that C has undertaken can be reversed in the same form, such as where there is a payment of money. For example, if C pays £1,000 to D in advance in exchange for D repairing C's motorcar, although dependent upon the precise circumstances, it will often be 'so obvious as to go without saying'[4] that D has impliedly promised to make restitution of the payment if it wrongly performs none of the repairs.

A case that provides some support for this interpretation, albeit where the claimants repudiated the contract, is *Dies v British and International Mining and Finance Corp*.[5] The claimants agreed to purchase 20,000 rifles with ammunition from the defendants. The price was £270,000, of which £100,000 was paid by the claimants in advance. The contract was later terminated due to the claimants having wrongly refused to accept delivery. Consequently, the defendants became entitled to £13,500 as liquidated damages. The claimants successfully recovered the £86,500 balance of their advance payment. Stable J held that the claimants' right to restitution 'derived from the terms of the contract'.[6] It is very difficult to see why the result should have been different if the defendants had been the repudiating party.

There are, however, cases where restitution for a failure of condition may be awarded that the implied promise theory cannot explain. An example is cases exemplified by *Pavey & Matthews Pty Ltd v Paul*,[7] the facts of which were set out in the previous chapter,[8] where there is a failure by the defendant to perform an unenforceable payment obligation following the claimant's performance of a service. An English case resembling *Pavey* is *Scarisbrick v Parkinson*.[9] The claimant entered into an unenforceable contract to work as the defendant's clerk for three years.

[4] *Marks & Spencer plc v BNP Paribas Securities Services Trust Co (Jersey) Ltd* [2016] AC 742, [23] (Lord Neuberger).

[5] *Dies v British and International Mining and Finance Corp* [1939] 1 KB 724.

[6] ibid 744.

[7] *Pavey & Matthews Pty Ltd v Paul* (1987) 162 CLR 221. See also *Deglman v Guaranty Trust Co of Canada and Constantineau* [1954] 3 DLR 785.

[8] Text to n 85.

[9] *Scarisbrick v Parkinson* (1869) 20 LT 175.

Following the performance of the work, the defendant wrongly refused to pay the agreed sum, and the claimant successfully brought an action for non-contractual quantum meruit. This quantum meruit award is now generally regarded as an award of restitution for a failure of condition.[10]

There are two difficulties with treating an implied promissory obligation to make restitution as justifying an award of restitution in cases such as *Pavey* and *Scarisbrick*, where C has performed services under an unenforceable contract in exchange for D's performance of a dependent payment obligation that D fails to perform. One is that to require D to perform a promissory obligation to make restitution would involve enforcing an unenforceable promissory obligation.[11]

Another difficulty is that the implication of such a promissory obligation would be an unusual construction of the parties' agreement. It would mean that D was promising to pay £y to C if it failed to pay £x, which is implausible as D would be promising to do almost exactly what it originally promised to do if the original promise was not performed. Similarly, if C transfers a title to a tractor to D in exchange for payment of £10,000, it would be strange to regard D as having promised to pay £x to C if it fails to pay £10,000 after the title to the tractor has been transferred.

A related objection is that the sum C is entitled to as restitution is capped at the market value of the performance C rendered.[12] Thus, imagine that C and D enter into a contract whereby C agrees to perform certain services on D's land in exchange for payment of £10,000 following substantial completion under an unenforceable contract. After C has substantially performed the services, D, in breach of contract, refuses to pay the agreed sum. The market value of the work is £9,000. In this scenario, the sum that C is entitled to as restitution is £9,000. If an implied promise is what justifies restitution for a failure of condition, this is perplexing. It cannot be that D promised to pay £10,000 for the work and promised that if it failed to perform its obligation to pay £10,000 it would pay £9,000 to C as restitution.

The implied promise theory is also not truly a theory of restitution for a *failure* of condition. Rather, what potentially triggers an entitlement to restitution under this account is the *fulfilment* of a condition precedent to D's promissory obligation to make restitution to C. Consider again a case where C makes an advance payment of £1,000 to D in exchange for D's performance of a dependent service obligation. According to the implied promise theory, in this scenario, D owes a promissory obligation to make restitution to C that is conditional upon D failing to substantially perform its dependent service obligation. It is therefore not the

[10] A Burrows, *The Law of Restitution*, 3rd edn (Oxford, Oxford University Press, 2011) 383.

[11] Professor Stoljar argued that, in cases involving the performance of services under an unenforceable contract, by awarding quantum meruit, courts were disregarding the formality requirement or treating the formality defect as cured by the executed consideration: Stoljar, *The Law of Quasi-Contract* (n 2) 203–04, 206.

[12] *Benedetti v Sawiris* [2014] AC 938.

failure of a condition that potentially obliges D to make restitution but the fulfilment of the condition precedent to D's restitutionary promissory obligation.

As the implied promise theory is not a theory of restitution for a failure of condition, limited further attention is given to this theory. But there is nothing in the agreement theory of failure of condition defended by this book that rules out the possibility that in certain cases the parties' agreement, properly interpreted, contains an implied promise by D to make restitution. The precise circumstances in which D impliedly promises to make restitution of a performance that C has undertaken are, however, not explored further. This is principally because in chapter 6 it is argued that a claim for restitution for a failure of condition should potentially be available in the alternative to an action for the agreed sum. On this view, even if D has come under a promissory obligation to make restitution, C may still be able to claim restitution for a failure of condition.[13]

It is also significant that where D has impliedly promised to make restitution of a performance C rendered if a certain state of affairs does not materialise or sustain itself, the parties' agreement, properly construed, will also implicitly provide that D's entitlement against C to the performance remained conditional upon this state of affairs materialising or sustaining itself. It would be contradictory for it to have been agreed that D is entitled against C to a performance rendered in circumstances where D has come under a promissory obligation to make restitution of the performance. So, suppose that C pays £300 in exchange for D's performance of an obligation to transfer a title to a bicycle via delivery and D promises that if the bicycle is not delivered by a certain date, it will make restitution of the advance payment. On the view just expressed, in addition to D's promissory obligation to make restitution being conditional upon D failing to deliver the bicycle, D's entitlement against C to the advance payment made will have been agreed to remain conditional upon the bicycle being delivered by a certain date, which may justify a non-promissory restitutionary claim if the bicycle is not delivered by that date.

The foregoing analysis suggests that in *Dies*, even if the claimants' right to restitution of the balance of its advance payment 'derived from the terms of the contract', the claimants should have had an alternative claim for non-contractual restitution. Although the defendants came under a promissory obligation to make restitution, the defendants' entitlement to the advance payment would also have been agreed to remain conditional upon the claimants having been transferred a title to the rifles and ammunition. This is practically significant because if the agreement had been unenforceable, such that the claimants were unable to enforce the defendants' restitutionary promissory obligation, the claimants would still have been entitled to non-contractual restitution.

[13] cf *Cadogan Petroleum Holdings Ltd v Global Process Systems LLC* [2013] EWHC 214 (Comm), [27] (Eder J).

III. The Absence Of Basis Theory

In his final work, Professor Birks argued:

> the failure of reciprocation can no longer be regarded as the immediate ground for restitution but only the sub-reason, at the base of the pyramid, why the master unjust factor operates. If you agree to build me a garage and I pay £10,000 in advance, and you then default your failure to build the garage invalidates the obligation under which I paid you. I have a power to terminate it and a right to recover my money. That is how the pyramid works: the failure of reciprocation invalidates the obligation and the invalidity of the obligation constitutes the absence of explanatory basis which renders the enrichment unjust.[14]

When discussing frustration, Birks claimed:

> We have to say that the failure of contractual reciprocation in circumstances of frustration brought about a failure of basis, in the form of supervening invalidity of the contract and, further, that the invalidity of the contract which was the basis of the payment was sufficient even though it was a termination and not a rescission ab initio.[15]

These passages suggest that Birks regarded a 'failure of reciprocation' resulting in the exercise of a power to terminate and termination for frustration in circumstances where there is a 'failure of reciprocation' as resulting in an absence of basis. Accordingly, where, for example, C performs a payment obligation in exchange for D's performance of a service obligation and the contract is terminated for frustration when D has performed no part of its service obligation, C may be entitled to restitution as C's payment obligation is 'invalidated' due to the termination of the contract for frustration in circumstances where C has not received the agreed counter-performance. Because of the 'invalidation' of C's payment obligation, there is an absence of basis for the payment. Such cases were referred to by Birks as involving a 'subsequent' as opposed to 'initial' absence of basis, because the basis for the payment ceased to exist after the payment was made.[16]

Although not describing it as such,[17] Birks' explanation for awarding restitution of an enrichment conferred in these circumstances can be understood as a theory of restitution for a failure of condition. Birks did not directly explain why, doctrinally, the exercise of a power to terminate following a 'failure of reciprocation' and termination for frustration in circumstances where there was a 'failure of reciprocation' resulted in an absence of basis. But on Birks' account, one explanation is that the juristic reason (or basis) for an enrichment conferred in the contract's performance was conditional upon the contract not being terminated when the agreed counter-performance had not been provided.

[14] P Birks *Unjust Enrichment*, 2nd edn (Oxford, Oxford University Press, 2005) 142.
[15] ibid 141.
[16] ibid 140–42.
[17] Although see Birks' discussion of gifts: (n 14) 150.

The problem with Birks' absence of basis theory is that neither a 'failure of reciprocation' nor termination rescinds a contract's obligations ab initio. Rather, the effect of termination is to discharge obligations that have not unconditionally accrued for performance.[18] Termination does not affect obligations that have unconditionally accrued, or which have previously been discharged. There is also no authority for the proposition that a 'failure of reciprocation' results in the rescission ab initio of a contractual obligation that has been performed. To fully understand why these observations are fatal to Birks' account, it is necessary to appreciate what it means for an obligation to be discharged and how this relates to whether there was a juristic reason for a contractual performance.

The juristic reason for a contractual performance is the contractual obligation to undertake the performance. Following the performance of a contractual obligation, the obligation is discharged. When an obligation is discharged, the obligation, while having existed up until the point of discharge, ceases to exist. In determining whether there was a juristic reason for a contractual performance, the relevant question is therefore whether there *was* an obligation to undertake the performance when the performance was provided. Consequently, unless the obligation performed is deemed to have never existed, there will have been a juristic reason for the performance. Unlike rescission ab initio, neither termination nor a 'failure of reciprocation' has the effect that a contractual obligation performed is deemed to have never existed, meaning they do not remove the juristic reason for the performance. It is therefore wrong to regard termination or a 'failure of reciprocation' as 'invalidating' an obligation performed in any meaningful sense.

A revised version of Birks' absence of basis theory has recently been advanced by Professor English.[19] According to English, the justification for restitutionary awards for a failure of condition is that the juristic reason for C's performance was subject to a condition subsequent that has now failed. Thus, suppose that C performs a contractual obligation to pay £1,000 to D in advance in exchange for D's performance of a dependent obligation to undertake certain building work. Under English's account, the parties should be regarded as having agreed that the payment obligation C performed, which provided the juristic reason for the £1,000 payment, remained conditional upon D's substantial performance of its dependent obligation. Consequently, if C makes the £1,000 advance payment but D wrongly performs none of the work, the payment obligation C performed is rescinded ab initio with the consequence that there is an absence of basis in respect of the payment.

In *Gray v Lavan*,[20] a similar version of the absence of basis theory appeared to receive support from the High Court of Australia. The Court said:[21]

> in these cases of an absence or failure of the condition upon which money was paid, restitution is awarded also because the obligation under which the money was paid can

[18] *McDonald v Dennys Lascelles Ltd* (1933) 48 CLR 457, 475–78 (Dixon J); *Holland v Wiltshire* (1954) 90 CLR 409, 416 (Dixon CJ); *Johnson v Agnew* [1980] AC 367, 396–98 (Lord Wilberforce).

[19] J English, *Discharge of Contractual Obligations* (Oxford, Oxford University Press, 2025) 298, 307.

[20] *Gray v Lavan* (n 1).

[21] ibid [37].

> no longer justify the defendant retaining the money: the retention of the money was dependent upon the absent or failed basis or condition of the obligation.

None of the cases cited by the High Court supports the proposition that 'the retention of the money was dependent upon the absent or failed basis or condition of the obligation',[22] which suggests that what is conditional is the obligation performed. Indeed, there is no previous case where this account of restitution for a failure of condition has been endorsed, and it should not be adopted in other jurisdictions.

First, and fundamentally, it is conceptually problematic to maintain that an obligation can remain conditional after it has been performed. Where an obligation is performed, the obligation is discharged. As observed, what it means for an obligation to be discharged is that the obligation, while having previously existed, no longer does. Given that an obligation no longer exists after it has been discharged, it cannot be that the obligation can remain conditional after the obligation has been discharged through performance. Something that no longer exists cannot remain conditional.

English has responded to this objection by suggesting that the:[23]

> performance of a contractual obligation does not make that obligation, or the duty of performance it creates, disappear. The performing party is discharged from their contractual obligation because the obligation no longer requires anything from that party. The obligation and the duty of performance still exist, but the obliged party has complied with their obligation by performing.

But it is wrong to say that the performance of an obligation does *not* mean that the obligation ceases to exist. Imagine that I owe my wife an obligation to pick her up from the gym at 7:00 pm. At 7:00 pm I pick my wife up from the gym, performing my obligation. It would be strange to say that, after I have picked my wife up (ie, performed my obligation), there still exists an obligation to pick my wife up from the gym at 7:00 pm. I cannot think of a single example where someone would be described as having an obligation to do X after they have performed their obligation to do X. Rather, where an obligation has been performed, one would say that someone *had* an obligation to do X and not that they *have* an obligation to do X. The past tense makes it clear that following the performance of the obligation, the obligation ceases to exist. English's account strains the word 'obligation' to the point of fiction.

Second, and relatedly, the absence of basis theory is based upon a version of the rescission fallacy. Following the performance of an obligation, the only way that a failure of condition could cause there to be an absence of basis is if the obligation performed is fictitiously deemed not to have existed at the time it was performed.

[22] *Baltic Shipping Co v Dillon* (1993) 176 CLR 344, 389; *Anderson v McPherson (No 2)* [2012] WASC 19, [235]; *Barton v Morris* [2023] AC 684, [78], quoting *Dargamo Holdings Ltd v Avonwick Holdings Ltd* [2022] 1 All ER (Comm) 1244, [79].

[23] English, *Discharge of Contractual Obligations* (n 19) 318.

That is the doctrine of rescission ab initio.[24] It would be remarkable if the law were to return to the view that a failure of contractual performance rescinds (some of) a contract's obligations ab initio.

Third, there are cases involving restitutionary awards for a failure of condition where it is unclear what the juristic reason was that was subject to a condition that has now failed. An example is the anticipated contract case of *William Lacey (Hounslow) Ltd v Davis*,[25] which was discussed in the previous chapter.[26] Another example is *British Steel Corp v Cleveland Bridge and Engineering Co Ltd*.[27] The defendants notified the claimants, who were iron and steel manufacturers, of their intention to enter into a contract with the claimants for the purchase of the steel nodes that the defendants required for a building project. Before the contract had been formed, the claimants, at the defendants' request, began manufacturing and supplying the steel nodes to the defendants. The contract anticipated by the parties was never formed. Robert Goff J held that the claimants were entitled to restitution even though the claimants were not obliged to perform the work they did manufacturing and delivering the nodes.[28] Given that the claimants were not obliged to perform the services, it is difficult to know what the juristic reason was that was subject to a condition that failed.[29]

Finally, the absence of basis theory does not, without further elaboration, identify a normative reason for restitution.[30] As observed, under this theory, the event that may entitle C to restitution against D is that the juristic reason for the performance C rendered was subject to a condition that has now failed. But this does not positively explain why D should potentially be required to make restitution where there is no juristic reason for the performance. Although this does not mean the theory is incorrect, it does suggest that it is incomplete in an important respect.

Part of the motivation for the absence of basis theory is undoubtedly a perceived tension between cases involving restitutionary awards of a performance of a valid contractual obligation for a failure of condition and the so-called 'obligation rule'. This has been said to be the rule that 'a claim in restitution cannot override a valid and subsisting legal obligation of the claimant to confer the benefit on the defendant'.[31] However, this statement of the rule does not make sense. Once a 'benefit' has been conferred, the obligation to confer the benefit ceases to exist, meaning

[24] *Johnson v Agnew* [1980] AC 367, 393.

[25] *William Lacey (Hounslow) Ltd v Davis* [1957] 1 WLR 932.

[26] Text to n 92.

[27] *British Steel Corp v Cleveland Bridge and Engineering Co Ltd* [1984] 1 All ER 504. It is arguable that the defendants had impliedly undertaken to pay for the steel nodes in the circumstances. However, this is not how the case was argued or decided by Robert Goff J.

[28] ibid 510–11.

[29] The juristic reason for the services that failed cannot have been a gift as there is no such thing as a gift of services.

[30] A Georgiou, 'Mistaken Payments, Quasi-Contracts, and the "Justice" of Unjust Enrichment' (n 2) 610–11.

[31] *Dargamo Holdings Ltd v Avonwick Holdings Ltd* (n 22) [70].

that there is no 'valid and subsisting legal obligation' for a subsequent award of restitution to 'override'.

Another interpretation of the obligation rule is that if a 'benefit' was conferred in the performance of a 'valid obligation', that benefit generally cannot be recovered because there is a juristic reason for the benefit's conferral. But it is difficult to reconcile this interpretation with cases where restitution for a failure of condition has been held to be available. For example, if C pays £10,000 to D in the performance of a valid contractual obligation in exchange for D repairing C's roof, it is well-established that C can generally recover that payment if D performs no part of the work.[32] This is inconsistent with the preceding interpretation of the obligation rule because C's payment was made in the performance of a valid contractual obligation.

Where the juristic reason for a performance was an obligation and that obligation did not exist, restitution should generally be available because there was no juristic reason for the performance. The flip side of this proposition – which on one view is the obligation rule – is that where the juristic reason for a performance was an obligation and that obligation existed at the time of the performance, then generally restitution is not justified. But this is not an absolute rule, as Carr LJ expressly acknowledged in *Dargamo Holdings Ltd v Avonwick Holdings Ltd*,[33] which contains the leading statement of the obligation rule in the failure of condition context. It is otherwise impossible to explain cases such as *Fibrosa Spolka Akcyjna v Fairbairn Lawson Combe Barbour Ltd*,[34] where restitution of a payment made pursuant to a valid contractual obligation was awarded for a failure of condition. In cases like *Fibrosa*, where the contract is terminated after the payment was made, the obligations that have been performed are not 'invalidated' because termination only discharges obligations that have not unconditionally accrued.

It may be objected that '[f]or centuries, an element of a claim for restitution in such cases has been that there is no justification – that is, no juristic reason – for the defendant to retain (or "detain[]") the benefit'.[35] Leaving to one side that this proposition cannot be reconciled with cases like *Fibrosa*, where a performance was rendered pursuant to a valid obligation, older cases need to be viewed in their historical context. As explained in chapter 1, part of this context was a belief that a failure of counter-performance could rescind (at least certain of) a contract's obligations ab initio. Following the elimination of that fallacy, it is no longer a plausible interpretation of the law that, in a failure of condition claim, it is necessary for there to be no juristic reason for the performance before restitution may be awarded. A better interpretation is that, while an absence of a juristic reason prima facie justifies restitution, the existence of a juristic reason for a performance does not necessarily prevent restitution for a failure of condition from being awarded.

[32] *Fibrosa Spolka Akcyjna v Fairbairn Lawson Combe Barbour Ltd* [1943] AC 32.
[33] *Dargamo Holdings Ltd v Avonwick Holdings Ltd* (n 22) [72].
[34] *Fibrosa Spolka Akcyjna v Fairbairn Lawson Combe Barbour Ltd* (n 32).
[35] *Gray v Lavan* (n 1) [37].

IV. The Qualified Intention Theory

The remainder of this chapter examines the prevailing academic account of restitutionary awards for a failure of condition: the qualified intention theory. The section begins by setting out the qualified intention theory. It is then argued that the theory has a poor fit with the positive law. Finally, it is demonstrated that the qualified intention theory does not provide a convincing justification for ordering a defendant to make restitution for a failure of condition.

A. Content

In *An Introduction to the Law of Restitution*,[36] Birks argued that a claimant was entitled to restitution where the claimant 'qualified his intention by specifying the event in which, or basis on which, he wanted the defendant to have [a] benefit', and the basis on which the benefit was conferred failed. The justification provided by Birks for awarding restitution here was that 'in the events which have happened [the claimant] did not mean the defendant to have the benefit'.[37] On this view, where, for example, C makes an advance payment in exchange for D's performance of a dependent obligation to provide certain services and D wrongly performs none of the services, the justification for awarding restitution is that C did not intend for D to be entitled to 'retain' the benefit conferred via its payment in the circumstances.

Birks' qualified intention theory has been widely endorsed by commentators and remains the prevailing academic explanation of these restitutionary awards.[38] In a recent chapter, Lord Burrows, a leading proponent of the qualified intention theory, has re-stated the theory in the following terms:

> the underlying idea behind [failure of condition] is clear. The claimant has conferred a benefit on the defendant conditionally on a performance or event that has not materialised. The parties may have dealt with the consequences of the non-fulfilment of the condition: e.g., there may be a contractual term requiring repayment of money paid. However, even if the parties have not dealt with that eventuality, the law of unjust enrichment requires there to be restitution because the claimant's intention to benefit the

[36] P Birks, *An Introduction to the Law of Restitution*, rev edn (Oxford, Oxford University Press, 1989) 101, 219.

[37] ibid 101.

[38] K Barker, 'Restitution of Passenger Fare: The Mikhail Lermontov' (1993) *Lloyd's Maritime and Commercial Law Quarterly* 291, 293; M McInnes, 'The Measure of Restitution' (2002) 52 *University of Toronto Law Journal* 163, 175; F Maher, 'A New Conception of Failure of Basis' (2004) 12 *Restitution Law Review* 96, 100; J Edelman and E Bant, *Unjust Enrichment*, 2nd edn (Sydney, Hart Publishing, 2016) 251; A Burrows, 'Conditional Intention as an Unjust Factor' in E Bant, K Barker and S Degeling (eds), *Research Handbook on Unjust Enrichment and Restitution* (UK, Edward Elgar Publishing, 2020) 346–47; C Mitchell, P Mitchell and S Watterson, *Goff & Jones on Unjust Enrichment*, 10th edn (UK, Sweet & Maxwell, 2022) 461, [12-01].

> defendant was conditional and that condition has not occurred. In the circumstances, the claimant did not intend the defendant to retain the benefit conferred, after the condition has failed, and the defendant should therefore make restitution of the value of the benefit.[39]

Despite what this passage at one point appears to suggest, it cannot be that C's conditional intention to *confer* a benefit upon D is what justifies restitution. Where a party has a conditional intention, their intention to do (or not to do) something, or for something to happen (or not to happen), is subject to one or more conditions. If C has conferred a benefit upon D, any conditions that C's intention to confer the benefit was subject to will, provided the benefit was not conferred due to a mistake or compulsion, have been satisfied.

When it is suggested that C's conditional intention to confer a benefit upon D may justify an award of restitution, what appears to be meant is that C intended for D's entitlement to *retain* a benefit C conferred to be conditional upon (or qualified by) a certain state of affairs materialising or sustaining itself. To the extent that at the time of conferring the benefit, C did not intend for D to be unconditionally entitled to retain the benefit, C may be described as having held a qualified or conditional intention to benefit D, and the language of qualified intention will be used here.

Statements of the qualified intention theory often contain slightly different formulations of what is required before D's entitlement to retain a benefit C conferred will be conditional. The most prominent is that at the time the benefit was conferred, C intended for D's entitlement against C to retain the benefit to be subject to a condition, and, when the benefit was conferred, D either knew of C's intention, or a reasonable person in D's position would have known of C's intention.[40] Ultimately, what is referred to here as the qualified intention theory is the thesis that the justification for restitution for a failure of condition relates to C having intended for D's entitlement to retain a benefit it conferred to be subject to a now failed condition.

There is some support for the qualified intention theory in the authorities. In *Fibrosa*,[41] which involved a claim to recover an advance payment, Lord Wright said that where there is a 'total failure of consideration' in respect of a payment, C will have had 'no intention to enrich [D] in the events which happened'.[42] Consistent with the qualified intention theory, Lord Wright links the justification for these restitutionary awards to C's intention. In *Gribbon v Lutton*,[43] Robert Walker LJ characterised the claim to recover a deposit in that case as 'arising out of a transfer

[39] Burrows, 'Conditional Intention as an Unjust Factor' (n 38) 346–47.

[40] Birks, *An Introduction to the Law of Restitution* (n 36) 142; A Burrows, *A Restatement of the English Law of Unjust Enrichment* (Oxford, Oxford University Press, 2012) 88. cf Burrows, 'Conditional Intention as an Unjust Factor' (n 38) 347.

[41] *Fibrosa Spolka Akcyjna v Fairbairn Lawson Combe Barbour Ltd* (n 32).

[42] ibid 65. See also ibid 61.

[43] *Gribbon v Lutton* [2002] 2 WLR 842.

which is non-voluntary because the intention to transfer [was] qualified'.[44] More recently, in *Dargamo*,[45] Carr LJ said that '[w]hilst failure of basis ranks alongside the unjust factors of mistake, duress and undue influence as a factor negativing consent, it differs in that it is concerned with qualification of consent'.[46]

There are also cases involving actions for non-contractual quantum meruit where courts have used language that accords with the qualified intention theory. In *Cobbe v Yeoman's Row Management Ltd*,[47] Lord Scott held that the claimant in that case, Mr Cobbe, was entitled to an award of non-contractual quantum meruit for services he had performed because the defendant company 'knew he was providing his services in the expectation of becoming the purchaser of the property under an enforceable contract'.[48] Actions for non-contractual quantum meruit in cases exemplified by *Cobbe*, where services are performed with an expectation that fails, are now generally regarded as claims for restitution for a failure of condition.[49] Thus understood, the foregoing passage provides some support for the qualified intention theory as Lord Scott apparently regarded an award of non-contractual quantum meruit as justified due to the defendant company's knowledge of Cobbe's expectation to be paid for his services in the circumstances.[50]

B. The Qualified Intention Theory as an Interpretation of the Positive Law

The focus of this section now turns to whether the qualified intention theory is a plausible interpretation of the positive law. It is argued that the theory has a poor fit with the positive law, because the qualification of C's intention to benefit D is neither necessary nor sufficient for restitution for a failure of condition to be awarded.

i. Qualified Intention is not Necessary

There are limited cases where consideration has directly been given to what, to use the language of the qualified intention theory, is required before D's entitlement to retain a benefit C conferred may be conditional. Historically, in an action for money had and received upon a consideration that failed, the question courts regarded themselves as addressing was whether the claimant payor had received part of the counter-performance for its payment. That issue was, without exception,

[44] ibid [60].

[45] *Dargamo Holdings Ltd v Avonwick Holdings Ltd* (n 22).

[46] ibid [79], citing Burrows, *The Law of Restitution* (n 10) 319.

[47] *Cobbe v Yeoman's Row Management Ltd* [2008] 1 WLR 1752.

[48] ibid [42].

[49] *Dargamo Holdings Ltd v Avonwick Holdings Ltd* (n 22) [77]–[101] (Carr LJ); Burrows, *The Law of Restitution* (n 10) 318–19; Mitchell, Mitchell and Watterson, *Goff & Jones* (n 38) 463, fn 11; Edelman and Bant, *Unjust Enrichment* (n 38) 467–68.

[50] See also *Lissack v Manhattan Loft Corporation Ltd* [2013] EWHC 128 (Ch), [88]–[89] (Roth J).

approached 'objectively',[51] in the sense that it was determined by considering the meaning of the parties' agreement to a reasonable bystander with knowledge of the relevant context.[52]

A case that illustrates this objective approach is *Biggerstaff v Rowatt's Wharf Ltd.*[53] The claimant contracted with the defendant to purchase 7,000 barrels of oil at a price of 3s 6d per barrel. The entire price was paid in advance. The defendant delivered only some of the promised barrels. The claimant brought an action for money had and received, arguing that there had been a total failure of consideration in respect of the part of its advance payment that had been made in consideration for the undelivered barrels. In response, the defendant argued that the advance payment was not severable between each barrel,[54] meaning there was not a total failure of consideration because some of the barrels had been delivered.[55] The Court of Appeal's approach was to consider whether, on the usual objective approach to contractual interpretation, the consideration for the payment was entire or severable.[56] It was held that the consideration was severable, such that there was a total failure of consideration in respect of the part of the payment made in exchange for barrels that had not been delivered.

A more recent case concerning the approach to be taken to determining whether D's entitlement to retain a benefit C conferred was subject to a condition is *Giedo van der Garde BV v Force India Formula One Team Ltd.*[57] There, Stadlen J held that 'although the question is to be answered from the perspective of the payer in the sense of identifying the essential bargain for which he contracted … it is a question [to] be answered objectively rather than by reference to evidence of his subjective motives'.[58] This analysis was endorsed by the Singapore Court of Appeal in *Benzline Auto Pte Ltd v Supercars Lorinser Pte Ltd*,[59] where Judith Prakash JA said that '[t]he basis of a transfer must be objectively determined based on what is communicated between the parties'. To similar effect, in *Barton v Morris*,[60] Lord Burrows said:

> failure of consideration or basis means 'that the state of affairs contemplated as the basis or reason for the payment has failed to materialise or, if it did exist, has failed to sustain

[51] The idea of construing an agreement 'objectively' is, strictly speaking, a misnomer. The opposite of subjective intention is not objective intention. Nor is the opposite of subjective (ie, speaker) meaning objective meaning.

[52] *Biggerstaff v Rowatt's Wharf Ltd* [1896] 2 Ch 93, 103 (Lopes LJ); *Rowland v Divall* [1923] 2 KB 500, 505 (Scrutton LJ), 506–07 (Atkin LJ).

[53] ibid.

[54] In other words, the defendant was arguing that its entitlement to any part of the advance payment remained conditional upon delivery of all 7,000 barrels.

[55] In other words, the defendant was arguing that its obligation to deliver the barrels was entire.

[56] *Biggerstaff v Rowatt's Wharf Ltd* (n 52) 103 (Lopes LJ).

[57] *Giedo van der Garde BV v Force India Formula One Team Ltd* [2010] EWHC 2373 (QB).

[58] ibid [286].

[59] *Benzline Auto Pte Ltd v Supercars Lorinser Pte Ltd* [2018] 1 SLR 239, [52] (Judith Prakash JA).

[60] *Barton v Morris* (n 22).

itself'.[61] Although that definition focuses on the restitution of money, it applies equally to the restitution of the value of other benefits, including services. Identifying the basis is a matter for objective interpretation.[62]

A recent illustration of this objective approach is *HEB Enterprise Ltd v Richards*.[63] The case concerned contracts for the sale of a title to two lots within a commercial development. Each contract provided for payment by the claimant purchaser of a deposit and the balance over 20 years in monthly instalments together with interest, following which a fee simple title to the lots would pass. After many years, during which the purchaser enjoyed possession of the lots and used them for commercial purposes, the contracts were terminated for the purchaser's repudiation. The question that arose was whether the purchaser was entitled to restitution of the interest payments made.[64] The approach taken by Lord Kitchin, giving the advice of the Privy Council, to determining whether there had been a 'failure of basis' in respect of the interest payments was to carefully construe the parties' contract via the usual objective analysis.[65] His Lordship concluded that, on the contract's proper construction, there was not a failure of basis with the consequence that restitution was denied.

It appears that the only case where it has been suggested that a subjective approach should be taken to determining whether D's entitlement to retain a benefit C conferred was subject to a condition is *David Securities Pty Ltd v Commonwealth Bank of Australia*.[66] In that case, a majority of the High Court of Australia said that 'to decide whether the appellants in this case have received consideration for payment of the additional moneys, we must ask what these particular appellants, in all the circumstances, thought they were receiving as consideration.'[67] The majority later added: 'as we have stated, the "state of affairs" existing in the appellants' minds was that the withholding tax was their liability.'[68] In support, the majority referred to *Rover International Ltd v Cannon Film Sales Ltd (No 3)*,[69] where Kerr LJ had endorsed the proposition that the consideration for a payment was to be assessed 'from the payer's point of view'.[70]

What appears to be meant when it is said that the consideration for a payment is to be assessed from 'the payor's point of view' is that the consideration for a payment is to be determined having regard to whether the claimant 'enjoyed

[61] Birks, *An Introduction to the Law of Restitution* (n 36) 223.

[62] *Barton v Morris* (n 22) [232] (Lord Burrows). See also [231], [233] (Lord Burrows).

[63] *HEB Enterprise Ltd v Richards* [2023] UKPC 7. See also *Stocznia Gdanska SA v Latvian Shipping Co* [1998] 1 WLR 574.

[64] There was no dispute that the buyer was entitled to recover the instalment payments, which was likely due to the decision in *Mayson v Clouet* [1924] AC 980.

[65] *HEB Enterprise Ltd v Richards* (n 63) [51]–[71].

[66] *David Securities Pty Ltd v Commonwealth Bank of Australia* (1992) 175 CLR 353.

[67] ibid 382 (Mason CJ, Deane, Toohey, Gaudron, and McHugh JJ).

[68] ibid 382 (Mason CJ, Deane, Toohey, Gaudron, and McHugh JJ).

[69] *Rover International Ltd v Cannon Film Sales Ltd (No 3)* [1989] 1 WLR 912.

[70] ibid 923–24, citing A Guest (ed), *Chitty on Contracts*, 25th edn (London, Sweet & Maxwell, 1983) 1091–92.

the benefit of any part of what he bargained for'.[71] But this does not, as Stadlen J observed in *Giedo*, necessarily mean that the consideration for a payment depends on a claimant's state of mind.[72] Another interpretation is that one asks what a reasonable bystander would regard as the benefit the claimant bargained for in exchange for the payment. On this interpretation, where, for example, C makes an advance payment to D, the consideration for the payment is to be assessed from C's 'point of view' in the sense that one considers what a reasonable bystander would regard C as having bargained for in exchange for the payment.

The subjective approach endorsed by the majority in *David Securities* has not subsequently been followed in Australia. In *Fostif Pty Ltd v Campbells Cash & Carry Pty Ltd*,[73] Mason P said that at least where a benefit is conferred in the performance of a contract, the conditions on D's entitlement to retain the benefit conferred are determined objectively.[74] In *Anderson v McPherson (No 2)*,[75] Edelman J similarly held that '[i]n cases involving bilateral (or exchange) transactions … the assessment of the condition or basis for a payment is objective; the focus is upon failure of an (objectively) manifested condition or basis.'[76] This objective analysis of conditions was also recently endorsed by the High Court of Australia in *Gray v Lavan*.[77]

If, as the authorities establish, an objective approach is to be taken to determining the existence and content of a condition in the context of restitutionary claims for a failure of condition, this suggests that C does not need to have held a qualified intention to benefit D before restitution may be awarded. Although it might appear on objective analysis that C's intention to benefit D was subject to a condition, this does not necessarily mean that C actually held such an intention. Further, the authorities do not suggest that C must prove that it subjectively intended for D's entitlement to retain a benefit conferred to be subject to a condition that has now failed before restitution may be awarded. If it is not necessary for C to have held a qualified intention to benefit D, nor for C to prove that it held such an intention, contrary to what the qualified intention theory maintains, C's intention cannot be the justification for the claim.

ii. Qualified Intention is not Sufficient

In addition to it not being necessary for C to have intended for D's entitlement to retain a benefit to be subject to a condition that has now failed for restitution to be awarded, it is also not sufficient. Rather, the authorities have variously held that

[71] ibid 924.
[72] *Giedo van der Garde BV v Force India Formula One Team Ltd* (n 57) [286].
[73] *Fostif Pty Ltd v Campbells Cash & Carry Pty Ltd* (2005) 63 NSWLR 203.
[74] ibid [225]–[233], [238]–[239].
[75] *Anderson v McPherson (No 2)* [2012] WASC 19.
[76] ibid [236]. See also *Nu Line Construction Group Pty Ltd v Fowler* [2012] NSWSC 587, [324] (Ward J).
[77] *Gray v Lavan* (n 1).

a reasonable person in D's position must have known of such an intention,[78] or that the condition must have been 'jointly understood'[79] or 'mutual'.[80] The idea that a condition cannot be unilaterally imposed by C's intention will be referred to here as the bilaterality requirement. It is now argued that proponents of the qualified intention theory have failed to convincingly explain the bilaterality requirement, and hence why C's qualified intention to benefit D is not sufficient to prima facie justify an award of restitution if the intended condition fails. This argument is developed by examining different explanations that have been, and which might be, provided by the theory for the bilaterality requirement.

a. Floodgates

One explanation that could be advanced by the qualified intention theory for the bilaterality requirement is that it prevents there from being an excessive number of restitutionary claims for a failure of condition. To elaborate, if C was prima facie entitled to restitution merely if C intended for D's entitlement to retain a benefit C conferred to be subject to a condition that has now failed (ie, there was no bilaterality requirement), C would frequently allege such an intention in cases where the parties' bargain turns out to be a bad one for C.

An initial objection to the floodgates justification is that it rests upon the idea that it is problematic for a certain number of restitutionary claims to arise. But without further elaboration, it is mysterious what that number of claims is and why. This does not mean that the floodgates justification is wrong, but it does suggest that in the form it is expressed above (which resembles how floodgates arguments are often put) the justification is incomplete in an important respect. Further, similar floodgate concerns arise with respect to mistaken payments, and yet, in that context, a reasonable person in D's position does not need to have known of C's mistake before restitution may be awarded.[81]

It is also doubtful that a floodgates problem would in fact arise in the absence of the bilaterality requirement. In this connection, two preliminary observations need to be made. The first is that a significant number of claims for restitution for a failure of condition involve attempts to recover what the qualified intention theory would refer to as benefits conferred in the performance of a contract. The

[78] *Cobbe v Yeoman's Row Management* (n 47) [42] (Lord Scott); *Lissack v Manhattan Loft Corporation* (n 50) [88]–[89] (Roth J); *Benedetti v Sawiris* (n 12) [86] (Lord Reed).

[79] *Featherwood Trading Ltd v Fraunteld Management Ltd* (2013) 85 WIR 308, [8] (Mitchell JA); *Spaul v Spaul* [2014] EWCA Civ 679, [46]–[47] (Rimer LJ); *School Facility Management Ltd v Governing Body of Christ the King College* [2020] WLR(D) 289, [419] (Foxton J); *London Trocadero (2015) LLP v Picturehouse Cinemas Ltd and others* [2021] EWHC 2591 (Ch), [82] (HHJ Robin Vos); *Hellfire Entertainment Ltd v Acimar Ltd* [2021] EWHC 1077 (Ch), [64] (Snowden J); *Dargamo Holdings Ltd v Avonwick Holdings Ltd* (n 22) [79] (Carr LJ).

[80] *Swynson Ltd v Lowick Rose LLP* [2018] AC 313, [30] (Lord Sumption).

[81] In the mistake context, floodgates concerns are addressed to some extent by the rule that mistakes in the form of mispredictions do not justify restitution: *Dextra Bank & Trust Co Ltd v Bank of Jamaica* [2002] 1 All ER 193.

second is that proponents of the qualified intention theory, consistently with the authorities,[82] maintain that a claim for restitution for a failure of condition should be denied if awarding restitution would be inconsistent with the parties' contract.[83]

As explained further in chapter 6, if the conditions stipulated in a contract that D's entitlement to retain a benefit C conferred in the performance of the contract were subject to have been fulfilled, then, according to the contract, D is almost always unconditionally entitled to the benefit. The only exception is where the agreement is silent on whether D is unconditionally entitled to the benefit in the circumstances. To treat D's entitlement to retain a benefit C conferred in the performance of the contract as subject to a condition because this is what C subjectively intended, will, if such a condition was not incorporated into the contract, therefore almost always be inconsistent with the contract. It follows that C's subjective intention would rarely be relevant, which substantially undermines any floodgates concern that might arise absent the bilaterality requirement.

Finally, if one were concerned with the number of restitutionary claims that would arise if C's qualified intention to benefit D could justify an award of restitution, it is extremely doubtful that the bilaterality requirement is the rule that one would adopt to alleviate this concern. A more obvious rule would be that an award of restitution of benefits conferred in the performance of a contract is unavailable, or that restitution will be denied if it would allow C to escape a bad bargain. This suggests that the reason for the bilaterality requirement is not to prevent there from being an excessive number of restitutionary claims for a failure of condition.

b. Security of Receipt

A further justification for the bilaterality requirement that has been advanced from the standpoint of the qualified intention theory is that the bilaterality requirement enhances the ability of recipients of benefits to securely make plans around having those benefits.[84] More specifically, if C's uncommunicated subjective intention could render D's entitlement to retain a benefit subject to a condition, D's ability to securely plan based upon having the benefit would be negatively affected because D's entitlement to the benefit could be defeated by facts that D reasonably did not know of.[85] Call this the security of receipt justification.

Although the security of receipt justification is probably the most plausible justification of the bilaterality requirement available to the qualified intention theory, it remains problematic. One difficulty is that proponents of the theory generally regard there as being a change of position defence to restitutionary

[82] *Re Richmond Gate Property Co Ltd* [1965] 1 WLR 335, 337 (Plowman J); *Pan Ocean Shipping Co Ltd v Creditcorp Ltd (The Trident Beauty)* [1994] 1 WLR 161, 164 (Lord Goff); *Taylor v Motability Finance Ltd* [2004] All ER 341, [25] (Cooke J).

[83] *Dargamo Holdings Ltd v Avonwick Holdings Ltd* (n 22) [75]–[76] (Carr LJ); Mitchell, Mitchell and Watterson, *Goff & Jones* (n 38) 50–52, [3-09]–[3-12].

[84] F Wilmot-Smith, *Failure of Condition* (DPhil thesis, University of Oxford, 2013) 153.

[85] ibid.

claims for a failure of condition.[86] Assuming there is a change of position defence in the failure of condition context, it is difficult to understand why issues relating to security of receipt are not adequately dealt with by such a defence, and further justify a bilaterality requirement. In this regard, it is also noteworthy that in the mistake context, where issues relating to the security of receipt are prevalent, there is no bilaterality requirement in addition to a change of position defence.

Another difficulty is that, as the qualified intention theory is typically expressed, a reasonable person in D's position must have known of C's qualified intention when the relevant benefit was conferred.[87] Consequently, if, sometime after receipt, a reasonable person in D's position would have come to know that C intended for D's entitlement to retain a benefit it conferred to be subject to a certain condition, C's intention cannot give rise to a claim for restitution for a failure of condition. But if protecting security of receipt is what justifies the bilaterality requirement, it is unclear why this should be the case. Rather, so long as C's intention was reasonably apparent to D before D made plans based upon having the benefit conferred, it would seem that C's qualified intention should be capable of justifying an award of restitution.

c. Risk-Taker

The most prominent explanation for the bilaterality requirement is that if a reasonable person in D's position would not have known of C's qualified intention when the benefit was conferred, then restitution should be denied because C is a risk-taker.[88] This argument, which will be referred to as the risk-taking justification, was originally advanced by Birks, who claimed that 'what distinguishes [C] from the risk-taking volunteer, who hopes that a particular state of affairs will eventuate', is that C 'stipulated' that it intended for D's entitlement to retain a benefit conferred to be subject to a condition.[89] Birks later clarified this argument via the following example:

> someone who cleans my windows while I am out, hoping for payment, can say that the benefit was intended to be conditional upon his being paid. But this volunteer can be driven back to bear the risk which he ran when he chose to do the work without specifying the conditions on which it was done.[90]

The risk-taking justification has more recently been expressed by Burrows as follows: 'the claimant's condition must be accepted by, or made clear to, the defendant. The explanation for this is that, in order to throw the relevant risk onto

[86] Burrows, *The Law of Restitution* (n 10) 545–46.
[87] Burrows, 'Conditional Intention as an Unjust Factor' (n 38) 347.
[88] Maher, 'A New Conception of Failure of Basis' (n 38) 100–01; HW Tang, 'An Unjust Enrichment Claim for the Mistaken Improver of Land' (2011) 75 *Conveyancer and Property Lawyer* 8, 22, 24.
[89] Birks, *An Introduction to the Law of Restitution* (n 36) 219.
[90] ibid.

the defendant, it is insufficient that the condition is merely, subjectively, in the claimant's mind.'[91]

As the concept of risk-taking is conventionally used, someone takes a risk if they expose themselves to a foreseeable eventuality that may negatively impact their interests. It is not always clear what those who advance the risk-taking justification regard as the risk that is taken where C does not communicate its qualified intention. One interpretation is that C takes the risk that the intended condition will fail.[92] But where C does communicate this intention, this is still a risk that C takes, in the sense that it remains a foreseeable eventuality that C is exposed to. This risk also does not disappear if D is under an obligation to undertake a performance that would fulfil the condition because that obligation may be unenforceable or because C may not have the resources to enforce the obligation or a secondary obligation arising from its breach.

Another interpretation of the risk that C takes is that it will be unable to recover the benefit it conferred upon D if the intended condition fails. However, to claim that C is not entitled to restitution because C took the risk that it would be unable to recover the benefit is circular: C can only be regarded as having taken this risk if C is not entitled to restitution.[93] It is also not obvious from a normative standpoint why someone who takes the risk that they will be unable to recover a benefit conferred should be denied restitution.[94]

C. The Qualified Intention Theory is Normatively Unconvincing

Unless one is prepared to accept that justifications for private law remedies can be entirely claimant-sided, which would also be to accept that it is legitimate for judge-made law to use defendants as a means to an end,[95] in addition to explaining why C should have a claim for restitution against D, it is necessary to explain why D should be required to make restitution to C.[96] It is now argued that the qualified intention theory has failed to identify a convincing reason for ordering D to make restitution for a failure of condition. This argument is developed by

[91] Burrows, *A Restatement of the English Law of Unjust Enrichment* (n 40) 88.

[92] J Goodwin, 'Failure of Basis in the Contractual Context' (2013) 21 *Restitution Law Review* 24, 29–30.

[93] F Wilmot-Smith, 'Replacing Risk-Taking Reason' (2011) 127 *LQR* 610, 613–14.

[94] For further criticisms of the risk-taking justification, see J Edelman, 'Liability in Unjust Enrichment Where a Contract Fails to Materialise' in A Burrows and E Peel (eds), *Contract Formation and Parties* (Oxford, Oxford University Press, 2010) 160–62.

[95] See also R Stevens, 'The Unjust Enrichment Disaster' (2018) 134 *LQR* 574, 581–82.

[96] Another view is that the same reason must simultaneously justify C having a claim against D and D being liable to C: see E Weinrib, *The Idea of Private Law*, 2nd edn (Oxford, Oxford University Press, 2012) 38–45 and ch 3. If this is correct, it is a fatal objection to the qualified intention theory because the theory rests upon there being different reasons for C being entitled to and D being obliged to make restitution.

considering justifications that might be provided by the theory for ordering D to make restitution.

i. The No-Loss Argument

A first argument for why C's qualified intention to benefit D may justify ordering D to make restitution is that, provided D has not changed its position, no loss would be caused to D if it were required to make restitution. This argument has some prominence in the literature on mistaken payments.[97] Professor Chambers, for example, has claimed:

> [t]he liability to return a mistaken payment has been compared with a duty to rescue. While repayment is generally regarded as the right thing to do, what justifies turning this 'imperfect moral duty' into a 'perfect legal duty' to make restitution? Unlike the witnesses to an emergency, the recipient of a mistaken payment is the only person in the world who can save the payer from loss without bearing the cost of doing so.[98]

However, the fact that D would not suffer a loss if it were ordered to make restitution to C does not identify a positive reason for ordering D to make restitution to C. As others have observed, the absence of loss is only capable of rebutting a reason that might be provided against ordering D to make restitution; it does not positively justify making such an order in the first place.[99]

ii. Enrichment at the Expense of

A second argument for why C's qualified intention to benefit D may justify ordering D to make restitution is that D has been enriched at C's expense in circumstances where C did not intend for D to be.[100] From this perspective, C's intention that D's entitlement to retain a benefit it conferred was to be subject to a now failed condition provides the claimant-sided reason for restitution, and D's enrichment at C's expense provides the defendant-sided reason for restitution.

In chapter 4, it is argued that what motivates the claim that D should need to have been enriched, in the sense that concept is understood by unjust enrichment theory, before restitution may be awarded, is that D should not be ordered to make restitution if D would, for lack of a better expression, be left 'worse off' as a result. To say D would be left 'worse off' means, in this context, that by making restitution D would be required to give up a benefit that is greater than the benefit it received from C. For example, if D was required to make restitution of £100 despite the

[97] Birks, *Unjust Enrichment* (n 14) 6; C Webb, *Reason and Restitution* (Oxford, Oxford University Press, 2016) 195.

[98] R Chambers, 'Proprietary Restitution and Change of Position' in A Dyson, J Goudkamp and F Wilmot-Smith (eds), *Defences in Unjust Enrichment* (Oxford, Hart Publishing, 2016) 119.

[99] F Wilmot-Smith, 'Should the Payee Pay?' (2017) 37 *OJLS* 844, 846–51; R Stevens, 'The Unjust Enrichment Disaster' (n 95) 578.

[100] A Burrows, 'In Defence of Unjust Enrichment' (2019) 78 *CLJ* 521, 541, fn 86.

value to D of the benefit it received from C being £0, such that D was not enriched, D would be left 'worse off' as a consequence of making restitution. The perceived reason that D should not be left 'worse off', which informs the enrichment requirement, is that restitutionary liability for unjust enrichment is not based on a breach of duty. As Professor McInnes has observed:

> the element of enrichment provides the primary means for ensuring that restitution does not unfairly affect the defendant. Liability for unjust enrichment is truly strict – it is not premised upon the breach of an obligation. There consequently is a danger that an innocent recipient may be compelled to pay for an unwanted benefit. Despite doing nothing wrong, the defendant may be left worse for wear. That risk is managed in several ways, but the primary solution lies in a specialised conception of enrichment.[101]

According to this understanding of enrichment, the enrichment at the expense of argument is no different from the no-loss argument. If one asks why D's enrichment at C's expense may justify ordering D to make restitution where C's intention to benefit D was qualified by a condition that has now failed, the answer must be that because D was enriched at C's expense, D 'can save [C] from loss without bearing the cost of doing so' provided D has not changed its position.[102] But as observed, the no-loss argument is flawed because it does not positively explain why C's qualified intention provides a good reason for ordering D to make restitution.

iii. Acceptance

Another possible explanation for why C's qualified intention to benefit D may justify ordering D to make restitution is that D accepted a benefit with the knowledge that C intended for its entitlement to retain this benefit to be subject to a condition. The most sophisticated version of this argument, which will be referred to as the acceptance argument, is advanced by Professor Weinrib, albeit with a focus on mistake.[103] Weinrib claims that the justification for potentially ordering D to make restitution of a mistakenly conferred benefit is that C made a 'transfer of value' to D 'without the intention to make a gift'[104] which D accepted as non-donatively given.[105] The absence of donative intent on C's side, and D's acceptance of the 'transfer of value' as non-donatively made, mark out what Weinrib calls 'the convergence of both parties' wills on the non-donativeness of the transfer' and

[101] M McInnes, 'Enrichment' in E Bant, K Barker and S Degeling (eds), *Research Handbook on Unjust Enrichment and Restitution* (UK, Edward Elgar Publishing 2020) 234.

[102] Chambers, 'Proprietary Restitution and Change of Position' (n 98) 119.

[103] E Weinrib, 'The Normative Structure of Unjust Enrichment' in R Grantham and C Rickett (eds), *Structure and Justification in Private Law: Essays for Peter Birks* (Oxford, Hart Publishing, 2008) 37; E Weinrib, 'Correctively Unjust Enrichment' in R Chambers, C Mitchell and J Penner (eds), *Philosophical Foundations of the Law of Unjust Enrichment* (Oxford, Oxford University Press, 2009) 42; E Weinrib, 'The Corrective Justice of Liability for Unjust Enrichment' in E Bant, K Barker and S Degeling (eds), *Research Handbook on Unjust Enrichment and Restitution* (UK, Edward Elgar Publishing, 2020) 175–79.

[104] Weinrib 'The Corrective Justice of Liability for Unjust Enrichment' (n 103) 175.

[105] ibid 177–79.

may justify ordering D to make restitution if the 'transfer of value' turns out to be donative.[106] Thus, for Weinrib, if C makes a payment to discharge a debt owed and D accepts the payment on this basis, C may be entitled to restitution if the debt turns out not to exist because there was a 'convergence of both parties' wills' on the non-donativeness of the payment.

Weinrib's acceptance argument can be re-formulated and applied to restitutionary claims for a failure of condition as follows. C intended for D's entitlement to retain a 'transfer of value' to be conditional upon a certain state of affairs materialising or sustaining itself. D accepted the 'transfer of value' on this basis. If the state of affairs that C intended for D's entitlement to retain the 'transfer of value' to be conditional upon fails to materialise or sustain itself, it would be unjust for D to retain the value transferred because a condition that D's entitlement to the transfer was subject to, upon which the parties' wills converged, has failed.

There are two reasons that it is problematic for the qualified intention theory to draw upon D's acceptance. One is that the theory expressly rejects the proposition that D must have accepted a benefit on a particular basis before restitution for a failure of condition may be awarded. As Burrows writes: 'the claimant's condition must be accepted by, *or* made clear to, the defendant.'[107] The other is that the acceptance argument collapses the qualified intention theory into an agreement theory of failure of condition. If C makes a 'transfer of value' on a specific basis, and D accepts the transfer on this basis, there will be an agreement that the 'transfer of value' was made on this basis. The justification for restitution would therefore no longer be based upon C's qualified intention to benefit D but rather the failure of an agreed basis.

V. Conclusion

This chapter has examined the leading alternative accounts of restitution for a failure of condition to the agreement theory defended by this book. The chapter began by examining the implied promise and absence of basis theories. As regards the implied promise theory, it was argued that this theory does not provide a convincing account of restitution for a failure of condition because it is inconsistent with restitution being awarded in cases involving the performance of unenforceable contract and because a defendant cannot, on an objective analysis, plausibly be regarded as having impliedly promised to make restitution in certain cases where restitution for a failure of condition may be awarded. As to the absence of basis theory, it was shown that this theory is conceptually problematic; based upon a flawed interpretation of contractual termination; cannot explain certain cases where there was not an obligation to undertake the relevant performance; and does not identify a normative reason for restitution.

[106] ibid 177.
[107] Burrows, *A Restatement of the English Law of Unjust Enrichment* (n 40) 88 (emphasis added).

Having considered the implied promise and absence of basis theories, the chapter examined the prevailing academic account of restitution for a failure of condition: the qualified intention theory. It was argued that the qualified intention theory has a poor fit with the positive law because C's qualified intention to benefit D is neither necessary nor sufficient to potentially justify an award of restitution. Finally, it was argued that the qualified intention theory has failed to identify a convincing defendant-sided reason why D should be ordered to make restitution in circumstances where C intended for D's entitlement to retain a benefit conferred to be subject to a condition that has now failed.

3

An Agreement Theory of Failure of Condition

I. Introduction

This chapter develops the foundations of a different account of restitution for a failure of condition. The account developed, which is referred to as the agreement theory, maintains that restitutionary awards for a failure of condition give effect to an agreement between C and D that D's entitlement against C to a performance rendered, or an act performed by C for D, remained subject to a condition and that condition has failed. The justification for restitution for a failure of condition is, on this view, to ensure that D is not entitled against C to a performance rendered or an act performed in circumstances where the parties agreed that D was not so entitled.

The chapter begins by setting out the content of the agreement theory and the central reasons for preferring this theory to the theories of restitution for a failure of condition discussed in the previous chapter. The relationship between failure of condition; failure of consideration; and no consideration as grounds for restitution is then discussed. Finally, the chapter examines certain implications of preferring the agreement theory to other theories of failure of condition.

II. The Agreement Theory

A. Justification

Under the agreement theory, the justification for restitutionary awards for a failure of condition is, as just observed, to ensure that D is not entitled against C to a performance C rendered or an act C performed for D in circumstances where the parties agreed that D's entitlement against C to the performance rendered or act performed remained subject to a condition that has now failed.[1] So, suppose that C makes an advance payment of £1,000 to D in exchange for D's performance of

[1] See R Stevens 'The Unjust Enrichment Disaster' (2018) 134 *LQR* 574, 585; R Stevens, *The Laws of Restitution* (Oxford, Oxford University Press, 2023) ch 7.

a dependent obligation to provide certain services, but D, in breach of contract, performs no part of its dependent service obligation. According to the agreement theory, the reason that C should generally be entitled to restitution of its £1,000 payment for a failure of condition is that the parties agreed that D's entitlement against C to the £1,000 payment made remained conditional upon D substantially performing its dependent service obligation. If restitution of the payment was not awarded, D would be entitled against C to the payment made despite the parties having agreed that D was not so entitled in the circumstances. The justification for awarding restitution is therefore to give effect to the parties' agreement.

This justification for restitution applies equally to services and transfers of rights. Suppose that C and D enter into a contract whereby C undertakes an entire obligation to perform certain building work on D's land in exchange for payment following substantial completion. When C has performed half of the work, D wrongly withdraws its consent to C entering its land to perform the work and C accepts D's repudiation. In this scenario, C will generally be entitled to restitution for a failure of condition.[2] For the agreement theory, the justification for awarding restitution here is that the parties agreed that D's entitlement against C to C's performance of any part of its service obligation remained conditional upon C not wrongly being deprived by D of an opportunity to substantially perform its service obligation. Due to D having withdrawn its consent to C entering its land, C was wrongly deprived of such an opportunity. An award of restitution is therefore justified to ensure that D is not entitled to C's performance of the services in circumstances where it was agreed that D was not so entitled.

Regarding transfers of rights, consider the following: C and D enter into a contract whereby C is obliged to transfer a title to a lorry to D via delivery in exchange for D's performance of certain services. After delivery, D wrongly fails to perform any of the services. In this scenario, the parties will generally have agreed that D's entitlement against C to the transfer of a title to the lorry remained conditional upon D's substantial performance of the services. When D failed to perform the services, a condition that D's entitlement to the transfer remained subject to therefore failed. An award of restitution is justified to ensure that D is not entitled against C to the transfer of title in circumstances where the parties agreed that D was not so entitled.[3]

The concepts of a performance and an act performed, which have been used above, are discussed in more detail in chapter 4. In summary, a performance is a legal event involving a tender by C and an acceptance by D.[4] An example is a payment. An act performed by C for D, on the other hand, refers to something that C can do for D without an acceptance and which is not necessarily a legal event. An example is a service. The sense in which a service is not a legal event is

[2] *Mann v Paterson Constructions Pty Ltd* (2019) 267 CLR 560.

[3] The availability of restitution for a failure of condition in the context of transfers of rights is discussed in chapter 7.

[4] For essentially the same view, see Stevens, 'The Unjust Enrichment Disaster' (n 1) 581; Stevens, *The Laws of Restitution* (n 1) 109–15.

that, unlike a payment or a transfer of a right, a service does not necessarily alter legal relations.

What the language of performance or performance of an act ultimately seeks to capture is that what restitutionary awards for a failure of condition reverse are, respectively, a legal event that has occurred between C and D or something that C has done for D. These concepts are also used to make clear that it should not, as chapter 4 argues, be necessary for D to have been enriched at C's expense for restitution for a failure of condition to be awarded. Reference to a performance or the performance of an act is, however, capable of causing confusion and, where possible, it is preferable to simply refer to restitutionary awards for a failure of condition as reversing a payment made, performance of a service, or transfer of a right.

B. Giving Effect to and Enforcing Agreements

It is critical to appreciate that the agreement theory does not maintain that restitutionary awards for a failure of condition *enforce* an agreement between the parties. Rather, in the view of this theory, these awards *give effect to* what the parties agreed. Although the enforcement of an agreement involves giving effect to an agreement, the converse is not necessarily true. To enforce something is to compel compliance with that thing. The enforcement of an agreement therefore denotes an order requiring D to perform an obligation that it agreed to be under.

Agreements are often given effect to in ways that do not involve the enforcement of the agreement. For example, where C and D form an agreement that is intended to create legal relations which provides that C is to have a specific right, power, immunity, or privilege, and D is to have the correlative duty, liability, disability, or no-right, the law will generally treat these relations as existing. Here, the law is giving effect to but not enforcing C and D's agreement because it is treating the agreement as affecting the legal relations between them but not ordering the performance of an obligation C or D agreed to be under. The general sense in which the agreement is being given effect to is that the law is making the world how the parties agreed it was to be.

A more specific example of an agreement being given effect to but not enforced is an agreement that D is to be discharged from an obligation to pay damages. Provided that such an agreement is supported by consideration, and perhaps even if it is not, the law will generally give effect to the agreement by treating D as discharged from its obligation to pay damages.[5] Another example of the law giving effect to but not enforcing an agreement is no-oral-modification clauses, which are clauses providing that a variation to a contract or particular terms of a contract must comply with a formality requirement to be valid. Following *MWB Business Exchange Centres Ltd v Rock Advertising Ltd*,[6] these clauses will generally be given

[5] *Tetley v Wanless* (1867) LR 2 Exch 275.

[6] *MWB Business Exchange Centres Ltd v Rock Advertising Ltd* [2018] 2 WLR 1603.

effect to, such that a contractual variation that does not comply with the formality requirement is invalid.

To restate, the sense in which restitutionary awards for a failure of condition give effect to an agreement is that these awards ensure that D is not entitled against C to a performance C rendered, or an act C performed for D, in circumstances where the parties agreed that such an entitlement remained subject to a now failed condition. If restitution was not available here, contrary to what was agreed, D would be entitled to the performance rendered or the act performed in the circumstances. Of course, restitutionary awards for a failure of condition, unlike the examples given above, involve giving effect to an agreement via an order for D to make restitution and to that extent are not entirely analogous. But what those examples do illustrate is a general preparedness on the law's part to give effect to agreements in ways that do not involve the enforcement of the agreement.

C. What is Conditional?

As discussed in chapter 1, for there to be a condition, there must be something that is conditional. Under the agreement theory, what is conditional is a question of construction of the parties' agreement. Generally, the most plausible construction of what is agreed to be conditional, and which may justify an award of restitution, is D's entitlement against C to a payment made by C to D, a performance of a service by C for D, or a transfer of a right from C to D.

Where, for example, C agrees to pay £1,000 to D in advance in exchange for D repairing C's roof, generally the proper construction of the agreement is that C is obliged to pay £1,000 to D on or by a certain date and that D's obligation to repair C's roof is to fall due (immediately or within a certain time) after the payment is made. But it is also generally implicit that D must do something to remain entitled against C to the payment after it has been made, which is to substantially repair C's roof by a certain time. In other words, it is D's *entitlement* against C to the payment made that is agreed to remain conditional upon D's substantial provision of the repair work.[7]

Essentially the same construction is also generally the most plausible in relation to the provision of a service or transfer of a right. Consider:

(1) C and D enter into an unenforceable contract whereby C undertakes to repair D's windows before the end of next week and D undertakes to pay £1,000 to C within a reasonable time after substantial completion of the work.

(2) C and D enter into an unenforceable contract whereby C undertakes to deliver 10 bicycles to D before the end of next week and D undertakes to pay £1,000 to C within a reasonable time after delivery. The parties intend for a title to the bicycles to transfer via delivery.

[7] *Baltic Shipping Co v Dillon (The Mikhail Lermontov)* (1993) 176 CLR 344, 390 (McHugh J).

The meaning of both of these agreements is that following C's performance of the services or the transfer of a title to the bicycles, for D to remain entitled against C to the performance of the services or the transfer of title, D must substantially[8] perform its dependent payment obligation.

It was argued in the previous chapter that what is conditional in the above examples is none of: a promissory obligation undertaken by D to make restitution; an obligation that C has performed; or C's intention to benefit D. It will be argued in the next chapter that what is conditional is not D's entitlement to an enrichment C conferred. If these arguments are accepted, then it is difficult to identify anything conditional in the above examples other than D's entitlement against C to the payment made, performance of the services, or transfer of the rights made. It also cannot be D's entitlement against C to retain or keep the payment made, the performance of the services, or the transfer of the rights that is conditional because payments, performances of services, and transfers of rights are not things or rights and are therefore incapable of being retained or kept.

The term 'entitlement' is often used interchangeably with (claim-)right. But it is incorrect to regard, for example, a payee as having a conditional right to a payment after the payment has been made.[9] This is because there is no corresponding duty the payor owes in respect of the payment after it has been made. The same is true regarding services and transfers of rights. What D's conditional entitlement to a payment made, the performance of a service, or transfer of a right denotes is what can alternatively be referred to as D's deservingness of the payment made, the performance of the service rendered, or the transfer of the right made, which is the other way entitlement is used. It is submitted that this is what courts really mean when they say that D's 'right to retain' a payment made,[10] or 'title to' a payment made,[11] is conditional.[12]

An objection that may be raised to this account of what is conditional is that it leads to a contradiction in cases involving the performance of contractual obligations. Imagine that parties enter into a contract whereby D undertakes to repair C's roof. The contract provides that C is obliged to make an advance payment of £1,000 on 6 April 2022 and that D is under an obligation to perform the work within a reasonable time after the payment has been made. The usual construction of such a contract is that it is a condition precedent to C's obligation to make the £1,000 advance payment that it is 6 April 2022. According to the present objection, once

[8] The most prominent situation where a payment obligation is only substantially performed is where the payment is made late.

[9] cf C Mitchell, P Mitchell and S Watterson, *Goff & Jones on Unjust Enrichment*, 10th edn (UK, Sweet & Maxwell, 2022) 461, [12-01].

[10] See, eg, *Fibrosa Spolka Akcyjna v Fairbairn Lawson Combe Barbour Ltd* [1943] AC 32, 65; *Baltic Shipping Co v Dillon* (1993) (n 7) 344 (Mason CJ), 385, 386 (Gaudron J), 388, 389, 391 (McHugh J).

[11] *McDonald v Dennys Lascelles Ltd* (1933) 48 CLR 457, 477 (Dixon J).

[12] As Professor English has explained, neither of these things can literally be what courts are suggesting is conditional: J English, *Discharge of Contractual Obligations* (Oxford, Oxford University Press, 2025) 301–04.

this condition has been fulfilled, D is entitled to the £1,000 payment.[13] Thus, if C performs the payment obligation but D then fails to perform the work, it cannot be said that the payment is recoverable because D's entitlement to the payment made was subject to a condition that has now failed.

The problem with this objection is that it conflates two senses in which D's entitlement against C to the payment is conditional. Where a condition precedent to C's duty to make an advance payment to D is fulfilled, D is entitled to the payment in the sense that D has a (claim-)right that the payment is made. But there is a difference between D having a right that a payment is made, and D remaining entitled to a payment that has been made. It is not contradictory to regard D's right to be paid £1,000 as subject to a condition precedent (eg, that it is 6 April 2022) and to regard D's entitlement against C to the £1,000 payment after it has been made as remaining subject to another condition (eg, that D substantially performs its dependent obligation to repair C's roof).[14] Further, if C is under a duty to pay £1,000 to D on 6 April 2022, what C is really obliged to do is tender £1,000 to D on this date. This is evident from the fact that if C tenders payment but D refuses to accept the tender, such that no payment is made,[15] C will not be in breach of contract.[16] Strictly speaking, then, where a payment obligation that C owes to D has fallen due, what D is entitled to is that C tenders the agreed sum.

Another objection, recently advanced by Professor English, is that 'English law does not have a concept of a defendant's "deservingness" to a payment and to the extent that the concept is simply suggesting that restitution ought to be made it is circular. This is because to say that a defendant is not deserving of a payment, or is only deserving conditionally, asserts what it seeks to prove.'[17] It is not entirely clear what the argument here is. The claim that 'English law does not have a concept of a defendant's "deservingness" to a payment' is a conclusion without an argument. As to the suggestion that 'to the extent that the concept [of deservingness] is simply suggesting that restitution ought to be made it is circular', this appears to misunderstand the argument that is being made. To restate, D's deservingness of the payment made remains conditional because the parties *agreed* that it was. If that

[13] Note, however, that where a payment obligation has fallen due, the obligation may still remain conditional: *McDonald v Dennys Lascelles Ltd* (n 11) 477 (Dixon J). For example, imagine that C and D enter into a contract for the sale of a fee simple title to land that provides that C is required to pay £100,000 to D in advance on 8 August. On 9 August, the contract is terminated for D's repudiation when C has not made the £100,000 payment. In this scenario, although C's payment obligation had fallen due, the payment obligation will generally be discharged because the obligation had not unconditionally accrued at the time of termination.

[14] For a similar argument, see R Stevens, 'Is there a Law of Unjust Enrichment' in S Degeling and J Edelman (eds), *Unjust Enrichment in Commercial Law* (Sydney, Lawbook Co, 2008) 26–28. See also *McDonald v Dennys Lascelles Ltd* (n 11) 477 (Dixon J).

[15] As discussed further in chapter 4, for a payment to be made there must be an acceptance by the payee: text to n 80.

[16] *Farquharson v Pearl Assurance Co Ltd* [1937] 3 All ER 124; G Harrison, *The Law of Tender* (London, Stevens & Sons, 1908) 15.

[17] English, *Discharge of Contractual Obligations* (n 12) 304.

condition fails, D is not deserving of the payment because the parties agreed that D was not deserving of the payment in the circumstances.

The plausibility of the claim that it is D's deservingness of the performance rendered that is agreed to remain conditional perhaps becomes clearer from examples slightly beyond the legal context. Imagine, for example, that C agrees to buy D a coffee if D returns the favour tomorrow. Here, (part of) what the parties have agreed is that D's deservingness of C's gift of a coffee is conditional upon D buying C a coffee tomorrow, which is just a more conceptually precise way of saying that the gift C made was made conditionally. The same is true if C makes a payment in exchange for D cleaning C's windows: D's deservingness of the payment made is conditional upon D cleaning C's windows, which is just a more precise way of saying that the payment was made conditionally.

D. The Kind of Agreement Required

i. Two Senses of Agreement

There are two principal senses in which the concept of agreement is used.[18] The first is an agreement in the active sense, which is something that parties make or enter into. For example, a friend and I might agree in the active sense that we will visit London this weekend. Here we have made an agreement. The second is an agreement in the stative sense, which is a state parties are in regarding some matter. For example, a colleague and I might agree in the stative sense that unjust enrichment theory is flawed. Here we are *in* agreement but have not *made an* agreement.

Under the agreement theory, for restitution for a failure of condition to be awarded there must be an agreement in the active sense. Where there is agreement in the stative sense, the parties in agreement, who might not even know of one another's existence, merely have a shared mental state regarding some matter. If the justification for restitution for a failure of condition related to a shared mental state, evidence of the parties' states of mind should, contrary to what the authorities suggest,[19] be relevant to determining the conditions that D's entitlement against C to a performance rendered or an act performed remained subject to.

The objective approach to determining whether D's entitlement against C to a performance rendered or an act performed remained subject to a condition is unsurprising if an agreement in the active sense is required. This is because the law takes an objective approach to determining the existence and content of agreements in the active sense. It is not necessary to examine why this approach is

[18] T Endicott, 'Objectivity, Subjectivity and Incomplete Agreements' in J Horder (ed), *Oxford Essays in Jurisprudence*: Fourth series (Oxford, Oxford University Press, 2000) 154. See also O Black, *Agreements: A Philosophical and Legal Study* (Cambridge, Cambridge University Press, 2012) 63.

[19] *Fostif Pty Ltd v Campbells Cash & Carry Pty Ltd* (2005) 63 NSWLR 203, [225]–[233], [238]–[239] (Mason P); *Giedo van der Garde BV v Force India Formula One Team Ltd* [2010] EWHC 2373 (QB), [286] (Stadlen J); *Benzline Auto Pte Ltd v Supercars Lorinser Pte Ltd* [2018] 1 SLR 239, [52] (Judith Prakash JA); *Barton v Morris* [2023] AC 684, [231]–[232] (Lord Burrows).

taken.[20] But one (partial) explanation is that whether an agreement has been made and what the content of the agreement is are, in ordinary life, objective questions, in the sense that they do not depend upon parties' subjective states of mind, and the law does not have a sufficiently good reason for adopting a fiction that the existence and content of agreements depend upon parties' mental states.[21]

ii. Intention to Create Legal Relations

Suppose that a father agrees with his adult son that he will cook dinner if his son mows the lawn in the morning. The father cooks dinner but the son, without any reasonable excuse, does not mow the lawn. No court would order the son to make restitution for a failure of condition despite the father having performed a service on an agreed condition that has now failed. Why?

A tempting answer is that the father and son did not, objectively considered, intend for their agreement to create legal relations. The difficulty with this answer is that there are cases that are best understood as involving restitutionary awards for a failure of condition where it is doubtful that there was an intention to create legal relations. An example is *Deglman v Guaranty Trust Co of Canada and Constantineau*.[22] The claimant and his aunt orally agreed that if he performed services she requested from time to time while he was staying with her, she would bequeath a title to one of her houses to him. The claimant performed the services, but his aunt died intestate. The claimant was awarded non-contractual quantum meruit for his services despite the agreement with his aunt being unenforceable. In general, informal agreements between family members are not treated as having been intended 'to be attended by legal consequences'.[23]

Another example is *Jennings v Rice*.[24] Around 1970, Mr Jennings started to work for Mrs Royle, an elderly widow, as a gardener on a part-time basis. As time went by, Jennings began to perform other errands for Royle that she requested or freely accepted. In the late 1980s, Royle stopped paying Jennings. Jennings challenged Royle on several occasions for her failure to pay him. Each time, her response was to the effect that 'he did not need to worry' or that 'he would be alright'. Royle also made statements to Jennings to the effect that 'this will all be yours one day'. These assurances led Jennings to reasonably believe that he was going to receive a title to Royle's house and its contents after she died. Consequently, Jennings continued to

[20] For discussion, see *Mihail Tartsinis v Navona Management Co* [2015] EWHC 57 (Comm), [87]–[99] (Leggatt J); G Leggatt, 'Making Sense of Contract: The Rational Choice Theory' (2015) 131 *LQR* 454; R Stevens, 'What is an Agreement?' (2020) 136 *LQR* 599, 600–01.

[21] See also Stevens, 'What is an Agreement?' (n 20) 601. cf *FSHC Group Holdings Ltd v Glas Trust Corp Ltd* [2020] Ch 365, [151] (Leggatt LJ); C Fried, *Contract as Promise: A Theory of Contractual Obligation* (Cambridge, Mass, Harvard University Press, 1981) 62–66; P Atiyah, *An Introduction to the Law of Contract*, 5th edn (Oxford, Clarendon Press, 1995) 82.

[22] *Deglman v Guaranty Trust Co of Canada and Constantineau* [1954] 3 DLR 785.

[23] *Balfour v Balfour* [1919] 2 KB 571, 579 (Atkin LJ).

[24] *Jennings v Rice* [2002] WTLR 367.

provide services for Royle without payment until she died intestate in 1997. The trial judge held that no contract had been formed as the agreement was insufficiently certain and not intended to create legal relations. Jennings was nevertheless awarded £200,000 based upon 'proprietary estoppel', which was the market value of the services he had provided over the last eight years of Royle's life.

It is difficult to regard *Jennings* as an estoppel case because there was nothing that Royle was stopped from.[25] The case is better understood as involving an award of restitution for a failure of condition. The assurances Royle made to Jennings must, at a certain point, have formed an agreement that Royle's entitlement to Jennings' performance of further services for her remained conditional upon her making a substantial gift to him. When Royle died intestate, there was therefore a failure of condition entitling Jennings to restitution of his performance of these services.

The question that arises is why restitution for a failure of condition may be awarded in cases such as *Deglman* and *Jennings*, but not in cases exemplified by the father and son example above. The preferable way of distinguishing these cases is that in *Deglman* and *Jennings*, although the parties did not intend for their agreement to create enforceable obligations – and in that sense to create legal relations – the agreement was not intended to be wholly without legal effect. Rather, on an objective analysis, the parties intended for their agreement that the services were performed on a condition to have legal effect. By contrast, in the father and son example, a reasonable bystander would not regard the father and son as having intended for their agreement to have any legal effects whatsoever.[26]

iii. Consideration

Restitution may be awarded where the agreement in which the condition that has failed is found is unsupported by consideration. In *Re Ames' Settlement*,[27] in contemplation of his son's marriage, a settlor agreed with trustees to settle a sum of money 'in consideration of the said intended marriage' within one year of solemnisation of the marriage. The marriage was solemnised, and the agreed sum was paid to the trustees, but the marriage was later declared void. Following the settlor's death, the trustees sought judicial advice regarding whether they ought to return the 'fund' to the settlor's executors. Vaisey J held that because the marriage was void, the money was 'paid on a consideration which failed', and declared that 'the trustees ought to pay and transfer the fund in their hand'.[28]

[25] See further Stevens, *The Laws of Restitution* (n 1) 276–87.

[26] For a similar argument, see ibid 113.

[27] *Re Ames' Settlement* [1946] Ch 217.

[28] ibid 223. Although the claimants argued that there was a resulting trust, Vaisey J does not appear to have made a declaration to that effect.

iv. Vagueness and Completeness

The concept of certainty in contract formation is often used to refer to (at least) two distinct reasons that an agreement may be unenforceable. The first is that the agreement is incomplete, which generally means the parties have failed to agree on everything that the law regards as essential before it is prepared to enforce the agreement. [29] The second, more appropriate, use of uncertainty is to refer to an agreement that is incurably vague, which means that the agreement 'fail[s] to evince any definite meaning on which the court can safely act'[30] regarding a matter which, if not agreed, would render the agreement incomplete. In *Brown v Gould*,[31] Megarry J explained that there are two circumstances in which an agreement will 'fail to evince any definite meaning'. One is where an essential part of the agreement is 'devoid of any meaning', in the sense that what was agreed is unintelligible.[32] The other is where there are a variety of meanings that are reasonably attributable to an essential part of the agreement but it is impossible to determine which is to be preferred.[33]

Incompleteness should be irrelevant to the availability of restitution for a failure of condition. If it is established that the parties agreed that D's entitlement against C to a performance rendered or an act performed remained subject to a condition that has now failed, the justification for awarding restitution is established. There is no good reason for it being necessary for the agreement in which the condition is found to be sufficiently complete to form a contract. This is supported by *Benedetti v Sawiris*.[34] Mr Benedetti and Mr Sawiris entered into a contract providing that Benedetti was to undertake services facilitating a corporate takeover in exchange for becoming a shareholder of the company if the takeover was successful. The contract was later abandoned but Benedetti continued to provide services 'on the basis that arrangements would be agreed for Benedetti to be rewarded, but no such arrangements eventuated.'[35] The takeover succeeded. A dispute then arose regarding Benedetti's remuneration for his services.

One of the claims brought by Benedetti was for restitution for a failure of condition. Although the claim failed due to Benedetti having been paid more than the market value of his services, it was assumed that if Benedetti had not been paid there would have been a failure of condition justifying restitution.[36] In other words, despite the agreement being incomplete because it was an agreement to

[29] Incompleteness is also sometimes used to refer to a situation where the parties do not intend for their agreement to be enforceable at the stage negotiations have reached between them: E Peel, *Treitel on the Law of Contract*, 15th edn (UK, Sweet & Maxwell, 2020) 56–60.

[30] *Scammell & Nephew Ltd v Ouston* [1941] AC 251, 268–69 (Lord Wright).

[31] *Brown v Gould* [1972] Ch 52, 61–62. See also *UYCF Ltd v Forrester* [2000] EWCA Civ 317, [9] (Potter LJ).

[32] *Brown v Gould* (n 31) 61.

[33] ibid 62.

[34] *Benedetti v Sawiris* [2014] AC 938. See also *DMA Resources v Brazilian Nickel* [2026] EWHC 833 (Ch).

[35] ibid [86] (Lord Reed).

[36] *Benedetti v Sawiris* (n 34) [10]–[11] (Lord Clarke), [86] (Lord Reed), [175]–[176] (Lord Neuberger).

agree to a price, it was assumed that there could still have been a failure of condition justifying an award of restitution.

Where the part of the agreement that is alleged to contain the relevant condition is incurably vague, this should not necessarily be fatal to a claim for restitution for a failure of condition. Consider a case where C performs a service for D in exchange for payment following substantial completion under an unenforceable contract. Suppose further that the method stated in the agreement regarding the calculation of the sum that C is entitled to is incurably vague. If C is not paid anything for its service following completion, C should still potentially be entitled to restitution. D's entitlement against C to the performance of the service was agreed to remain conditional upon payment of a certain sum, which did not occur. In those circumstances, the justification for restitution is established even if it is not possible to safely determine the sum that D was obliged to pay under the agreement.

Where, however, the agreement is so vague that it is not possible to determine whether D's entitlement against C to a performance rendered or an act performed was agreed to remain conditional, restitution should be denied. This is because C will have failed to prove an essential element of the claim. So, in the example just given, if it was impossible to determine whether or not D's entitlement to C's performance of the service was agreed to remain conditional upon payment, restitution should be denied: C will not have established that D's entitlement to the performance of the service remained subject to a now failed condition.

Another situation where restitution should be denied on the grounds of vagueness is where it is apparent that the performance rendered was conditional, but due to the vagueness of the condition it is not possible to say whether the condition has failed or not. An example would be where C makes an advance payment on the condition of D's performance of certain work but it is not possible to determine the scope of the work that D was required to perform to unconditionally earn the payment made.

v. Capacity

Where one (or both) parties lack the capacity to enter into a contract, the contract is generally voidable or void. Thus, contracts entered into by public authorities that are ultra vires are generally void.[37] Before the introduction of section 39(1) of the Companies Act 2006, a contract that a company lacked the capacity to enter into was also generally void.[38] Contracts entered into by mentally incapable people who retain control of their affairs are voidable if the other party knew (or perhaps reasonably ought to have known)[39] of their incapacity.[40] It is argued below

[37] *Westdeutsche Landesbank Girozentrale v Islington London Borough Council* [1994] 4 All ER 890, 915 (Hobhouse J).

[38] *Ashbury Railway Carriage and Iron Co v Riche* (1875) LR 7 HL 653.

[39] *Dunhill v Burgin* [2014] 1 WLR 933, [1], [25] (Lady Hale).

[40] *Imperial Loan Co Ltd v Stone* [1892] 1 QB 599, 602–03 (Fry LJ).

that where a contract is void or has been avoided, failure of condition is generally not the ground for restitution, and there does not appear to be any English case involving a claim for restitution against or by a mentally incapable person of a performance of a contract that has not been avoided.

The position regarding contracts with minors[41] is complex. Contracts with minors in relation to necessary goods sold and delivered to the minor;[42] the provision of necessary services for the minor;[43] apprenticeships;[44] education;[45] and employment[46] are prima facie enforceable against the minor.[47] Certain contracts with minors are voidable at the minor's option. Examples include contracts to subscribe for shares[48] and for the purchase of a fee simple title by a minor.[49] Voidable contracts with minors appear to fall into two further categories.[50] The first are those that can be enforced against the minor unless and until the minor has repudiated the contract while a minor or within a reasonable time after attaining their majority. The second are contracts that are unenforceable against the minor unless and until the minor ratifies the contract after attaining their majority. A contract with a very young child is almost certainly void.[51]

It is important to distinguish between cases involving claims for restitution for a failure of condition against a minor and those involving claims by a minor. The leading case involving a claim for restitution *against* a minor of a performance of a contract that was unenforceable against the minor and which had not been avoided is *Cowern v Nield*,[52] which is difficult to defend. The claimant buyer entered into a contract with a minor for the sale of hay and clover. The claimant paid the price in advance. The minor failed to deliver the hay, and the clover that he delivered was rejected. Although the contract was voidable by the minor, it was never avoided. The claimant failed in his action for money had and received upon a consideration that failed. The basis for rejecting the claim seems to have been that to allow recovery of the payment would have involved enforcing the contract against the minor.[53] But restitutionary awards for a failure of condition do not enforce a contract, meaning this is not a plausible explanation for the result. Where a minor can make restitution of a performance on a condition that has now failed in the same form, it is very difficult to identify a good reason for denying

[41] A person under the age of 18: Family Law Reform Act 1969, s 1.
[42] Sale of Goods Act 1979, s 3.
[43] *De Stacpoole v De Stacpoole* (1887) 37 Ch D 139.
[44] *Walter v Everard* [1891] 2 QB 369.
[45] *Roberts v Gray* [1913] 1 KB 520.
[46] *Clements v London and North Western Rly Co* [1894] 2 QB 482.
[47] This list is not exhaustive.
[48] *Newry and Enniskillen Ry Co v Coombe* (1849) 3 Ex 565; 154 ER 970.
[49] *Whittingham v Murdy* (1889) 60 LT 956. See also *Orakpo v Manson Investments Ltd* [1978] AC 95, 106 (Lord Diplock).
[50] S Whittaker, 'Personal Incapacity' in H Beale (ed), *Chitty on Contracts*, 36th edn (UK, Sweet & Maxwell, 2025), [12-007], referring to *R v Oldham Metropolitan BC, ex parte Garlick* [1993] 1 FLR 645, 662.
[51] *R v Oldham Metropolitan BC, ex parte Garlick* (n 50), 662 (Scott LJ).
[52] *Cowern v Nield* [1912] 2 KB 419.
[53] ibid 422–23 (Phillimore J), 424 (Bray J).

restitution. Restitution of a performance will be capable of being made in the same form where D can make restitution to C via a performance of the same kind as the performance that C is attempting to recover. For example, restitution of a payment by C can be made by D in the same form because D can make restitution of the payment by also making a payment to C.

The most difficult cases regarding minors are those involving the provision of services for a minor on a condition that has now failed. Professor Birks argued that '[w]here a defendant relies on his contractual incapacity to refuse to pay for non-necessary goods or services, a claim in unjust enrichment for their reasonable value would stultify, or at best transform, the contractual protection.'[54] This concern has been echoed by courts, albeit in cases where the ground for restitution should not be regarded as failure of condition as the contract had been avoided.[55] To clarify Birks' point, suppose that a minor enters into a contract with D for the provision of services in exchange for payment by the minor following substantial completion. Assume the contract is unenforceable against the minor. D substantially performs the services but the minor wrongly refuses to pay. To require the minor to make restitution would, according to Birks, be objectionable because the minor would effectively be being required to pay for the services.

The difficulty with this argument is that restitutionary awards for a failure of condition have been made of services performed under unenforceable contracts in circumstances where such an award places the service provider in the same, or a very similar, position to the position that it would have been in if the agreement had been enforced. Consider a case where C and D enter into an unenforceable contract whereby C agrees to perform certain services for D in exchange for payment of the market value of the services following substantial completion. C performs the services but D refuses to pay. In this scenario, the authorities suggest that C is often entitled to restitution.[56] The effect of such an award is that C is placed in a very similar position to the position that it would have been in if D's payment obligation had been enforced. It would therefore seem that refusing to order a minor to make restitution on the basis that such an award would, in practice, require the minor to pay for the service C provided treats alike cases differently. If it is justifiable to reject a claim against a minor for restitution of a performance of service, the justification must be that such an award would undermine the policy behind treating certain contracts for services as unenforceable against a minor.

There does not appear to be any case involving a claim for restitution for a failure of condition *by* a minor of a performance of a contract that is unenforceable against the minor but which has not been avoided.[57] As discussed below, where a contract has been avoided, the ground for restitution should be regarded as failure

[54] P Birks, *An Introduction to the Law of Restitution*, rev edn (Oxford, Clarendon Press, 1989) 436.

[55] *R Leslie Ltd v Sheill* [1914] 3 KB 607, 621 (Kennedy LJ). See also Birks, *An Introduction to the Law of Restitution* (n 54) 436.

[56] *Scarisbrick v Parkinson* (1869) 20 LT 175; *Pavey & Matthews Pty Ltd v Paul* (1987) 162 CLR 221.

[57] For cases where the contract was avoided, see *Steinberg v Scala (Leeds) Ltd* [1923] 2 Ch 452; *Pearce v Brain* [1929] 2 KB 310.

of juristic reason and not failure of condition. But it would be surprising if a claim for restitution for a failure of condition was not available to a minor because of the minor's incapacity. Thus, imagine that a minor enters into a contract with an adult, D, for the provision of building work by D. The contract is unenforceable against the minor. The minor pays part of the price in advance before the contract is terminated by the minor's acceptance of D's repudiation. At the time of termination, D has performed none of the work. If a minor's lack of capacity prevented an agreement from justifying an award of restitution for a failure of condition, the minor would not have a claim for restitution, which seems the incorrect result.

E. Subject to Contract

Where an agreement is expressed as 'subject to contract', although certain cases suggest that an award of restitution for a failure of condition generally will not be available,[58] the use of these words should not necessarily be fatal to such a claim. The effect of 'subject to contract' is always a question of construction. Depending on the circumstances, 'subject to contract' can reasonably be understood as having one of (at least) the following meanings.[59] The first is that the agreement is not to have any legal effects whatsoever until it is set out in a more formal executed document. Secondly, the agreement is to be unenforceable until it is set out in a more formal executed document.[60] Thirdly, the agreement is to be enforceable but one or more of the obligations contained in the agreement is not to fall due until the agreement is set out in a more formal executed document.[61] Finally, the agreement is to be enforceable but the parties intend for the agreement to be 'restated in a form which will be fuller or more precise but not different in effect'.[62]

As noted above, for a claim for restitution for a failure of condition to potentially arise, it should suffice that the parties formed an agreement containing a condition that was, objectively considered, intended to have legal effect. It follows that unless the first construction of 'subject to contract' is preferred, a claim for restitution for a failure of condition should be possible. This receives some support from *Cobbe v Yeoman's Row Management Ltd*.[63] The defendant landowner formed an oral agreement with the claimant developer that was not intended to be contractually binding at the stage negotiations had reached between them.[64]

[58] *Regalian Properties Plc v London Dockland Development Corp* [1995] 1 WLR 212, 231 (Rattee J).

[59] For a similar interpretation, see *Masters v Cameron* (1954) 91 CLR 353, 360–61 (Dixon CJ, McTiernan and Kitto JJ).

[60] *Pagnan SPA v Feed Products Ltd* [1987] 2 Lloyd's Rep 601, 619 (Lloyd LJ); *Cheverney Consulting Ltd v Whitehead Mann Ltd* [2006] EWCA Civ 1303, [42] (Sir Andrew Morritt C).

[61] *Masters v Cameron* (n 59) 360 (Dixon CJ, McTiernan and Kitto JJ).

[62] ibid.

[63] *Cobbe v Yeoman's Row Management Ltd* [2008] 1 WLR 1752. See also *Countrywide Communications Ltd v ICL Pathway Ltd* [2000] CLC 324, 349 (Nicholas Strauss QC); *Astra Asset Management UK Ltd v Co-operative Bank Plc* [2019] EWHC 897 (Comm), [172]–[178] (Andrew Henshaw QC).

[64] If there had been a contract, the contract would have been void due to s 2 of the *Law of Property (Miscellaneous Provisions) Act 1989* as the agreement was oral.

Under the agreement, which it can be said was impliedly agreed to be 'subject to contract' the developer was to seek planning permission at his own expense for the erection of six houses on land belonging to the landowner. In the event that planning permission was obtained, it was agreed that the landowner would sell his title to the land to the developer for £12 million. It was further agreed that if the developer made a gross profit exceeding £24 million, the profits over £24 million would be shared. The developer obtained planning permission. The landowner then refused to sell at the agreed price and sought to renegotiate the agreement, but the developer was unwilling to renegotiate. It was held that the developer was entitled to an award of non-contractual quantum meruit for the services he had performed obtaining planning permission. This quantum meruit award is now widely interpreted as an award of restitution for a failure of condition.[65]

F. Reasons for Preferring the Agreement Theory

As discussed in the previous chapter, the leading alternative accounts of restitution for a failure of condition are the implied promise; absence of basis; and qualified intention theories. The agreement theory should be preferred to each of these theories as an interpretation of the positive law. Starting with the implied promise theory, as discussed in chapter 2, this theory (which is not truly a theory of failure of condition) claims that restitutionary awards for a failure of condition enforce an implied promissory obligation owed by D to make restitution to C. An objection raised to the implied promise theory was that if an award of restitution for a failure of condition enforces an implied promissory obligation, then, contrary to what the authorities suggest,[66] C should never be entitled to restitution of a performance of an unenforceable contract as this would involve enforcing an unenforceable promissory obligation to make restitution. For the agreement theory, it is not problematic for restitution of a performance of an unenforceable contract to be awarded for a failure of condition because, under this theory, these restitutionary awards do not enforce but instead give effect to an agreement.

As regards the absence of basis theory, recall that this theory claims that restitution for a failure of condition is awarded in response to the failure of a condition that the juristic reason for an enrichment was subject to. Often, this juristic reason for the enrichment will be the obligation to confer the enrichment. An objection raised to this theory was that it is inconsistent with the prevailing understanding of the effect of a failure of contractual counter-performance and termination. This understanding is that a failure of counter-performance and termination do not affect

[65] A Burrows, 'Conditional Intention as an Unjust Factor' in E Bant, K Barker and S Degeling (eds), *Research Handbook on Unjust Enrichment and Restitution* (UK, Edward Elgar Publishing, 2020) 356–57.

[66] *Scarisbrick v Parkinson* (n 56); *Deglman v Guaranty Trust Co of Canada and Constantineau* [1954] 3 DLR 785; *Pavey & Matthews Pty Ltd v Paul* (n 56).

contractual obligations that have previously been performed, but only potentially discharge obligations that have not unconditionally accrued. It was explained that for there to be an absence of basis in respect of an enrichment conferred by C in the performance of a contractual obligation due to a failure of counter-performance by D or termination, D's failure of counter-performance or termination would need to rescind the obligation C performed ab initio. This is because, unless the obligation C performed is rescinded ab initio, there will be a juristic reason for the enrichment C conferred. However, it is well-established that a failure of counter-performance and termination do not rescind obligations that have been performed.

Under the agreement theory, it is not necessary to depart from the orthodox position that a failure of counter-performance and termination do not rescind ab initio certain of a contract's obligations. To take a simple example, suppose that C makes an advance payment of £1,000 to D in the performance of a contractual payment obligation in exchange for D's performance of a dependent service obligation. The contract is later terminated by C's acceptance of D's repudiation when D has performed none of the services. For the agreement theory, what justifies restitution here is that D's entitlement against C to the £1,000 payment made was agreed to remain conditional upon D's substantial performance of its dependent service obligation. The reason that C should potentially be entitled to restitution despite the payment obligation C performed not having been rescinded, and hence despite there having been a juristic reason for the payment, is that to deny C restitution would undermine the parties' agreement. The fact that there was a juristic reason for the performance rendered does not necessarily mean that there is not a good reason for restitution. It was also observed above that it is not contradictory to maintain that D's entitlement to a performance C has undertaken remains conditional despite D having had a now discharged right to C undertaking that performance. There is a difference between having a right that someone does something and being entitled to what they have done after that right has been discharged. The fact that D had a right that C undertakes (or, more commonly, tenders)[67] a performance does not necessarily mean that D should be treated as unconditionally entitled to the performance after it has been rendered.

Turning to the qualified intention theory, recall that this theory maintains that the justification for restitution for a failure of condition is that C did not intend for D to be entitled to retain a benefit C conferred in the circumstances. The agreement theory should be preferred to the qualified intention theory as an interpretation of the law for the following reasons. First, although there are cases containing dicta supporting the proposition that the justification for restitution for a failure of condition relates to C's qualified intention to benefit D, the authorities have more often suggested that the condition must be 'jointly understood'[68] or

[67] As observed, where C is under an obligation to pay a sum of money to D, what this really means is that C is under an obligation to tender payment of that sum to D.

[68] *Spaul v Spaul* [2014] EWCA Civ 679, [46]–[47] (Rimer LJ); *Hellfire Entertainment Ltd v Acimar Ltd* [2021] EWHC 1077 (Ch), [64] (Snowden J); *School Facility Management Ltd v Governing Body of Christ*

'mutual',[69] which is extremely similar to the condition needing to have been agreed. Where a reasonable person in D's position merely knows of C's qualified intention, which the qualified intention theory claims is all that is required,[70] it is difficult to describe C's intention as jointly understood or mutual as D's mere knowledge of C's intention does not involve the adoption of that intention by D.

Secondly, C's intention that D's entitlement to retain a benefit conferred was to be subject to a condition that has now failed is not sufficient to prima facie justify an award of restitution. As just observed, the authorities suggest that the condition must have been jointly understood or mutual. Furthermore, in chapter 2, it was demonstrated that the qualified intention theory has failed to convincingly explain why C's qualified intention to benefit D is not sufficient to justify restitution. From the perspective of the agreement theory, the reason that such an intention is not sufficient is that the justification for these awards does not relate to C's qualified intention to benefit D but rather to an agreement between the parties.

Finally, C does not need to have intended for D's entitlement to retain a benefit that C conferred to be subject to a condition that has now failed for restitution for a failure of condition to be awarded. Rather, the cases establish that they are determined objectively.[71] In other words, whether a condition was, to use the language of the authorities, jointly understood or mutual depends upon whether a reasonable bystander would regard the condition as such. Consequently, C's qualified intention to benefit D is not necessary before restitution may be awarded because the objective appearance that a condition was jointly understood or mutual does not necessarily mean that C subjectively intended for D's entitlement to a benefit conferred to remain subject to this condition. By contrast, the objective approach to determining conditions is unsurprising if conditions must be found in an agreement. This is because the law takes an objective approach to determining the existence and content of agreements.

III. Distinguishing Failure of Condition from Other Grounds for Restitution

This section argues that failure of condition is a distinct ground for restitution, separate from 'failure of consideration' and 'no consideration'. In advancing this argument, the section responds to a further objection that may be raised to the agreement theory, which is that the theory cannot explain cases involving restitutionary awards of payments made under void contracts. This, claims the objection,

the King College [2020] WLR(D) 289, [419] (Foxton J).

[69] *Swynson Ltd v Lowick Rose LLP* [2018] AC 313, [30] (Lord Sumption).

[70] A Burrows, *A Restatement of the English Law of Unjust Enrichment* (Oxford, Oxford University Press, 2012) 88; Burrows, 'Conditional intention as an Unjust Factor' (n 65) 347.

[71] See the cases cited at n 19 above.

is because to treat the parties' agreement as rendering D's entitlement to a performance as conditional in circumstances where their contract is void would mean that the parties' contract was not truly void because their agreement would still have legal effects on the parties' entitlements.

The response developed to this objection is that, where the parties' contract is void in the sense that their agreement is a complete legal nullity, the ground for restitution is not failure of condition but what has variously been referred to in the cases as 'no consideration';[72] 'absence of consideration';[73] or 'without consideration'.[74] Where, however, the parties' contract is void in the sense that the obligations that their agreement purported to create are a nullity, although failure of condition may sometimes provide the ground for restitution, restitution is also generally awarded for 'no consideration'. These arguments imply that failure of condition is the ground for restitution in a narrower range of cases than is conventionally believed.[75]

A. Failure of Consideration

Failure of consideration is often alternatively referred to as 'failure of basis'.[76] Nothing of substance turns upon this choice of terminology, and the language of failure of consideration will be used here. The consideration for something is the reason for that thing.[77] As observed in chapter 1, historically the consideration for a performance was generally understood as the juristic reason for the performance, such as a contractual obligation. More recently, in the restitutionary context, consideration has come to be understood as a jointly understood reason for C conferring an enrichment upon D.[78]

There are scenarios where it is possible, as a matter of English, to describe there as having been either a failure of consideration or a failure of condition. Consider a case where C and D enter into a contract whereby C undertakes to pay £100 to D in advance in exchange for D's performance of a dependent obligation to provide certain gardening work. After C's payment obligation has been performed, the contract is terminated for D's repudiation. Here, C will generally be entitled to restitution of the advance payment, and failure of consideration has been treated as

[72] *Re Phoenix Life Assurance Company (Burges and Stock's Case)* (1862) 2 J & H 441, 448; 70 ER 1131 (Ch D), 1134 (Sir Page Wood VC); *South Tyneside Metropolitan Borough Council v Svenska International* [1995] 1 All ER 545, 558 (Clarke J).

[73] *Westdeutsche Landesbank Girozentrale v Islington London Borough Council* (n 37) 930 (Hobhouse J).

[74] *Strickland v Turner* (1852) 7 Exch 208, 219; 155 ER 919, 924 (Pollock CB).

[75] For a broader interpretation of when failure of condition justifies restitution, see A Burrows, *The Law of Restitution*, 3rd edn (Oxford, Oxford University Press, 2011) ch 15; Mitchell, Mitchell and Watterson, *Goff & Jones* (n 9) chs 12 and 13.

[76] *Barton v Morris* (n 19) [78] (Lady Rose), [231]–[232] (Lord Burrows).

[77] *Barnes v Eastenders Cash & Carry plc* [2015] AC 1, [106]–[107] (Lord Toulson).

[78] *Barton v Morris* (n 19) [231]–[232] (Lord Burrows); Mitchell, Mitchell and Watterson, *Goff & Jones* (n 9) 461, [12-01].

the applicable ground for restitution.[79] This might seem unusual. If one asks what the reason for C's payment was, the most natural answer is that C was obliged to make the payment. Given that following termination the obligation C performed is not rescinded ab initio, one might therefore be tempted to conclude that there was not a failure of the consideration for the payment. But it does seem possible, albeit slightly strained, to say that there was a failure of a reason for the payment in the sense that a jointly understood reason for which the payment was made failed. More specifically, it was on an objective analysis jointly understood that the reason C made the payment was to obtain D's performance of certain gardening work, which C never received. Thus, although there was not a failure of the juristic reason for the payment (ie, the payment obligation), there was a failure of a non-juristic reason for the payment (ie, the promised counter-performance) and in that sense a failure of consideration.

Where there is a failure of a jointly understood reason for a performance, there will also generally be a failure of an agreed condition in respect of the performance. This is because the parties will normally have agreed that D's entitlement against C to the performance rendered remained conditional upon this reason substantially being fulfilled. So, in the gardening work example above, D's entitlement against C to the payment made is plausibly construed as having been agreed to remain conditional upon the jointly understood reason for the payment being substantially fulfilled, with this reason being D's performance of the promised gardening work.

Where there is a failure of a jointly understood reason for a performance, the ground for restitution is better understood as failure of condition and not failure of consideration. One reason for this is the fact that there is a failure of a jointly understood reason for a performance does not point towards a normative explanation for awarding restitution. By contrast, the concept of failure of condition directs attention to what justifies restitution, which is to give effect to an agreement that D's entitlement to the performance rendered remained subject to a now failed condition. If there is a choice regarding the label to be used for a ground for a legal response, that label should focus attention on what justifies the response. Further, the concept of consideration in the context of contract formation is not synonymous with a jointly understood reason for a performance, which is ripe to cause confusion regarding the scope of failure of consideration as a ground for restitution.[80]

There are, however, cases where it is plausible to regard restitution as being awarded in response to a failure of consideration, in the sense of a failure of the juristic reason for a performance, but not a failure of an agreed condition: it is submitted that if the concept of failure of consideration is to be used, it ought to be confined to these cases. An example is cases involving the performance of a contractual obligation that has been rescinded ab initio. Where a contract

[79] Burrows, 'Conditional Intention as an Unjust Factor' (n 65) 345–46.
[80] ibid.

is rescinded ab initio, the legal relations the agreement gave rise to are deemed to have never existed.[81] If restitution was awarded in this circumstance on the grounds of a failure of condition, the rescinded contract would still be being treated as rendering D's entitlement against C to a performance as conditional, and to that extent still affecting the legal relations between them. Further, even if a narrower interpretation of rescission ab initio is adopted, whereby rescission ab initio does not completely wipe out the parties' agreement, it is still implausible to regard failure of condition as the ground for restitution. This is because there is no authority for the proposition that the claimant must plead and prove that an agreed condition has, as a consequence of rescission, failed before restitution is awarded. Rather, rescission alone suffices to justify restitution of a performance of the now rescinded contract.

By contrast, it is possible to regard a failure of consideration (in the sense of the failure of the juristic reason for a performance) as justifying restitution where there is a performance of an obligation that has been rescinded ab initio.[82] To explain why, it is helpful to consider the example of rescission for fraudulent misrepresentation. Where a contract is rescinded because of a fraudulent misrepresentation, it has never been suggested in the authorities that for C, the representee, to be entitled to restitution, C must prove that its performance of the contract, in addition to entry into the contract, was caused by the misrepresentation. Nor has it ever been held that if C's performance of the contract was undertaken due to the misrepresentation, but the contract is not rescinded, C will be entitled to restitution of any performance of the contract.[83] This suggests that where C performs a contractual payment obligation that is subsequently rescinded due to D's fraudulent misrepresentation, restitution is not awarded in response to D's misrepresentation but the rescission of the contract's obligations.[84] In these circumstances, failure of consideration and not failure of condition is appropriately regarded as the ground for restitution. The juristic reason (ie, consideration) for the performance was C's contractual obligation to undertake the performance. When the performance was undertaken, there was a juristic reason for the performance in the form of a contractual obligation. Following rescission, that juristic reason was nullified, making it possible to speak of the juristic reason and hence consideration for the performance as having failed.

It would, however, almost certainly cause confusion to treat failure of condition and failure of consideration as distinct grounds for restitution due to the widespread perception that these grounds for restitution are either synonymous

[81] *Mackender v Feldia AG* [1967] 2 QB 590, 603 (Diplock LJ); *Johnson v Agnew* [1980] AC 367, 393 (Lord Wilberforce); *Islington London Borough Council v Uckac* [2006] 1 WLR 1303, [26] (Dyson LJ).

[82] D O'Sullivan, S Elliott and R Zakrzewski, *The Law of Rescission*, 2nd edn (Oxford, Oxford University Press, 2014) 292.

[83] *Portman Building Society v Hamlyn Taylor Neck* [1998] 4 All ER 202, 208 (Millett LJ). There may be some doubt about this proposition due to the comments (at [90]) of Lord Burrows and Lady Rose in their dissenting judgment in *Moses v Moses* [2022] UKPC 42.

[84] See also Stevens, *The Laws of Restitution* (n 1) 83–84.

or that failure of consideration has developed into a ground for restitution that should now be understood as failure of condition. For this reason, where restitution is awarded in response to a failure of the juristic reason for a performance, it is preferable to refer to failure of juristic reason as opposed to failure of consideration as the ground for restitution.

An implication of this argument that should be mentioned is that Birks was correct to regard a 'subsequent absence of basis' as justifying restitution. The error by Birks was to use this concept to explain restitutionary awards in too many cases. As argued in chapter 2, contrary to what Birks claimed, restitution is not available in response to a 'subsequent absence of basis' in cases involving the performance of a terminated contract or the performance of an unenforceable contract. But a 'subsequent absence of basis', in the sense of a failure of the juristic reason for a performance after the performance has taken place, is plausibly regarded as justifying restitution where the juristic reason for a performance, such as a contractual obligation, has been rescinded ab initio.

B. No Consideration

i. *The Case for No Consideration*

As foreshadowed, an objection that may be raised to the agreement theory is that the theory cannot explain cases involving restitutionary awards of payments made under void contracts. This is because to award restitution for a failure of condition where a contract is void would mean that the parties' contract was not truly void, as their agreement would still be affecting the legal relations between them.

However, as discussed in chapter 1, there is no logical reason why the parties' agreement should be treated as a complete nullity in every case where their contract is void. It will depend upon the interpretation of the statute or the general law rule rendering the contract void. Sometimes, only the obligations intended to be created by the agreement should be regarded as a nullity, meaning that it will still be possible for the agreement reached, including the conditions forming part of that agreement, to be recognised as a matter of fact and to have legal effects. In such cases, there is nothing problematic with treating the failure of an agreed condition as potentially justifying an award of restitution.[85] That being said, as discussed below, it will usually be more straightforward for restitution to be claimed on the grounds of 'no consideration'.

But this does not eliminate the objection raised. This is because, as also observed in chapter 1, there are plausibly cases where what it means for the parties' contract to be void is that their agreement (in addition to the obligations that agreement purported to create) is a complete nullity. In response, it is now argued that the ground for restitution

[85] Although, as will become apparent below, restitution should also be possible on the grounds of 'no consideration'.

in such cases is not failure of condition but what the cases have often referred to as 'no consideration', which denotes the absence of a juristic reason for a performance at the time it was rendered.[86] In other words, it is claimed that a failure of condition is not the reason for restitution in certain cases involving payments made under a void contract (ie, those where the contract is void in the sense that the parties' agreement is a complete legal nullity). However, it is shown that this is not problematic for the agreement theory because the cases are consistent with there being another reason for restitution here, which is that there was no juristic reason for the payment.

As a matter of principle, the reason that failure of condition does not provide the ground for restitution in cases involving the performance of a contract that is a complete nullity is that if the parties' agreement could still render D's entitlement against C to a performance rendered subject to one or more conditions, the parties' contract would not be a complete nullity as their agreement would still be affecting the legal relations between them. It follows that, under the agreement theory, failure of condition should not be regarded as the applicable ground for restitution. The question arises whether this view can be reconciled with the authorities.

As discussed in chapter 1, there are numerous nineteenth century decisions where no consideration was regarded as justifying an action for money had and received in respect of a payment made under a void contract. It was also observed that the consideration for a payment was, in this context, originally understood as the obligation to make the payment. The difference between no consideration and failure of consideration was that no consideration provided the basis for an action for money had and received where there was no juristic reason for a payment when it was made.[87] On the other hand, where there was a juristic reason for a payment when it was made but that reason subsequently ceased to exist because, for example, the payment obligation was rescinded ab initio, failure of consideration justified an action for money had and received.[88] To reiterate, this is no longer how failure of consideration is typically understood. Rather, the prevailing interpretation is that in the restitutionary context, a failure of consideration denotes a failure of a jointly understood reason for C conferring an enrichment upon D.

Despite the older decisions where no consideration was regarded as justifying the recovery of a payment made under a void contract, the question arises whether following the incorporation of unjust enrichment into English law in *Lipkin Gorman v Karpnale Ltd*,[89] it remains possible to understand restitutionary awards of payments made under void contracts as awarded for no consideration. The reason the recognition of unjust enrichment is significant to no consideration is that the unjust factors model of unjust enrichment, which English courts

[86] *Westdeutsche Landesbank Girozentrale v Islington London Borough Council* (n 37) 953 (Leggatt LJ).

[87] *Jaques v Golightly* (1746) 2 Black W 1073; 96 ER 632; *Strickland v Turner* (n 74); *Re Phoenix Life Assurance Co* (n 72).

[88] *Giles v Edwards* (1797) 7 TR 181; 101 ER 920.

[89] *Lipkin Gorman v Karpnale Ltd* [1991] 2 AC 548.

have arguably adopted at least in part,[90] apparently denies that the absence of a juristic reason for a performance justifies restitution.[91] It is also noteworthy that no current textbook treats no consideration as a basis for restitution.

The leading case following *Lipkin Gorman* involving a claim for restitution of a payment made under a void contract is *Westdeutsche Landesbank Girozentrale v Islington London Borough Council*.[92] The claimant bank paid £2,500,000 to the defendant council under an interest rate swap. The defendant council also made payments to the bank under the swap totalling £1,354,474. When the swap was still open, it was discovered that the contract was void as ultra vires and the bank sought restitution of the balance of its £2,500,000 payment.

At first instance, Hobhouse J held that the bank was entitled to restitution because there was an 'absence of consideration and not [a] failure of consideration' for the payment.[93] In the Court of Appeal, Dillon LJ considered that there was 'no consideration for the payment by the bank of the £2.5m and therefore the balance which has not so far been repaid by the council can be recovered'.[94] Leggatt LJ held that '[t]here can have been no consideration under a contract void ab initio. … As it was, they were not performing the contract even in part: they were making payments that had no legal justification, instead of affording each other mutual consideration for an enforceable contract.'[95] Each of these statements supports no consideration as the ground for restitution.

In the House of Lords, Lord Goff, without reviewing the authorities or having the benefit of argument on the point, suggested that there was force in the academic criticisms that had been made of no consideration.[96] The criticisms Lord Goff was referring to are discussed below; none are persuasive. Lord Goff went on to observe that 'it may be right to regard the ground of recovery as failure of consideration'.[97] The only other member of the House of Lords to comment on the ground for restitution was Lord Browne-Wilkinson, who suggested, in passing, that the bank had an 'action at law to recover the moneys paid as on a total failure of consideration'.[98] It is unclear what Lord Browne-Wilkinson meant by a total failure of consideration, and whether his Lordship regarded total failure of consideration as distinct from what Hobhouse J and the Court of Appeal had respectively referred to as absence of consideration and no consideration.

[90] *Deutsche Morgan Grenfell v Inland Revenue Commissioners* [2007] 1 AC 558; *Samsoondar v Capital Insurance Company Ltd* [2021] 2 All ER 1105.

[91] A Burrows, 'Absence of Basis: The New Birksian Scheme' in A Burrows and A Rodger (eds), *Mapping the Law: Essays in Memory of Peter Birks* (Oxford, Oxford University Press, 2006) ch 2; G Virgo, *Principles of the Law of Restitution*, 4th edn (Oxford, Oxford University Press, 2024) ch 6.

[92] *Westdeutsche Landesbank Girozentrale v Islington London Borough Council* (n 37).

[93] ibid 930.

[94] ibid 944.

[95] ibid 953.

[96] *Westdeutsche Landesbank Girozentrale v Islington London Borough Council* [1996] AC 669, 683.

[97] ibid.

[98] ibid, 714.

Almost every textbook now takes the position that failure of consideration, in the sense of a failure of a jointly understood reason as opposed to the juristic reason for an enrichment, generally provides the ground for restitution of a payment made under a void contract.[99] The case that is usually cited for that proposition is *Guinness Mahon & Co Ltd v Kensington and Chelsea Royal London Borough Council*.[100] The claimant bank entered into an interest rate swap with the defendant council. After the swap had closed, it was discovered that the contract was void as ultra vires and the bank successfully claimed restitution of payments it had made under the swap.

Morritt LJ characterised the ground for restitution as a 'total failure of consideration'.[101] In support, his Lordship referred to the Court of Appeal's decision in *Westdeutsche* and suggested that restitution had there been awarded 'on the basis of a total failure of consideration'.[102] This part of Morritt LJ's judgment is difficult to interpret. As observed, in *Westdeutsche* the Court of Appeal awarded restitution to the bank based on no consideration and not total failure of consideration. Morritt LJ must either have failed to appreciate that the Court of Appeal had regarded no consideration and total failure of consideration as distinct grounds for restitution or, more likely, have been using total failure of consideration to mean there was no juristic reason for the payment, which is what the Court of Appeal in *Westdeutsche* had labelled no consideration.

Waller LJ suggested that there was 'force in the argument that "absence" consideration as opposed to "failure" of consideration should not by itself be a ground for restitution'.[103] But his Lordship went on to observe that '[no consideration] has in fact been approved by the Court of Appeal [in *Westdeutsche*] and we are bound by it'.[104] Waller LJ therefore did not decide the case based on a failure of consideration.

Robert Walker LJ agreed with Leggatt LJ's statement in *Westdeutsche* that where a payment is made under a void contract, there is no consideration for the payment.[105] His Lordship later observed that the bank was entitled to restitution because there was a 'total failure of consideration, in that neither side to the supposed contract undertook any valid obligation, or there was, in Hobhouse J's preferred expression, absence of consideration'.[106] One reading of this passage is that Robert Walker LJ did not consider no consideration and total failure of consideration distinct grounds for restitution. Another is that Robert Walker LJ regarded either failure of consideration or no consideration as the ground for restitution. Irrespective of which interpretation is correct, Robert Walker LJ did not

[99] See, eg, Burrows, *The Law of Restitution* (n 75) 385–97; Virgo, *Principles of the Law of Restitution* (n 91) 367–68.

[100] *Guinness Mahon & Co Ltd v Kensington and Chelsea Royal London Borough Council* [1998] 3 WLR 829.

[101] ibid 841.

[102] ibid 834, 838.

[103] ibid 842.

[104] ibid 844.

[105] ibid 850.

[106] ibid 850.

decide that failure of consideration as opposed to no consideration provided the ground for restitution.

There are several cases following *Guinness Mahon* containing dicta to the effect that a payment made under a void contract is generally recoverable for a failure of consideration or what courts, following certain commentators, have occasionally referred to as 'failure of basis'.[107] An example is *DD Growth Premium 2X Fund v RMF Market Neutral Strategies (Master) Ltd*, where Lord Sumption and Lord Briggs, without considering the authorities, suggested that where a payment is made under a void contract, the payment is generally recoverable as there is a 'failure of basis'.[108]

The cases following *Lipkin Gorman* cannot be regarded as having established that failure of condition is the applicable ground for restitution of a payment made under a void contract. A previously well-established doctrine such as no consideration does not cease to exist because it has been forgotten or its meaning lost for a short period. There has also not been a proper review of the authorities concerning the applicable ground for restitution following the decisions in *Westdeutsche* at first instance and in the Court of Appeal,[109] where, after considering many of the relevant authorities, both courts concluded that no consideration justified restitution.

Although the language of no consideration has some pedigree in the cases, given the confusion it has engendered in the context of payments made under void contracts and the ambiguity in the concept of consideration, it is best avoided. A preferable label for this ground for restitution is 'no juristic reason', which makes clear that restitution is being awarded in response to there having been no juristic reason for the payment.

ii. Objections to No Consideration

As Lord Goff observed in *Westdeutsche*, there have been criticisms of the view that no consideration, or what has just been suggested is better labelled no juristic reason, provides the ground for restitution of a payment made under a void contract. Although it is not strictly necessary to examine these criticisms, they are worth discussing because they help to elucidate why commentators have been resistant to no consideration. One objection to no consideration is that there is little support for it as a ground for restitution in the authorities.[110] As discussed in chapter 1, this is incorrect: there are numerous nineteenth century decisions where no consideration was regarded as justifying an action for money had and received.

[107] *Haugesund Kommune v Depfa ACS Bank* [2012] QB 549, [62] (Aikens LJ); *Sharma v Simposh* [2013] Ch 23, [20]–[25] (Toulson LJ).

[108] *DD Growth Premium 2X Fund v RMF Market Neutral Strategies (Master) Ltd* [2018] Bus LR 1595, [60].

[109] This is also true of *Guinness Mahon & Co Ltd v Kensington and Chelsea Royal London Borough Council* (n 100).

[110] A Burrows, 'Swaps and the Friction between Common Law and Equity' [1995] 3 *Restitution Law Review* 15, 17.

A second objection is that if no consideration was a ground for restitution, every gift would be prima facie recoverable.[111] But this objection misunderstands no consideration, which is not synonymous with an absence of consideration of the kind required to form a contract. As Leggatt LJ observed in *Westdeutsche*, in the restitutionary context no consideration refers to the absence of a legally recognised justification for a performance,[112] and it is well-established that a gift provides such a justification.[113]

A third objection is that there is no compelling reason for awarding restitution of a payment made under a void contract if the contract has been fully 'performed' on both sides or where the payor has received the counter-performance for the payment, which would be a consequence of recognising no consideration as a ground for restitution.[114] But no consideration does not necessarily lead to this result. Where a void contract has been fully performed, or the payor has received the counter-performance for the payment, there is a countervailing reason against awarding restitution. This reason is that the payor has consented to the position they find themselves in, in the sense that the payor expected to and agreed to end up in substantially the same position that it is now in relative to the payee, making the payor undeserving of restitution.[115]

A final objection is that the underlying justification for awarding restitution of payments made under a void contract is not that there was no juristic reason for the payment but that D was unjustly enriched because C's intention to benefit D was defective.[116] However, it remains intensely controversial whether a defect in C's intention to benefit D provides a convincing reason for ordering D to make restitution.[117]

iii. No Consideration and Services

There is a question as to whether no juristic reason provides a ground for restitution of a performance of services under a void contract. This question arises because services are not always a juristic event. Unlike payments or transfers of rights, the provision of services does not necessarily alter the legal entitlements of the service provider and recipient of the services. It is therefore possible that no juristic reason does not justify restitution of a performance of services because non-juristic events do not require a juristic justification.

[111] ibid 17.

[112] *Westdeutsche Landesbank Girozentrale v Islington London Borough Council* [1994] 1 WLR 938, 953.

[113] *Garland v Consumers' Gas Co* (2004) 237 DLR (4th) 385, [44] (Iacobucci J).

[114] Birks, *An Introduction to the Law of Restitution* (n 54) 216–27.

[115] Stevens, *The Laws of Restitution* (n 1) 76–78, 369–70. For some judicial support for this analysis, see *Linz v Electric Wire Co of Palestine Ltd* [1948] AC 371, 377 (Lord Simonds).

[116] Burrows, 'Swaps and the Friction between Common Law and Equity' (n 110) 17.

[117] F Wilmot-Smith, 'Should the Payee Pay?' (2017) 37 *OJLS* 844; Stevens, *The Laws of Restitution* (n 1) ch 4.

In cases involving services performed under a void contract, courts have generally justified awarding quantum meruit on the basis that C's services were 'freely accepted' by D.[118] But the fact that services were 'freely accepted' does not identify a reason (let alone a good reason) for awarding quantum meruit to D, and free acceptance is not a ground for restitution in English law.[119]

One view is that, in void contract cases, quantum meruit may be awarded to enforce a genuine implied promise to pay the reasonable value of the services that arose due to D's free acceptance of the services in circumstances where, objectively considered, the services were performed in the expectation of payment by C. But where a contract is void, this does not mean that, factually, the parties' agreement does not exist. This is important because it is implausible to regard there as being a separate agreement existing alongside the void contract containing an enforceable implied promise to pay for the services performed pursuant to the void contract.

A different explanation for awarding restitution of a performance of services under a void contract (in the sense of an agreement that is a complete legal nullity) is that although it is unnecessary for there to be a juristic reason for a performance of services, in circumstances where the parties objectively intend for there to be a juristic reason for a performance of services, the absence of this juristic reason may justify restitution. Thus, where C performs a service under a void contract, the parties intend for there to be a juristic reason for C's performance of the services in the form of C's contractual obligation to provide the services. If that obligation turns out not to exist, restitution should generally be awarded because the parties objectively intended for there to be a juristic reason for the services but that juristic reason does not exist.

IV. Implications

The focus of this chapter now turns to certain implications of preferring the agreement theory of failure of condition to the absence of basis and qualified intention theories.[120] This section demonstrates that the adoption of the agreement theory has consequences for when failure of condition is the applicable ground for restitution; when counter-restitution should be required; whether it is necessary for a contract to have been terminated before restitution may be awarded; and the availability of a change of position defence. Further consequences of preferring the agreement theory to other theories of failure of condition are discussed in subsequent chapters.

[118] *Craven-Ellis v Canons Ltd* [1936] 2 KB 403, 409 (Greer LJ), 414 (Greene LJ).
[119] *Barton v Morris* (n 19) [230].
[120] The implied promise theory is not discussed further because it is not a theory of failure of condition.

A. Applicable Ground for Restitution

One of the implications of preferring the agreement theory to the absence of basis and qualified intention theories concerns the circumstances in which failure of condition is the applicable ground for restitution, which in turn has consequences for which cases should be regarded as materially alike. This point is most easily explained having regard to the following examples:

(1) C pays £10,000 to D in the performance of a void contractual payment obligation.

(2) C pays £10,000 to D in the performance of a contractual payment obligation in exchange for D's performance of a dependent obligation to undertake certain work on C's land. Before D has started performing the work, C elects to rescind the contract ab initio for D's fraudulent misrepresentation.

(3) C pays £10,000 to D in the performance of a contractual payment obligation in exchange for D's performance of a dependent obligation to undertake certain work on C's land. Before D has started performing the work, C terminates the contract for D's repudiation.

In each scenario, C is prima facie entitled to restitution of its £10,000 payment from D. But there is a difference between what the agreement; absence of basis; and qualified intention theories of failure of condition regard as the event triggering that entitlement. In the previous section, it was argued that under the agreement theory, restitution should generally be regarded as being awarded in each scenario in response to different events. In scenario (1), such an award responds to there having been no juristic reason for the payment when it was made. In scenario (2), restitution is awarded in response to the juristic reason for the payment, which was C's contractual payment obligation, being deemed to have never existed following the rescission of the contract ab initio. In scenario (3), restitution is awarded in response to the failure of a condition that the parties agreed D's entitlement against C to the payment made remained subject to.

Under the absence of basis theory, at a general level, restitution is awarded in response to the same event in each scenario, with this event being the absence of a juristic reason for the payment. But only in scenario (3) does a failure of condition cause there to be an absence of a juristic reason for the payment. In scenario (1), there was never a juristic reason for the payment, meaning one cannot regard the failure of a condition as causing the absence of juristic reason. In scenario (2), following the rescission of the contract, the payment obligation C performed is deemed to have never existed, with the consequence that there was an absence of any juristic reason for the payment. In scenario (3), as explained in chapter 2, for an absence of basis to provide the ground for restitution, C's payment obligation must be treated as having been conditional upon D not repudiating the contract when D had not substantially performed its dependent obligation.

For the qualified intention theory, restitution is awarded in response to the same event in scenarios (1) and (3). This event is that C intended for D's entitlement to the benefit conferred via its payment to remain subject to a condition that has now failed, and a reasonable person in D's position would have known that C intended for D's entitlement to the benefit conferred to remain subject to this condition. In scenario (1), D's entitlement to the benefit C conferred is generally regarded as having been conditional upon the benefit having been conferred in the performance of a valid obligation[121] or, on a slightly different view, on the condition that D was obliged to counter-perform.[122] Those who endorse the qualified intention theory also sometimes suggest that C may alternatively be entitled to restitution in this circumstance on the basis that C's mistaken belief that it was obliged to make the payment caused C to make the payment.[123] In scenario (3), the condition that is generally regarded as failing is that D failed to perform its dependent obligation.[124] As regards scenario (2), proponents of the qualified intention theory usually reject failure of condition as the ground for restitution and maintain that restitution is awarded due to the mistake induced by D's misrepresentation.[125]

One reason these competing characterisations of the ground upon which restitution is awarded are practically significant concerns the cases that are appropriate to analogise from. So, there is authority suggesting that in cases involving the performance of void contracts, counter-restitution is generally required.[126] For the qualified intention theory, like cases being treated alike, this suggests that counter-restitution should (at least generally) be required in other contexts where failure of condition is believed to be the ground for restitution, such as scenario (3), where there is a claim to recover a performance of a contract that has been terminated. For the absence of basis theory, such authority suggests that counter-restitution should generally be required in scenarios (2) and (3).

In contrast, given that according to the agreement theory restitution is not awarded in scenario (1) in response to a failure of condition, cases holding that counter-restitution should be required in a claim to recover a performance of a void contract have little bearing upon whether counter-restitution is required where there is a failure of an agreed condition. And from the standpoint of the agreement theory, counter-restitution often should not be required because it would undermine the parties' agreement. Consider this example: C makes an advance payment of £10,000 in exchange for D's performance of an entire obligation to provide certain building work on C's land. The agreement is unenforceable. When D has performed half of the work, the agreement is terminated for D's repudiation. Under the agreement theory, D should not be entitled to counter-restitution. As D's obligation to provide the work was entire, to become unconditionally entitled

[121] Burrows, *The Law of Restitution* (n 75) 386.

[122] J Goodwin, 'Failure of Basis in the Contractual Context' [2013] 21 *Restitution Law Review* 24, 41.

[123] See eg, P Birks, 'No Consideration: Restitution after Void Contracts' (1993) 23 *University of Western Australia Law Review* 195, 198–99; Burrows, *The Law of Restitution* (n 75) 386.

[124] Birks, *An Introduction to the Law of Restitution* (n 54) 223.

[125] Burrows, *The Law of Restitution* (n 75) 246–48.

[126] *Hicks v Hicks* (1802) 3 East 17; 102 ER 502; *School Facility Management v Governing Body of Christ the King College* (n 68).

to any part of C's advance payment, D had to substantially perform the work.[127] To require C to make counter-restitution of the part of the work that D performed would undermine that agreement because it would, in practice, mean that D was unconditionally entitled to part of C's advance payment, despite it having been agreed that D was not so entitled in the circumstances.

B. Necessity of Termination

Another example:[128]

> C and D enter into a contract whereby D agrees to provide 10 security guards to protect C's office buildings each month for three years at a price of £100,000 per month, with £1.2 million payable annually in advance. After the first year, C discovers that due to an oversight no guards were provided for June. C does not terminate the contract but brings a claim for restitution of £100,000 for a failure of condition.

According to the absence of basis theory advanced by Birks, in cases where C undertakes a contractual performance in exchange for D's provision of a counter-performance which D wrongfully fails to provide, what may justify restitution is that a failure of counter-performance conferring a power to terminate 'invalidates' the obligation C performed, thereby resulting in an absence of basis.[129] As far as I am aware, Birks never directly addressed what the position was where a failure of counter-performance conferred a power to terminate that was not exercised. His analysis does, however, suggest that a claim for restitution should be denied here. For Birks, 'nullity, termination, terminability, and voidability' were what meant that an enrichment conferred in the performance of a contract may have no 'valid basis'.[130] Where a party has a power to terminate but elects not to exercise that power, the contract is no longer 'terminable'. It would therefore seem that for Birks there is a 'valid basis' for the enrichment in such circumstances. If this is the correct interpretation, given that in the above example C refrained from exercising any power to terminate it might have had, there is a 'valid basis' for C's £100,000 payment for June, meaning that there is no justification for restitution. C would therefore be limited to a claim for damages.

Whether termination should be required under the qualified intention theory is not straightforward. Where a benefit is conferred in the performance of a contractual obligation, there will have been a juristic reason for the conferral of the benefit. It is an underexplored question within unjust enrichment theory

[127] See further chapter 5, text to n 46.

[128] This example is taken from R Stevens, 'Private Law and the Form of Reasons' in A Robertson and J Goudkamp (eds), *Form and Substance in the Law of Obligations* (Oxford, Hart Publishing, 2019) 140–41.

[129] P Birks, *Unjust Enrichment*, 2nd edn (Oxford, Oxford University Press, 2005) 142.

[130] ibid 126.

whether, and if so when, restitution of benefits conferred in the performance of an obligation, arising from a contract or otherwise, should be available and why.[131] But there now generally seems to be an acceptance that where there was a juristic reason for the conferral of a benefit, this usually provides a good reason against awarding restitution.[132] This is significant because, as Lord Burrows has observed in his academic writing:

> [o]ne might think that to allow restitution [for a failure of condition of a benefit conferred in the performance of a valid contract] is inconsistent with the general rule that an unjust factor does not render an enrichment at the claimant's expense unjust where the enrichment was owed to the defendant by the claimant under a valid contractual obligation. In other words, one might here say that there should be no restitution because despite the unjust factor of failure of condition, there is a justifying factor because of the existence of the contract.[133]

Although Burrows recognises that termination does not rescind a contract's obligations ab initio, he claims that 'it would appear that, in relation to unjust enrichment, a terminated or unenforceable contract is not being treated in the same way as a fully valid contract'[134] when it comes to whether there was a juristic reason for the conferral of a benefit. Burrows therefore appears to be (tentatively) claiming that: (1) where there was a juristic reason for the conferral of a benefit, restitution for 'unjust enrichment' should generally be denied; and (2) where a benefit is conferred in the performance of a contract, to remove the juristic reason for a benefit conferred in the performance of the contract, it is necessary for the contract to have been terminated.[135]

The difficulty is that it is not clear how termination removes the juristic reason for a contractual performance without doing violence to the idea that termination only discharges obligations that have not unconditionally accrued. Further, following the performance of a contractual obligation, the obligation performed (and hence juristic reason for the performance) ceases to exist. Unless termination rescinds the obligation performed ab initio, it is therefore unclear how termination can remove the juristic reason for a performance. If it is necessary for a contract to be terminated before restitution for a failure of condition may be awarded, the reason for this cannot be that termination removes the juristic reason for a contractual performance.

The foregoing is equally true regarding the performance of unenforceable contracts. As discussed in chapter 1, unenforceable contracts still confer legally recognised rights, duties, powers, etc, upon the parties to the agreement.

[131] Although see KV Krishnaprasad, *Unjust Enrichment and Countervailing Obligations* (Oxford, Hart Publishing, 2025).

[132] Mitchell, Mitchell and Watterson, *Goff & Jones* (n 9) chs 3 and 4; Burrows, 'Conditional Intention as an Unjust Factor' (n 65) 348–49.

[133] Burrows, 'Conditional Intention as an Unjust Factor' (n 65) 349.

[134] ibid.

[135] cf Burrows, *The Law of Restitution* (n 75) 327.

Consequently, where an unenforceable contract is performed, the party undertaking the performance will, despite the agreement's unenforceability, still have owed an obligation to undertake the performance,[136] meaning there will have been a juristic reason for the performance. It is mysterious why the fact that the parties to an unenforceable contract do not have a right against a court to an order enforcing the obligations the agreement created has the effect that those obligations do not provide a juristic reason for a performance of the agreement. In addition, if the unenforceability of an agreement meant that the obligations created by an unenforceable contract do not provide a juristic reason for a performance of the agreement, contrary to what the authorities suggest,[137] every payment made in the performance of an unenforceable contract should prima facie be recoverable.

Under the agreement theory of failure of condition, depending on the construction of the contract, C should potentially be entitled to restitution of £100,000 in the above example, despite the contract not having been terminated. The most plausible construction of the contract is that each month D's entitlement against C to £100,000 out of the £1.2 million annual advance payment remained conditional upon the services D was obliged to perform that month being substantially provided. Consequently, if D failed to substantially perform its service obligation for one month, there would be a failure of condition in respect of D's entitlement against C to £100,000 out of the £1.2 million advance payment, entitling C to restitution.

C. Change of Position Defence

Another consequence of preferring the agreement theory to other theories of failure of condition concerns the possibility of a change of position defence. It is now argued that from the standpoint of the absence of basis and qualified intention theories, it is plausible to regard change of position as a defence to restitutionary claims for a failure of condition. By contrast, according to the agreement theory, there should never be a change of position defence to such claims.

i. Authorities

The possibility of a defence of change of position to at least certain claims for restitution was first explicitly recognised by the House of Lords in *Lipkin Gorman*. In that case, Lord Goff held that there may be a change of position defence where D's 'position has so changed that it would be inequitable in all the circumstances to require him to make restitution, or alternatively to make restitution in full'.[138] Subsequent decisions suggest that the defence may be available to a party, D, whose

[136] An exception is where the agreement is unilateral.
[137] *Thomas v Brown* (1876) 1 QBD 714.
[138] *Lipkin Gorman v Karpnale Ltd* (n 89) 580.

position has changed in good faith[139] following the receipt of, or in the anticipation of receiving,[140] an enrichment so that D would suffer detriment[141] if D was required to make restitution to C of the whole of, or a part of, the enrichment.[142] Where the defence applies, D is excused from being required to make restitution to the extent of its change of position.[143]

The prevailing view is that change of position is a defence to all or most claims for restitution within the law of unjust enrichment, including failure of condition.[144] An example provided by Burrows where the defence should be available in response to a claim for restitution for a failure of condition is as follows:[145] C makes an advance payment of £5,000 to D in exchange for D's performance of an obligation to provide certain work on C's house. Due to the payment, and before the work has commenced, D spends £3,000 in good faith purchasing materials required to perform the work and £2,000 on a trip to Australia. D's obligation to perform the work is then frustrated. According to Burrows, D 'ought to have a change of position defence which includes the expenses of the holiday'.[146]

There is some support for a change of position defence to restitutionary claims for a failure of condition.[147] For example, in *School Facility Management Ltd v Governing Body of Christ the King College*, the claimant school made payments under a void finance lease. In anticipation of receiving these payments, the defendant payee made payments to a third party in good faith. [148] The school later sought restitution of the payments it had made for a 'failure of basis'. Foxton J rejected the school's claim, among other reasons, because the payee had changed its position in anticipation of receiving the payments.[149] In *Banca Intesa Sanpaolo SPA v Comune Di Venezia*,[150] Foxton J re-iterated his view that change of position is a defence to restitutionary claims for a failure of condition, rejecting certain arguments to the contrary. However, in both of these cases the parties' contract was void. It may therefore be that the applicable ground for restitution ought to have

[139] ibid 580 (Lord Goff); *Niru Battery Manufacturing Co v Milestone Trading Ltd* [2003] 2 All ER 706, [135] (Moore-Bick J).

[140] *School Facility Management Ltd v Governing Body of Christ the King College* (n 68). See also *Dextra Bank & Trust Co Ltd v Bank of Jamaica* [2002] 1 All ER 193, [38] (Lord Goff).

[141] *Lipkin Gorman v Karpnale Ltd* (n 89) 580 (Lord Goff); *David Securities Pty Ltd v Commonwealth Bank of Australia* (1992) 175 CLR 353, 385 (Mason CJ, Deane, Toohey, Gaudron, and McHugh JJ); *Australian Financial Services and Leasing Pty Ltd v Hills Industries Ltd* (2014) 253 CLR 560, [77] (Hayne, Crennan, Kiefel, Bell, and Keane JJ).

[142] Whether the defence only applies in these circumstances remains an open question.

[143] *Lipkin Gorman v Karpnale Ltd* (n 89) 580 (Lord Goff).

[144] ibid 579–80 (Lord Goff); *Haugesund Kommune v Depfa ACS Bank* (n 107) [122] (Aikens LJ); *David Securities Pty Ltd v Commonwealth Bank of Australia* (n 141) 385 (Mason CJ, Deane, Toohey, Gaudron, and McHugh JJ); J Edelman and E Bant, *Unjust Enrichment*, 2nd edn (Sydney, Hart Publishing, 2016) 352.

[145] Burrows, *The Law of Restitution* (n 75) 546. See also Edelman and Bant, *Unjust Enrichment* (n 144) 352.

[146] ibid. The parties' entitlements in this scenario would be governed by the Law Reform (Frustrated Contracts) Act 1943.

[147] *Haugesund Kommune v Depfa ACS Bank* (n 107) [122] (Aikens LJ).

[148] *School Facility Management Ltd v Governing Body of Christ the King College* (n 68).

[149] ibid [499]–[500].

[150] *Banca Intesa Sanpaolo SPA v Comune Di Venezia* [2022] EWHC 2586 (Comm), [393]–[402].

been 'no consideration', in which case there can be no objection to a change of position defence.[151]

Other cases tend to suggest that if change of position does provide a defence to restitutionary claims for a failure of condition, it has a narrow operation. In *Haugesund Kommune v Depfa ACS Bank*,[152] the claimant bank entered several swap contracts with Norwegian public authorities. The public authorities lacked the capacity to enter into the swaps, which it was held meant the swaps were void.[153] The bank sought restitution of payments it had made under the swaps for a total failure of consideration. In response, the public authorities argued that they had a change of position defence because they had suffered losses on investments made with the funds the bank had advanced. The Court of Appeal rejected the defence on the basis that, by investing the money, the public authorities had taken the risk that they would not be able to repay the sum the bank had advanced.[154]

A case that is sometimes regarded as casting doubt upon the existence of a change of position defence in the failure of condition context is *Goss v Chilcott*.[155] A company loaned $30,000 to the defendants on the security of a mortgage. In a separate transaction, the defendants on-lent the $30,000 to a director of the company. The director fraudulently altered the mortgage instrument, which had the effect of discharging the defendants' obligation to repay the principal sum advanced. The company's liquidator later sought restitution of the $30,000 for either a failure of consideration or mistake. One of the arguments made by the defendants, rejected by the Privy Council, was that they had a change of position defence.[156] However, change of position only appears to have been raised as a defence to the mistake claim.[157]

ii. Position in Principle

Ultimately, whether there should be a change of position defence to restitutionary claims for a failure of condition depends upon whether the justification for the change of position defence provides a good reason for the defence's recognition in this context. Several justifications have been provided for the defence, the most prominent of which are as follows. The first is that the defence ensures that a defendant who has acted in good faith is only required to make restitution of the part of an enrichment it still has.[158] Call this the disenrichment justification.

[151] *South Tyneside Metropolitan Borough Council v Svenska International* (n 72).

[152] *Haugesund Kommune v Depfa ACS Bank* (n 107).

[153] It is difficult to justify such contracts being void as opposed to unenforceable.

[154] *Haugesund Kommune v Depfa ACS Bank* (n 107) [125]–[126] (Aikens LJ). This is circular as the public authorities can only be regarded as having taken this risk if they in fact had no change of position defence.

[155] *Goss v Chilcott* (1996) AC 788.

[156] ibid 798.

[157] ibid 798–99.

[158] Burrows, *The Law of Restitution* (n 75) 526–27. See also *Test Claimants in the FII Group Litigation v Her Majesty's Revenue and Customs Commissioners (No 5)* [2015] STC 1471, [354], [413] (Henderson J).

A second justification is that the change of position defence ensures blameless defendants are not left worse off.[159] Call this the protecting blameless defendants justification.

A final justification is that the defence ensures equal protection is given to the parties' interests.[160] Call this the equality of treatment justification.[161] To clarify this justification, imagine that C makes a payment of £50 in the mistaken belief that it owed this sum to D. Due to the payment, D spends £50 in good faith on a dinner that it would not otherwise have purchased. In this scenario, the equality of treatment justification maintains that C is 'unjustly disenriched' by £50 because of its mistaken payment and that D is also unjustly disenriched by £50 because it changed its position by spending £50 in the mistaken belief that it was not liable to make restitution to C. To require D to make restitution would, the justification claims, fail to afford equal protection to D of the interest underlying C's mistake claim.[162]

The plausibility of these justifications for the change of position defence does not need to be examined. It suffices to consider whether any of them provides a good reason for recognising the defence in the failure of condition context. As foreshadowed, the preferable view is that the answer differs depending upon which theory of failure of condition is adopted. To demonstrate why, another example is helpful. Suppose that C performs an obligation to pay £10,000 in advance in exchange for D's performance of a dependent obligation to construct and deliver a boat to C. It is also agreed that D's entitlement to any part of the £10,000 payment is to remain conditional upon D's construction and delivery of the boat, and that title to the boat is to remain with D until delivery. Assume further that C knows that D needs this sum to purchase the materials required to perform the work. Due to C's advance payment, D changes its position by spending £10,000 on materials required. The contract is then terminated for C's repudiation.[163] The value of the partly built boat plus the materials D purchased is £6,000, meaning that D has changed its position to the extent of £4,000.

From the perspective of the qualified intention theory, each of the preceding justifications for the change of position defence applies. Following D's good faith purchase of the materials and part performance of the work, D's enrichment was

[159] C Webb, *Reason and Restitution: A Theory of Unjust Enrichment* (Oxford, Oxford University Press, 2012) 219–21; Stevens, *The Laws of Restitution* (n 1) 354–56; *Australian Financial Services and Leasing Pty Ltd v Hills Industries Ltd* (n 141) [157] (Gageler J). The 'irreversible detriment' rationale for the defence also appears to be informed by the idea that innocent defendants should not be left worse off: see E Bant, *The Change of Position Defence* (Oxford, Hart Publishing, 2009) 130–37; *Australian Financial Services and Leasing Pty Ltd v Hills Industries Ltd* (n 141) [24] (French CJ).

[160] J Edelman, 'Change of Position: A Defence of Unjust Disenrichment' (2012) 92 *Boston University Law Review* 1009; R Grantham 'Change of Position-Based Defences' in E Bant, K Barker and S Degeling (eds), *Research Handbook on Unjust Enrichment and Restitution* (UK, Edward Elgar Publishing, 2020) ch 21.

[161] Edelman refers to this justification as 'unjust disenrichment': (n 160) 1011, 1022, 1033.

[162] It is controversial what this interest is.

[163] Unless an advance payment is a deposit, a repudiating party is generally able to recover the payment if it has become impossible for the repudiating party to earn the agreed counter-performance: *Mayson v Clouet* [1924] AC 980.

reduced from £10,000 to £6,000, meaning D was disenriched by £4,000. The protecting blameless defendants rationale is also applicable, as D changed its position in good faith by spending part of the advance payment in preparation for the performance of the contract and would be left worse off by £4,000 if it made restitution of the whole of the £10,000 payment. As to the equality of treatment justification, it can be said that D, to a reasonable person in C's position's knowledge, intended for the expenditure D incurred acquiring the materials to be conditional upon D not being wrongly deprived by C of an opportunity of performing its obligation to undertake the work.[164] When the contract was terminated, that condition failed, with the consequence that D was unjustly disenriched.

The position is slightly more complex regarding the absence of basis theory. Recall that under this theory what justifies restitution is that there is a failure of a condition that the juristic reason for the conferral of an enrichment was subject to. It is difficult to see how this justification could undermine the protecting blameless defendants rationale for the change of position defence. As to the disenrichment justification, insofar as D must have been enriched at C's expense for restitution for a failure of condition to be awarded, this justification also appears applicable. Equality of treatment cannot, however, justify a change of position defence under the absence of basis theory. Rather, where, for example, D has changed its position by conferring an enrichment on a third party, T, and there is no juristic reason for T's enrichment, this should not give D a defence against C but a claim for restitution against T.

Under the agreement theory, change of position should never be a defence to restitutionary claims for a failure of condition. If D could rely upon such a defence, D would be treated as entitled against C to a performance rendered, or part of a performance rendered, despite the parties having agreed that D was not so entitled in the circumstances.[165] So, in the above example, despite D having changed its position in good faith, this should not provide D with a defence as it would mean that D was unconditionally entitled to £4,000 out of the £10,000 payment despite the parties having agreed that D's entitlement to any part of the £10,000 payment made remained conditional upon D's construction and delivery of the boat to C.[166]

For the agreement theory, cases where a change of position defence might be thought to apply should be dealt with having regard to whether the parties' agreement provided that, in circumstances where D changed its position in a particular way, D was to become unconditionally entitled to either the whole of the performance rendered by C to D, or to the performance rendered to the extent of D's change of position. To clarify, consider a case where C and D enter into a contract whereby D is obliged to build C a house. Under the contract, C is obliged

[164] This appears to be Edelman's analysis of such a scenario: see Edelman, 'Change of Position: A Defence of Unjust Disenrichment' (n 160) 1023–24, 1031.
[165] See also Stevens, 'The Unjust Enrichment Disaster' (n 1) 587.
[166] Note that D will still have a claim for damages arising from C's breach of contract.

to pay £50,000 to D in advance, which C does. The payment is not a deposit. Now compare these two possible subsequent events:

(1) D changes its position by spending £30,000 on materials required to perform the work. The contract is then terminated for C's repudiation.

(2) D changes its position by spending £30,000 paying off a gambling debt. The contract is then terminated for C's repudiation.

Under the agreement theory, whether C is entitled to restitution in either scenario depends upon whether it was agreed that D was unconditionally entitled to the part of the payment it spent, or the payment to the extent of its change of position in circumstances where D changed its position by spending part of the sum paid on materials or paying off a gambling debt. It is unlikely that it was agreed that if D changed its position by spending the money paying off a gambling debt, D was to become unconditionally entitled to any part of the payment made, but it is a reasonable possibility in a case where D changed its position by purchasing materials required to do the work.

V. Conclusion

This chapter began by explaining that the justification for restitutionary awards for a failure of condition is to ensure that D is not entitled against C to a performance rendered by C or an act performed by C for D, in circumstances where the parties agreed that D was not so entitled. Consideration was next given to the requirements that must be satisfied for an agreement to render D's entitlement to a performance undertaken or an act performed conditional, and therefore capable of justifying an award of restitution. In this regard, it was shown that before restitution for a failure of condition may be awarded, the parties should, on an objective analysis, need to have intended for their agreement that D's entitlement against C to a performance rendered or an act performed was to remain subject to a condition to be legally effective.

The chapter then clarified the difference between failure of condition; failure of consideration; and no consideration, and the circumstances in which they should be regarded as justifying restitution. It was explained that failure of condition should not be treated as the ground for restitution of a performance of a contract that has been rescinded ab initio or which is void in the sense of a complete nullity. Instead, in cases involving a performance of a rescinded contract, failure of consideration, or what is better labelled failure of juristic reason, should be regarded as the ground for restitution. In cases involving a performance of a void contract, it was suggested that no consideration, or what is better labelled no juristic reason, should generally be the ground for restitution. It was further explained that failure of condition should not provide a ground for restitution if the parties' contract is void in the sense that their agreement is a complete nullity, and only potentially an alternative ground where the contract is void in the sense that only the obligations the parties' agreement purported to create are a nullity.

Finally, the chapter examined certain implications of preferring the agreement theory to the absence of basis and qualified intention theories. It was demonstrated that there is a divergence between these theories regarding when failure of condition is the applicable ground for restitution; the circumstances in which counter-restitution should be required; whether it should be necessary for a contract to have been terminated before restitution may be awarded; and the existence of a change of position defence to restitutionary claims for a failure of condition.

4

Enrichment at The Expense of

I. Introduction

This chapter argues that D should not need to have been enriched at C's expense before C may be entitled to restitution for a failure of condition. Rather, it should suffice that there has been a payment by C to D, a performance of a service by C for D, or a transfer of a right from C to D on an agreed condition that has now failed.

The chapter begins by examining whether D must be, and should need to be, enriched at C's expense in a claim for restitution for a failure of condition. Consideration is then given to what should be required if enrichment and at the expense of are not elements of the claim. Finally, the implications of D not having to be enriched at C's expense in the failure of condition context are discussed.

II. Enrichment

A. Meaning

The prevailing view is that, in the law of unjust enrichment, an enrichment is something capable of being exchanged for money that was of value to D at the time of receipt.[1] Something is generally regarded as of value to D if it is something that D wanted.[2] This interpretation of enrichment does not track the ordinary meaning of enrichment. To be enriched is the opposite of suffering a loss. To suffer a loss is to be made worse off relative to a particular baseline. To be enriched is to be made better off relative to a particular baseline.[3] Sometimes enriched is used to mean that someone is better off than they previously were. This is a historical

[1] P Birks, *Unjust Enrichment*, 2nd edn (Oxford, Oxford University Press, 2005) ch 3; M McInnes, 'Enrichment' in E Bant, K Barker and S Degeling (eds), *Research Handbook on Unjust Enrichment and Restitution* (UK, Edward Elgar Publishing, 2020) 238–44; C Mitchell, P Mitchell and S Watterson, *Goff & Jones on Unjust Enrichment*, 10th edn (UK, Sweet & Maxwell, 2022) 86–94, [4-03]–[4-29]. The most extensive discussion of enrichment is contained in A Lodder, *Enrichment in the Law of Unjust Enrichment and Restitution* (Oxford, Hart Publishing, 2012) chs 1–5.

[2] J Edelman, 'The Meaning of Loss and Enrichment' in R Chambers, C Mitchell and J Penner, *Philosophical Foundations of the Law of Unjust Enrichment* (Oxford, Oxford University Press, 2009) 211–12; A Burrows, *The Law of Restitution*, 3rd edn (Oxford, Oxford University Press, 2011) 51–52, 56–57.

[3] See also R Stevens, *The Laws of Restitution* (Oxford, Oxford University Press, 2023) 57.

baseline. If, for example, C repairs D's fence, D may be better off than it was before C performed the repair work and, in that sense, enriched. But enriched is also used to mean that D is counterfactually better off. So, if C repaints D's house, D may be better off than it would have been if its house had not been repainted and, in that sense, enriched. Something may enrich D relative to a historical baseline but at the same time cause D a loss relative to a counterfactual baseline, and vice versa.

It is also worth observing that D may be enriched relative to a certain baseline at a particular time, but at another time D is not. In the view of unjust enrichment theory, whether D has been enriched is to be assessed at the time of receipt of a payment, performance of a service, or transfer of a right.[4] It has never been satisfactorily explained why this is the case. Indeed, it is odd for the law to disregard subsequent events in the context of enrichment, given that subsequent events are generally relevant to determining loss.

The idea that for D to be enriched D must have received something capable of being exchanged for money that was of value to D at the time of receipt is, as a definition of enrichment in ordinary English, underinclusive. Some things enrich us that are not capable of being exchanged for money, such as love and friendship. Such a definition is also overinclusive. Assessed against a counterfactual baseline, the fact that D received something of value to it does not necessarily mean that D is enriched. Suppose, for example, that C and D enter into a contract whereby C undertakes to repair D's fence in exchange for payment of £1,000 following substantial completion. After the contract has been formed, but before the work has begun, X, an experienced builder, offers to repair D's fence for free as a favour. D declines the offer because of its contract with C. X responds that if C does not do the work, he would still be happy to do it. C repairs D's fence as promised. In this example, D has received something of value to it (ie, the repair work it wanted), but from a counterfactual standpoint, D has not been enriched as D could have obtained the work from X for free. Indeed, D is counterfactually worse off[5] due to C having performed the work, because D has come under a £1,000 payment obligation that it otherwise would not have.

It is also not difficult to construct examples where D has received something that it wanted where D is not, due to having received this thing, better off relative to a historical baseline. Imagine that D asks C to paint its house cyan in exchange for payment of £10,000 in the belief that painting the house this colour will increase its value. C paints D's house cyan and D pays the agreed sum. Due to the horrendous colour, which D also does not like following completion, D's house decreases in value by £50,000. In this example, D has received something from C that it wanted (ie, the work painting its house cyan). However, D is not better off relative to a historical baseline. Before D had its house repainted, the house's value was £1,000,000. After the house was repainted, the house's value is £950,000. D has also paid C £10,000. D is therefore worse off than it was before the house was painted.

[4] Edelman, 'The Meaning of Loss and Enrichment' (n 2) 224–25.

[5] At least at the time of completion of the work.

The authors of *Goff & Jones on Unjust Enrichment* claim that the concept of enrichment, as it is used in the law of unjust enrichment, is a 'term of art'.[6] That is, according to the authors, it 'is a technical legal question whether a defendant has received an "enrichment" that is capable of forming the subject matter of a claim'.[7] This interpretation of enrichment has some support in the authorities. In *Barnes v Eastenders Cash & Carry Plc*, for example, Lord Toulson said that 'the words "unjust" and "enrichment" are both in some respects terms of art'.[8]

There are serious difficulties with using enrichment as a term of art.[9] First, unless enrichment is the concept that most accurately describes the subject matter of the restitutionary claim, it is difficult to understand why this language should be used.[10] Secondly, given that the word enrichment is prominent in ordinary language, for the law to use enrichment in a way that does not conform with ordinary usage is likely to lead to confusion and error. Finally, to maintain that enrichment is a term of art opens unjust enrichment theory up to the objection that the concepts it is using suffer from the same flaw as those used by the quasi-contractual theory it sought to replace, which is that they do not accurately identify what is justifying the claim.

B. Applicability to Failure of Condition: The Authorities

Academic and judicial discussions of enrichment have generally taken place when considering claims for restitution for mistake. Limited attention has been given to whether enrichment is and should be an element of claims for restitution on other grounds, such as failure of condition. The remainder of this section examines whether D must be, and should need to be, enriched before restitution for a failure of condition may be awarded. In the next section, the relevance of at the expense of to restitutionary claims for a failure of condition is discussed. Together, these sections argue that although recent cases do suggest that D must be enriched at C's expense for C to be entitled to restitution for a failure of condition, this is not justified.

i. Authorities that Support Enrichment as an Element of the Claim

Following the decision in *Banque Financière v Parc (Battersea) Ltd*,[11] where the House of Lords first gave support to the idea that enrichment and at the expense of are elements of at least certain restitutionary claims, there are several cases

[6] Mitchell, Mitchell and Watterson, *Goff & Jones* (n 1) 86, [4-04]. See also McInnes, 'Enrichment' (n 1) 238.

[7] Mitchell, Mitchell and Watterson, *Goff & Jones* (n 1).

[8] *Barnes v Eastenders Cash & Carry Plc* [2015] AC 1, [100] (Lord Toulson).

[9] See also Stevens, *The Laws of Restitution* (n 3) ch 4.

[10] In support of the view that this is the most accurate terminology, see A Burrows, 'In Defence of Unjust Enrichment' (2019) 78 *CLJ* 521, 532.

[11] *Banque Financière v Parc (Battersea) Ltd* [1999] 1 AC 221, 227.

containing statements to the effect that D must have been enriched before C may be entitled to restitution for a failure of condition.[12] There are also cases at appellate level that support this requirement.[13]

An example is *Bellis v Challinor*.[14] The defendant firm of solicitors received into its client account payments from the claimants, who were a group of investors in a scheme. The total amount paid to the client account was £2.28 million. Most of that sum was paid on by the solicitors to the Royal Bank of Scotland to reduce a debt that Albemarle Fairoaks Ltd (AFL) owed on a bridging loan. The solicitors also transferred part of the sum that the investors had paid from their client account to their office account to discharge a debt that AFL owed. AFL later became insolvent, and a claim was brought by the investors for restitution of payments made to the solicitors for either mistake or failure of condition.[15]

Briggs LJ held that an insurmountable obstacle to the investors' claim was that the solicitors were not enriched because, from the moment of receipt, the solicitors held the funds on trust for AFL.[16] His Lordship also thought that the transfer to the office account did not enrich the solicitors. Although Briggs LJ did not decide whether there was a failure of condition, given that failure of condition was one of the grounds upon which the investors put their claim and his Lordship regarded the fact that the solicitors had not been enriched as fatal to that claim, Briggs LJ's judgment supports the need for an enrichment.

The Supreme Court case that comes closest to holding that D must be enriched before C may be entitled to restitution for a failure of condition is *Benedetti v Sawiris*.[17] The facts that are presently relevant, and which were not set out in the previous chapter, were that Mr Benedetti was paid €67 million by Mr Sawiris for services he had performed in relation to a successful corporate takeover. Benedetti regarded this sum as inadequate. Sawiris later offered to pay Benedetti a further €75.1 million for his services. The offer was rejected, and Benedetti sought restitution for a failure of condition.[18] At first instance, Benedetti was awarded €75.1 million. The Court of Appeal reduced this sum to €14.52 million. In the Supreme

[12] See, eg, *Cobbe v Yeoman's Row Management Ltd* [2008] 1 WLR 1752, [40] (Lord Scott); *Barnes v Eastenders Cash & Carry plc* (n 8) [101] (Lord Toulson); *Benedetti v Sawiris* [2014] AC 938, [10]–[11] (Lord Clarke); *Menelaou v Bank of Cyprus UK Ltd* [2016] AC 176, [21]–[24] (Lord Clarke); *Barton v Morris* [2023] AC 684, [78] (Lady Rose), [231] (Lord Burrows); *Attorney General of Trinidad and Tobago v Trinsalvage Enterprises Ltd* [2023] UKPC 26, [18]–[21] (Lord Burrows); *H & P Advisory Ltd v Barrick Gold (Holdings) Ltd* [2025] EWHC 562 (Ch), [174], [176]–[196]. See also the earlier decision in *Cantiare San Rocco SA v Clyde Shipbuilding and Engineering Co* [1924] AC 226, 235 (Lord Birkenhead LC).

[13] A first instance case where it was part of the *ratio* is *H & P Advisory Ltd v Barrick Gold (Holdings) Ltd* (n 12).

[14] *Bellis v Challinor* [2015] EWCA Civ 59.

[15] ibid [111].

[16] ibid [114]–[115].

[17] *Benedetti v Sawiris* (n 12).

[18] At first instance and in the Court of Appeal, the claim was framed as one for restitution for 'free acceptance'. However, as Lord Burrows has argued, free acceptance is not a ground for restitution in English law: *Barton v Morris* (n 12) [229]–[231] (Lord Burrows). See also A Burrows, 'Free Acceptance in the Law of Restitution' (1988) 104 *LQR* 567.

Court, Benedetti sought to have the €75.1 million award restored and Sawiris the €14.52 million award reduced to nothing.

The difficulty Benedetti confronted was that despite having been paid €67 million, his services only had a market value of €36.3 million. To overcome this hurdle, Benedetti argued, first, that a principle of 'subjective devaluation' should be recognised, which provided that if D subjectively valued C's services at less than the market value, the sum C is entitled to as restitution should be reduced below market value to reflect the value D placed on the services. Benedetti then argued that if subjective devaluation was permissible, 'subjective revaluation' also should be,[19] meaning that D should be required to make restitution of an amount exceeding the market value of C's services if D subjectively valued the services over market value.

Lord Clarke, with whom Lord Kerr and Lord Wilson agreed, held that the starting point in determining the sum C is entitled to as restitution is the market value, but that the sum awarded could be reduced if D could prove that it subjectively valued the services below market value.[20] His Lordship was, however, unprepared to recognise subjective revaluation.[21] Lord Reed rejected the possibility of subjective revaluation[22] and expressed serious doubt over subjective devaluation.[23] Lord Neuberger considered it difficult to envisage any scenario where subjective revaluation should be possible[24] and refrained from expressing a concluded view on whether subjective devaluation should be recognised.[25] Due to the court's rejection of subjective revaluation, Benedetti's appeal failed and the €14.52 million he had been awarded was reduced to nothing.

The ratio of *Benedetti v Sawiris* is that C is not entitled to restitution for a failure of condition in an amount exceeding the market value of services performed on a condition that has now failed if D subjectively valued the services over market value. That proposition does not require a conclusion that for C to be entitled to restitution for a failure of condition D must have been enriched at C's expense. However, when examining how the sum that is awarded as restitution should be determined, a majority of the court did give support to a principle of subjective devaluation. If the subject matter of a claim for restitution is not D's enrichment, it is very difficult to justify subjective devaluation. This is because subjective devaluation is premised on the idea that what restitutionary awards reverse is an enrichment, and that whether and to what extent D has been enriched depends upon the subjectivity of value.[26]

[19] As Lord Clarke observed (at [18]): 'The present case does not, of course, concern subjective devaluation, but that is the hook on which Mr Howard seeks to hang the principle of "subjective revaluation".'

[20] *Benedetti v Sawiris* (n 12) [15]–[18].

[21] ibid [29].

[22] ibid [120]–[121].

[23] ibid [110]–[119], [122]–[123].

[24] ibid [195]–[198].

[25] ibid [188].

[26] Burrows, *The Law of Restitution* (n 2) 47.

Despite there now being cases that support the proposition that D must be enriched before C is entitled to restitution for a failure of condition, there is no case where direct consideration has been given to this issue – such a requirement has simply been assumed. As the Court of Appeal observed in *Regina (Kadhim) v Brent London Borough Council Housing Benefit Review Board*,[27] 'a subsequent court is not bound by a proposition of law which, although part of the ratio of an earlier decision, had been assumed to be correct by the earlier court and had not been the subject of argument before, or consideration by, that court.' This point is apposite because there are prominent cases, which are now discussed, that are inconsistent with the proposition that D must have been enriched before C is entitled to restitution for a failure of condition, even on unjust enrichment theory's own (flawed) interpretation of enrichment.

ii. Authorities Against Enrichment as an Element of the Claim

In *Planché v Colburn*,[28] the defendants, Mr Colburn and Mr Bentley, who were partners in a publishing business, decided to publish a series of children's books. The claimant, Mr Planché, was commissioned to write two volumes on the history of costume in exchange for payment of £100 following the writing and delivery of each completed volume. The publishers later decided to abandon the series, by which time Planché had undertaken considerable work on the first volume. Planché never tendered either volume, and the contract was abandoned. Planché later brought an action for non-contractual quantum meruit and was awarded £50.

From a modern perspective, the most plausible interpretation of the non-contractual quantum meruit award in *Planché* is that it was an award of restitution for a failure of condition.[29] On this analysis, the condition that failed was that Planché was wrongly deprived by the publishers of an opportunity of earning a contractual right to payment for his work. The reason the award to Planché cannot be regarded as damages is that the court considered one of the critical issues before it, which it answered in the negative, as being whether the contract remained on foot.[30] This was significant because at the time the case was decided an award of non-contractual quantum meruit was unavailable for work undertaken in the performance of a contract that had not been rescinded ab initio.[31]

Before the development of unjust enrichment theory, *Planché* was uncontroversial. The reason the case has become so widely discussed is that the result is extremely difficult to reconcile with the idea that D must have been enriched

[27] *Regina (Kadhim) v Brent London Borough Council Housing Benefit Review Board* [2001] QB 955, [35].

[28] *Planché v Colburn* (1831) 8 Bing 14; 131 ER 305. In addition to the case discussed, see *Menetone v Athawes* (1764) 3 Burr 1594; 97 ER 998.

[29] See also Stevens, *The Laws of Restitution* (n 3) 132. cf Burrows, 'Free Acceptance in the Law of Restitution' (n 18) 588–89.

[30] *Planché v Colburn* (n 28) 15–16; 305–06 (Tindal CJ).

[31] *Hulle v Heightman* (1802) 4 Esp 75; 170 ER 647. See also J Barton, 'Contract and Quantum Meruit: The Antecedents of Cutter v Powell' (1987) 8 *Journal of Legal History* 48, 54–55; T Baloch, *Unjust Enrichment and Contract* (Oxford, Hart Publishing, 2009) 132–35.

for C to be entitled to restitution for a failure of condition. As Lord Burrows has observed in his academic work, to regard the publishers as enriched would involve 'an unrealistic and over inclusive notion of benefit'.[32] Justice Edelman and Professor Bant have also claimed that the publishers were not enriched because what the publishers requested was 'the completed manuscript' and not the 'service of writing' the manuscript.[33]

Professor Birks was more receptive to the idea that the publishers had been enriched.[34] For Birks, this turned upon whether Planché had 'conferred part of the contractual performance or merely put himself to preparatory trouble and expense'.[35] If the latter interpretation was correct, Birks thought the publishers were not enriched. However, if the proper construction of the contract was that the publishers had commissioned the work researching and writing the book, as well as the book itself, Birks considered it plausible to regard the publishers as enriched.

Professor McInnes has gone further and argued that the publishers were enriched. He suggests that 'the mere fact that the parties ultimately contemplated a manuscript is no reason to deny that the publisher was enriched by the services themselves. The manuscript would have constituted an enrichment, but so too did the underlying services.'[36] It is not clear what the argument is here. It can be accepted that where C performs a service towards the production of an end product, the service might sometimes enrich D if the end product is not produced, but that does not explain why on the facts of *Planché* the publishers were enriched.

The better view is that the publishers were not enriched. As observed, the prevailing view among unjust enrichment theorists is that D is enriched where D receives something of monetary value that was of value to it at the time of receipt. If a publishing business commissions someone to write and deliver a book to issue the book for sale, what the publisher generally wants and is of value to the publisher is the completed book that it commissioned so that it can publish and sell the book. Although the research and writing Planché did before the contract was abandoned may have been a valuable thing, this is not the same as the work having been of value to the publishers.

It might be objected that Planché's obligations were to spend time writing a book *and* to deliver the book. To the extent that Planché had performed part of his obligation to write the book, the publisher received something of value. The implicit premise of this objection is that if C spends time doing something that C owed an obligation to D to do, then D is enriched by C doing that thing. That premise cannot be accepted, as *Planché* itself demonstrates. If one poses the question

[32] Burrows, *The Law of Restitution* (n 2) 46.

[33] J Edelman and E Bant, *Unjust Enrichment*, 2nd edn (Sydney, Hart Publishing, 2016) 151. See also C Mitchell and C Mitchell, '*Planché v Colburn* (1831)' in C Mitchell and P Mitchell (eds), *Landmark Cases in the Law of Restitution* (Oxford, Bloomsbury Publishing, 2006) 92.

[34] P Birks, 'In Defence of Free Acceptance' in A Burrows (ed), *Essays on the Law of Restitution* (Oxford, Clarendon Press, 1991) 140–41.

[35] ibid 140.

[36] McInnes, 'Enrichment' (n 1) 260–61.

of whether the publisher received something of value to it from Planché merely spending time writing the manuscript, unless the thought of such a book being written was somehow of value to a commercial publisher, the answer must be 'no'.

Another case involving what would now be regarded as an award of restitution for a failure of condition where the defendant was not enriched is *Pulbrook v Lawes*.[37] The parties entered into an unenforceable contract whereby the claimant agreed to take a lease of the defendant's house if the defendant made certain improvements and alterations to the house, which the claimant agreed to pay £75 towards. Before the lease had been granted, and with the defendant's permission, the claimant made some of the improvements and alterations himself. Due to the defendant's failure to complete the improvements and alterations within a reasonable time, the claimant refused the lease. Blackburn J held that the claimant was entitled to an award of non-contractual quantum meruit for the part of the alterations he had carried out. In reaching that conclusion, his Lordship drew an analogy between the present case and an action for money had and received upon a consideration that failed.[38]

As Burrows observes, 'there are serious difficulties' with regarding the defendant in *Pulbrook v Lawes* as enriched.[39] The defendant, Burrows points out, 'did not request [the "improvements"] but merely permitted the claimant to carry them out' and there was no 'evidence that he was incontrovertibly benefited by realising, or being very likely to realise, the value of the improvements'.[40] Burrows concludes that the case, which he considers should now be understood as involving an award of restitution for a failure of condition, belongs 'alongside several other cases in which the courts have apparently ignored subjective devaluation in treating land improvements as beneficial'.[41]

A more recent case which casts doubt upon D having to be enriched is *Brewer Street Investments Ltd v Barclays Woollen Co Ltd*.[42] The defendants, who were prospective tenants, reached an agreement with the claimant prospective landlords for a lease of premises that was expressed as subject to contract. Before a formal lease had been executed, the parties formed a separate agreement whereby the claimants agreed to make certain alterations to the premises in exchange for reimbursement of the cost of the alterations. Prior to the separate agreement having been formed, the defendants had requested the inclusion of an option to purchase, which the claimants refused. A lease was never granted because the defendants insisted on the option. By this time, substantial work on the alterations had been completed and paid for by the claimants.

[37] *Pulbrook v Lawes* (1876) 1 QBD 284.
[38] ibid 289.
[39] Burrows, *The Law of Restitution* (n 2) 384.
[40] ibid.
[41] ibid 384.
[42] *Brewer Street Investments Ltd v Barclays Woollen Co Ltd* [1954] 1 QB 428.

Somervell and Romer LJJ, in separate judgments, held that the claimants were entitled to be paid the costs they had incurred in having the alterations made, even though the alterations were incomplete.[43] The reason Somervell and Romer LJJ regarded the claimants as entitled to be paid despite the agreement for the lease having been subject to contract is that their Lordships treated the agreement in respect of the alterations as separate from the agreement for the lease.

Denning LJ thought that the defendants had only agreed to pay for the alterations following their completion.[44] As the alterations were incomplete, the defendants' payment obligation had not accrued, with the consequence that the claimants did not have an action for the agreed sum. But Denning LJ held that the claimants were entitled to restitution because the alterations were paid for on 'a fundamental assumption – that the lease would be granted', which turned out to be false.[45] Given that the alterations were carried out on the claimants' land, which the defendants never occupied or received a proprietary interest in, it is implausible to regard the defendants as having received something of value to them and therefore as having been enriched.[46]

C. Applicability to Failure of Condition: Principle

i. *Justification for Enrichment*

The argument made by Birks in support of the proposition that enrichment was an element of restitutionary claims commenced from a belief that there should be 'symmetry' between claims for restitution of payments of money and benefits in kind.[47] For Birks, for the law to be coherent, the same event had to trigger an entitlement to restitution regardless of the form in which a 'transfer of value' took. Thus, if C made a transfer of value to D by mistake, Birks regarded it as incoherent if what C had to prove to be entitled to restitution differed depending upon whether the 'transfer of value' was in the form of a payment of money or the provision of a benefit in kind.

In addition to arguing that it was incoherent for different events to justify a claim for restitution of payments of money and benefits in kind, Birks wanted to demonstrate that this was a viable interpretation of the positive law. A difficulty he confronted was that it appeared the law was more willing to award restitution of transfers of value in the form of payments of money than the provision of benefits in kind.[48] The introduction of enrichment as an element of the claim provided the

[43] ibid 432–35 (Somervell LJ), 438–39 (Romer LJ).
[44] ibid 435.
[45] ibid 436.
[46] cf Birks, 'In Defence of Free Acceptance' (n 34) 283–85.
[47] P Birks, *Restitution – The Future* (Sydney, Federation Press, 1992) 86–91.
[48] P Birks, *An Introduction to the Law of Restitution*, rev edn (Oxford, Clarendon Press, 1989) 112–14.

solution to this perceived problem. Birks argued that the reason the law seemed more prepared to award restitution of payments of money was not that different events triggered an entitlement to restitution depending upon the form of the 'transfer of value', but that where C made a payment of money this was almost always of value to D.[49] By contrast, where C provided a benefit in kind, it was less clear that D had received something of value to it. The introduction of the enrichment requirement was therefore what enabled Birks to maintain that the same event prima facie justified restitution of a 'transfer of value' regardless of the form it took.

The justification provided by Birks, and most other unjust enrichment theorists, for why D should need to have been enriched before C may be entitled to restitution is the protection of D's 'freedom of choice'.[50] As the editors of *Goff & Jones on Unjust Enrichment* observe:

> [t]he common law 'places a premium on the right to choose how to spend one's money', and this right could be unfairly compromised if a defendant were forced to make restitution of the objective value of a benefit which he would only have bought himself at a lower price, or which he would not have bought at all, if he had had a free choice.[51]

The protection of D's freedom of choice is not a convincing justification for the enrichment requirement. Where, for example, C mistakenly performs a service for D, the fact that the service was of value to D does not mean that ordering D to make restitution of the performance of the service does not interfere with D's freedom of choice. D never agreed to pay for the service that C provided or to make restitution, meaning that ordering D to make restitution still interferes with D's freedom of choice. Indeed, even if D had agreed to pay for the service, requiring D to make restitution would interfere with D's freedom of choice because D is being compelled to do something that it might otherwise not have done.

A more plausible justification for enrichment is that, if ordered to make restitution, D should not be left 'worse off', in the sense of being required to give up something of greater value to it than what it directly received from C.[52] So, imagine that while D is away on holiday, C mistakenly repaints D's house. D did not want its house repainted because it could not afford to pay for the work and did not want its house the colour that it was painted. If D was required to make restitution, D would, despite not having committed a wrong, be left 'worse off' in the sense that D would be required to pay a monetary sum to C as restitution exceeding the value to D of what D received.

[49] ibid 116–17.

[50] Birks, *Unjust Enrichment* (n 1) 50, 54–56, 58–59, 62. See also Burrows, *The Law of Restitution* (n 2) 44; Lodder, *Enrichment in the Law of Unjust Enrichment and Restitution* (n 1) 49–51, ch 6; Edelman and Bant, *Unjust Enrichment* (n 33) 16.

[51] Mitchell, Mitchell and Watterson, *Goff & Jones* (n 1) 93, [4-25], quoting *Peel Regional Municipality of Peel v Ontario* [1992] 3 SCR 762, [25] (McLachlin J).

[52] McInnes, 'Enrichment' (n 1) 238. See also *BMW Australia Ltd v Brewster* (2019) 269 CLR 576, [194] (Edelman J).

ii. Enrichment and the Agreement Theory

The difficulty with enrichment as an element of restitutionary claims for a failure of condition is that it may lead to D being treated as unconditionally entitled to a performance C rendered in circumstances where C and D agreed that D was not so entitled. Consider:

> C and D enter into an unenforceable contract whereby C undertakes an entire obligation to manufacture and deliver 10 tractors in exchange for payment of £100,000 following delivery of the tractors. The agreement provides that a title to the tractors is to pass via delivery. After C has manufactured five tractors, but before any of them have been delivered, D repudiates the agreement. C accepts D's repudiation.

In this example, it is implausible to regard the services C provided as being of value to D as D did not receive a title to or use of any of the tractors. D was therefore not enriched. But in general, the proper construction of the agreement in this example is that D's entitlement against C to any part of C's performance of the services remained conditional upon D not wrongly depriving C of an opportunity of earning the agreed counter-performance for C's services. This condition will have failed because there cannot be a delivery of the tractors without a give-and-take.[53] To refuse to award restitution because D was not enriched would be inconsistent with the parties' agreement that D's entitlement to C's performance of the services remained subject to a condition that has now failed. There is no other area where the law refuses to give effect to an agreement on the basis that it would leave one party to the agreement 'worse off', which, as observed, is the best explanation for the enrichment requirement. It follows that in the above example, provided that an award of restitution would not undermine the policy of the statute rendering the agreement unenforceable, C should be entitled to restitution.

There are also cases where it would give rise to something of a legal black hole if restitution for a failure of condition was denied on the basis that D was not enriched. Suppose that C and D enter into an unenforceable contract whereby C, in contemplation of a lease being granted to D, undertakes to make certain improvements to the land in exchange for payment following substantial completion. D never promises to take the lease and does not represent or encourage a belief that a lease has been executed or that there is a lease. After the improvements are complete, D fails to pay the agreed sum and refuses to take the lease. In this example, C would not have an action for the agreed sum, an action for specific performance, or a claim for damages, because the agreement is unenforceable. There would also not be an evidential (ie, common law) or equitable estoppel. If C was not entitled to restitution because D was not enriched, C would therefore be left without any recourse, which is a difficult result to accept.

[53] Sale of Goods Act 1979, ss 31(2), 37(1)–(2), 61(5).

The argument that is generally made in support of the proposition that D must have been enriched for C to be entitled to restitution for a failure of condition is that if D must be enriched for C to be entitled to restitution for mistake, like cases being treated alike, D should also need to be enriched for C to be entitled to restitution for a failure of condition.[54] The problem with this argument is that once it is recognised that the justification for restitution for a failure of condition is to give effect to an agreement, one cannot safely analogise from restitutionary claims for mistake to restitutionary claims for a failure of condition, as the justification for awarding restitution on these grounds is different. As observed in chapter 1, on the orthodox view, the justification for restitution for mistake relates to C's intention to enrich D having been defective, which is a quite different reason for restitution to giving effect to an agreement.

III. At the Expense of

If enrichment is not an element of a claim for restitution for a failure of condition, it might seem unusual that at the expense of could be. There is force in this observation. But it is at least conceivable that for C to be entitled to restitution, D must have received something at the expense of C, whether or not that is an enrichment. For completeness, this section therefore examines whether at the expense of is and should be an element of restitutionary claims for a failure of condition. It is argued that although such a requirement now probably exists, it cannot be justified.

A. Meaning

The leading examination of the content of at the expense of is contained in *Investment Trust Companies (in liq) v Her Majesty's Revenue and Customs Commissioners*.[55] In that case, Lord Reed held that D's enrichment will not necessarily be at C's expense if D 'directly' receives an enrichment from C.[56] Rather, C must generally 'incur a loss through the provision of the benefit'[57] via 'direct dealings' with D or D's property.[58] Lord Reed did, however, recognise that exceptions might develop[59] and regarded there as being situations that should be treated as equivalent to 'direct dealings'.[60] These exceptions included cases involving the interposition of an agent between the parties; intervening transactions that are a

[54] Birks, *Unjust Enrichment* (n 1) ch 1; Burrows, 'In Defence of Unjust Enrichment' (n 10) 541–42.
[55] *Investment Trust Companies (in liq) v Her Majesty's Revenue and Customs Commissioners* [2018] AC 275 ('*ITC*').
[56] ibid [52].
[57] ibid.
[58] ibid [46], [52].
[59] ibid [50].
[60] ibid [47], [50].

sham; related transactions that are in reality a single scheme; the receipt of a right by D from a third party that C 'can trace an interest' to; and the assignment of a restitutionary right by C to a third party.[61]

The definition of at the expense of provided in *ITC* does not correspond to the ordinary meaning of at the expense of.[62] If something is done or happens at the expense of someone or something else, the thing that has been done or which has happened is to the detriment of someone or something else. For example, a tax cut might benefit the rich at the expense of the poor, or the success of one industry might come at the expense of another. What the words 'at the expense of' therefore mean in the phrase 'enriched at the expense of' in ordinary English is that D has been enriched to C's detriment. The principal difference between this definition of at the expense of and the definition in *ITC* is that it does not contain a requirement of 'direct dealings'.

B. Applicability to Failure of Condition: The Authorities

Until recently, it was difficult to find cases where it formed part of the ratio that at the expense of is an element of a claim for restitution for a failure of condition. However, there has been a recent flurry of first instance decisions involving claims for restitution for a failure of condition, in some of which courts have been called upon to decide whether the defendant's enrichment was at the claimant's expense.[63] In all of these cases, it has simply been assumed that at the expense of is an element of claims for restitution for a failure of condition.

An example is *H&P Advisory Ltd v Barrick Gold (Holdings) Ltd*.[64] The claimant investment bank did substantial work on a merger between two gold mining companies. During this time, the claimant pursued a contractual service agreement, but a contract was never formed. The claimant successfully brought a claim for restitution of the services it provided for a failure of condition and was awarded $2 million. The court rejected an argument that the defendant's enrichment was not at the claimant's expense because the bulk of the work was done by two people, neither of whom was an employee of the claimant at the relevant time.

A Supreme Court case that comes close to holding that at the expense of is an element of restitutionary claims for a failure of condition is *Menelaou v Bank of Cyprus UK Ltd*.[65] The Menelaou parents held a fee simple title to land known as Rush Green Hall. The Bank of Cyprus UK Ltd had a fixed charge over the parents' title. The parents decided to sell Rush Green Hall and use the proceeds to purchase a fee simple title to land known as Great Oak Court. Due to an undertaking by the

[61] ibid [48].
[62] This was recognised by Lord Reed in *ITC*: ibid [41].
[63] See, eg, *H&P Advisory Ltd v Barrick Gold (Holdings) Ltd* (n 12) [197]–[198]; *Tokyo Industries (Live) Ltd v Orbit Tickets Ltd* [2025] EWHC 2074 (Ch), [242]–[245].
[64] *H&P Advisory Limited v Barrick Gold (Holdings) Limited* (n 12) [197]–[198].
[65] *Menelaou v Bank of Cyprus UK Ltd* (n 12).

parents that the bank would be granted a fixed charge over the title it acquired to Great Oak Court, the bank released its charge. The parents registered Great Oak Court in their daughter Melissa's name, who refused to grant the bank the charge.

A majority of the Supreme Court held that the bank was subrogated to an unpaid vendor's lien over Great Oak Court to reverse Melissa's unjust enrichment at the bank's expense.[66] Lord Clarke, with whom Lord Kerr and Lord Wilson generally agreed, regarded Melissa as having been enriched because 'the value of [Great Oak Court] to Melissa was considerably greater than it would have been but for the avoidance of the charge and the Bank was left without the security which was central to the whole arrangement'.[67] His Lordship thought that Melissa's enrichment was clearly unjust, and suggested the applicable 'unjust factor' was either mistake or failure of condition.[68] For Lord Clarke, the real question raised by the case, which his Lordship answered in the affirmative,[69] was whether Melissa's enrichment was at the bank's expense.

Lord Neuberger agreed that the bank was entitled to be subrogated to an unpaid vendor's lien to reverse Melissa's unjust enrichment at the bank's expense.[70] But his Lordship was doubtful that the bank would have had a claim for monetary restitution against Melissa.[71] Lord Kerr and Lord Wilson also considered it 'preferable to leave the availability of a personal claim against Melissa entirely open'.[72] Lord Carnwath decided the case via the application of what his Lordship regarded as 'the traditional rules of subrogation' rather than through the lens of unjust enrichment.[73]

Although Lord Clarke considered the applicable unjust factor to be either mistake or failure of condition, *Menelaou* does not definitively establish that at the expense of is an element of restitutionary claims for a failure of condition. First, subsequent cases have cast serious doubt upon whether subrogation is a response to (or prevents) unjust enrichment.[74] Secondly, it is extremely doubtful that subrogation is a restitutionary response.[75] Thirdly, none of their Lordships in fact decided that the bank's subrogation to an unpaid vendor's lien was justified by a failure of condition. Fourthly, the court did not hold that the bank would have had a monetary restitutionary claim against Melissa for a failure of condition and expressed doubt over whether such a claim would have been available. Finally,

[66] ibid [18] (Lord Clarke), [59], [79], [94]–[96] (Lord Neuberger).
[67] ibid [24].
[68] ibid [21].
[69] ibid [24]–[27].
[70] ibid [95]–[96].
[71] ibid [80]–[82].
[72] ibid [141].
[73] ibid [107].
[74] *Swynson Ltd v Lowick Rose LLP* [2018] AC 313, [30] (Lord Sumption); *Prudential Assurance Co Ltd v Her Majesty's Revenue and Customs Commissioners* [2019] AC 929, [68] (Lord Mance, Lord Reed and Lord Hodge). See also R Gregson, 'Is Subrogation a Remedy for Unjust Enrichment?' (2020) 136 *LQR* 481.
[75] Stevens, *The Laws of Restitution* (n 3) 153–54, 252–56.

there was no dispute concerning whether for restitution for a failure of condition to be awarded D must have been enriched at C's expense.

C. Applicability to Failure of Condition: Principle

i. *Justification for At The Expense Of*

The justification for at the expense of, as it was conceived in *ITC*, is notoriously difficult to pin down.[76] The argument made here is that informing the at the expense of requirement is the idea that D should only be liable for restitution if D was partly responsible for C's provision of the relevant enrichment.[77] D will be partly responsible for C's provision of the enrichment, in the relevant sense, if D was a 'direct cause' of C conferring the enrichment. For present purposes, it is sufficiently precise to say that D is a 'direct cause' of X where something D has done (or refrained from doing) is the temporally most immediate but-for cause by a legal person of X.

One of the principal effects of at the expense of is to limit who C is entitled to restitution against. Compare:

(1) C mistakenly pays £100 to D in cash.

(2) C mistakenly pays £100 to X in cash, who gifts £100 in cash to D the next day. X would not have made the gift to D but for C's mistaken payment.

In both scenarios, D has been enriched due to C's mistaken payment. In scenario (1), C is generally entitled to restitution from D.[78] In scenario (2), C will not be entitled to restitution from D because D's enrichment was not at C's expense.[79] What explains this difference in result?

Where C mistakenly pays X, D will not be a direct cause of C having made the payment. That is, D's conduct will not be the temporally most immediate but-for cause of the mistaken payment. By contrast, where D is the recipient of a mistaken payment, D will be a direct cause of the payment and hence C's conferral of the enrichment. This is because for a payment to be made, there must be an acceptance by the payee or someone acting on the payee's behalf.[80] As Dr Mann famously observed:

> The physical or ministerial aspect of payment involves the delivery of money by one person to another. Where the two persons meet face to face and the debtor seeks to

[76] This is not intended as a criticism of *ITC*.

[77] It is not claimed that this is a good justification but only that this justification has the best fit with the positive law.

[78] *Kelly v Solari* (1841) 9 M&W 54; 152 ER 24.

[79] *Relfo Ltd (in liq) v Varsani* [2014] EWCA Civ 360, [78] (Arden LJ), [114] (Floyd LJ); *ITC* (n 55) [51] (Lord Reed).

[80] *TSB Bank of Scotland plc v Welwyn Hatfield DC* [1993] 2 Bank LR 267, 271 (Hobhouse J); *Commissioners of Customs and Excise v National Westminster Bank plc* [2002] EWHC 2204 (QB), [9]-[10] (Judge Rich QC); *Canmer International Inc v UK Mutual SS Assurance Association (Bermuda) Ltd* [2005] 2 Lloyd's Rep 479, [53] (Gloster J).

> hand to the creditor legal tender, the physical act of delivery, in the absence of some misrepresentation or mistake, will not be achieved without the concurrence of the debtor. Where the relevant contract or the terms of the debt require payment to be made in a particular way as, for example, by payment into an identified account at a particular branch of a named bank, the payment will be effected by payment into that account. Prior authority has been given to discharge the debt or other obligation in that way. The debtor has authorised the bank, or other relevant person, to receive and accept the money on his behalf.[81]

In scenario (1) above, the role played by D in C's conferral of the enrichment is therefore that, but for D's acceptance of C's tender of payment, there would not have been a mistaken payment by C. This will also be the case if the payment C made was via bank transfer. As explained further below, for a payment to be made via bank transfer, there must be an acceptance by D's bank of an instruction by C to credit D's account.[82] The bank's acceptance is attributed to D as the bank is authorised by D as agent to accept instructions to credit its account.[83]

The foregoing interpretation of at the expense of also helps to explain why restitution will be denied in two further situations. The first is where X, who is not acting on C's behalf, mistakenly pays D £100 when, objectively considered, X intended to pay C. Here, C will not be entitled to restitution from D because D's enrichment is not at C's expense.[84] This is consistent with the explanation for at the expense of provided above, as D will not be a direct cause of C's provision of an enrichment to it. Instead, D was a direct cause of X's provision of an enrichment to it.

The second situation is where D receives an 'incidental benefit'. An incidental benefit is a benefit that D obtains as a contingent consequence of something that C has done.[85] An example is an increase in the value of D's property due to C having mistakenly destroyed its own property. Restitution of incidental benefits is generally denied on the basis that such benefits are not at the expense of C,[86] which is again consistent with the above explanation of at the expense of. If, for example, C mistakenly cuts down a tree on its land, thereby increasing the value of D's land due to an improved view,[87] D will generally not be a direct cause of C cutting down the tree. Similarly, if C mistakenly leaves its heater on while it is away on holiday, thereby saving D the cost of using the heater in its upstairs flat,[88] D will generally not have been a direct cause of C heating its flat.

[81] F Mann, *The Legal Aspect of Money*, 5th edn (Oxford, Oxford University Press, 1992) 75.

[82] *Momm v Barclays Bank International Ltd* [1977] QB 790, 803 (Kerr LJ); *Tayeb (Hosni) v HSBC Bank Plc* [2004] EWHC 1529 (Comm), [47] (Colman J).

[83] *Royal Products Ltd v Midland Bank Ltd* [1981] 2 Lloyd's Rep 194, 198 (Webster J); *PT Berlian Laju Tanker TBK v Nuse Shipping Ltd* [2008] EWHC 1330 (Comm), [67] (Christopher Clarke J).

[84] *ITC* (n 55) [50] (Lord Reed).

[85] ibid [52].

[86] ibid [52]–[58].

[87] *Ruabon Steamship Co v London Assurance* [1900] AC 6, 12 (Lord Halsbury LC).

[88] *Edinburgh and District Tramways Ltd v Courtenay* (1909) SC 99, 105 (Lord President Dunedin).

ii. At the Expense Of and the Agreement Theory

It is difficult to envisage many cases where C confers an enrichment upon D on an agreed condition that fails where D is not a direct cause of C's provision of the enrichment. In other words, the at the expense of requirement will almost always be satisfied where C has conferred an enrichment upon D on an agreed condition that has now failed. One example involving a failure of condition where D's enrichment is not at C's expense might be as follows. C performs a service for D on a condition that subsequently fails. The evidence reveals that the service would have been performed by C in the absence of the parties' agreement or anything else done by D. If D's enrichment must have been at C's expense, then, in this example, restitution should be denied because D was not a direct cause of C's provision of the services. It is, however, extremely difficult to see why the fact that D was not a direct cause of C providing the service is a good reason for not giving effect, via a restitutionary award, to the parties' agreement that D's entitlement against C to the performance of the service remained subject to a condition that has now failed. At the expense of should not be an element of a claim for restitution for a failure of condition.

IV. Replacing Enrichment at the Expense of

If enrichment and at the expense of are rejected as elements of restitutionary claims for a failure of condition, a question that arises is what they should be replaced by. It cannot be that a failure of condition alone can justify restitution; there must be something that has occurred and which these awards seek to reverse. This section argues that before C may be entitled to restitution for a failure of condition, C must have made a payment to D, performed a service for D, or transferred a right to D. It is further suggested that, at a higher level of generality, payments, performances of services, and transfers of rights can be classified as either a performance or an act performed.[89]

A. Performance or an Act Performed

For C to be entitled to restitution for a failure of condition against D, it should, as just observed, be sufficient that C has made a payment to D, performed a service for D, or transferred a right to D on an agreed condition that has now failed. Where, for example, C performs a service for D on an agreed condition that has now failed, if the performance of the service was not reversed, D would be entitled against C to the performance of the service despite the parties having agreed that D was not so entitled in the circumstances. Similarly, if C transfers a right to D

[89] cf Stevens, *The Laws of Restitution* (n 3) ch 3.

and the parties agreed that D's entitlement against C to the transfer of the right was subject to a condition that has now failed, if the transfer was not reversed, D would be entitled to the transfer despite the parties having agreed that in the circumstances D was not so entitled.

At a more general level, payments, performances of services, and transfers of rights can be classified as either a performance or an act performed. It is for this reason that previous chapters have (cumbersomely) occasionally referred to D's entitlement against C to a performance rendered or an act performed as remaining conditional. Taking the concept of a performance first, a performance denotes the category of legal event that occurs where C makes a tender to D that is accepted by D.[90] An example is a payment. Where a payment is made in cash, there is a tender of title to the cash by the payor and an acceptance of that tender by the payee. Where a payment is made via bank transfer, assuming the payor and payee's accounts are with different banks, what occurs is the payor instructs its bank to debit its account by a certain sum and to instruct the payee's bank to credit the payee's account by that sum.[91] Upon receiving the instruction, the payor's bank will debit the payor's account. The payor's bank will then instruct the payee's bank to credit the payee's account. If the payee's bank accepts the instruction, there will be a payment. The essential steps in a payment via bank transfer are the same as a payment in cash: the payor's bank's instruction to the payee's bank to credit the payee's account constitutes a tender on the payor's behalf, and the payee's bank's crediting of the payee's account constitutes an acceptance of that tender by the bank on the payee's behalf.

There are, however, cases where restitution for a failure of condition may be awarded where what is reversed is not a performance between C and D but an act that has been performed by C for D. An example is cases involving the provision of a service. One reason a service is not a performance, as performance has been defined, is that for C to provide a service for D, it is unnecessary for there to have been an acceptance by D. For example, if someone comes and repairs my mountain bike without my request or knowledge while I am visiting my parents in New Zealand, they will have provided me with a service even though I did not accept the service. This is not to deny that in virtually every case where C is entitled to restitution of a performance of a service for a failure of condition, there will have been an acceptance by D. The point is that for C to perform a service for D, it is not necessary for there to have been an acceptance.

Another difference between a performance and the mere performance of an act is that the former is a legal event while the latter is not. The sense in which a performance is a legal event is that where a performance takes place, the legal relations of the parties to the performance are necessarily affected. This is illustrated by the example of a transfer of a right. For a right to be transferred from C to D,

[90] For a similar interpretation, see Stevens, *The Laws of Restitution* (n 3) 36–50.
[91] M Bridge and R Cox, *Law of Bank Payments*, 5th edn (UK, Sweet & Maxwell, 2017) 49, [3-004].

there must generally (although not always)[92] be a tender of the right by C to D and an acceptance of that tender by D. When a right is transferred from C to D, C loses a right and D acquires a right. The parties' legal relations are therefore altered.

Where C makes a payment to D, the parties' legal relations are necessarily affected. If C makes a payment to D in cash, C loses a right and D acquires a right to the cash used to make the payment. If C makes a payment to D via bank transfer, both parties acquire a new right against their respective banks.[93] So, if C pays D £1,000 in circumstances where, before the payment, C's credit balance was £2,000 and D's was £3,000, before the payment was made C was owed £2,000 by its bank and D was owed £3,000 by its bank. After the payment, C is owed £1,000 and D is owed £4,000. A right an account holder has against its bank to payment of £1,000 on demand is not the same as a right to payment of £2,000, and a right to payment of £3,000 on demand is not the same as a right to payment of £4,000. The parties have therefore acquired new rights against their banks by virtue of the payment.

By contrast, where C performs a service for D, the parties' legal relations might not be affected by the service's performance. For example, if C gratuitously repairs D's broken laptop, there is unlikely to be a change to the parties' legal relations.

Burrows has argued that the language of performance is:

> odd in the vast majority of restitution cases where one is talking about a (non-contractual) payment by C to D. The language of performance is fine where there has been a request in advance or even, if no request, where services are being rendered. However, it is a very odd use of the English language in a straightforward payment case to talk of performance.[94]

There is force in this argument. As Burrows observes, one would not ordinarily describe a payment that a party was not obliged to make as a performance. It is, however, doubtful that there is any terminology that is apt to describe payments, performances of services, and transfers of rights at a higher level of generality. Burrows suggests 'benefit'.[95] However, as explained, payments, performances of services, and transfers of rights are not necessarily benefits. Further, as discussed above, there are cases where restitution has been awarded where it is implausible to regard the defendant as having received a 'benefit'. Despite being imperfect, the language of performance has been used throughout this book principally to try to make it clear that for C to be entitled to restitution for a failure of condition, D should not need to have been enriched at C's expense. The imperfection of this language must nevertheless be acknowledged, and it is worth repeating that, where

[92] Sometimes a right can be transferred subject to a power to disclaim.

[93] *Commissioner of the Australian Federal Police v Tjongosutiono* [2018] NSWSC 48, [159] (Adams J); *Lordianto v Commissioner of the Australian Federal Police* (2019) 266 CLR 273, [76] (Kiefel CJ, Bell, Keane, and Gordon JJ).

[94] Burrows, 'In Defence of Unjust Enrichment' (n 10) 531–32.

[95] ibid 532.

possible, it is preferable to simply refer to restitution as reversing a payment made, the performance of a service, or the transfer of a right.

B. The Performance must be between C and D

For C to be entitled to restitution of a performance for a failure of condition, it should be necessary for the performance to have been between C and D. If there is a performance between C and X, C should not have a claim for restitution against D. This is because an order requiring D to pay a monetary sum to C to reverse the performance would not be an order for restitution. Thus, suppose that C donates £1,000 to X via bank transfer. The payment was made on an agreed condition between C and D that has now failed. In this scenario, C should not be entitled to restitution for a failure of condition against D. Where C makes a payment of £1,000 to X via bank transfer, a debit of £1,000 is made to C's account and a credit of £1,000 is made to X's account. To require D to pay £1,000 to C where C has paid £1,000 to X cannot be characterised as an award of restitution of the payment, because X will still be in a position where its account has been credited £1,000. That is, from X's perspective, the world will still be the same as if a payment of £1,000 had been made to it by C, which means the payment will not have been reversed if D is ordered to pay £1,000 to C.

C. Act C Performed must have been for D

If the agreement relates to an act performed by C (eg, a service), as opposed to a performance, it should be necessary for the act that C has performed to have been performed *for* D before C may be entitled to restitution for a failure of condition from D. Imagine that X asks C to perform certain work on X's farm gratuitously. C accepts. D, who is not acting on X's behalf, offers to pay £1,000 to C upon completion of the work C undertook to perform on X's farm. C accepts. Assume that the agreement between C and D is unenforceable. After C completes the work, D refuses to pay. The work would have been performed by C even if D had not promised to pay for the work. In this scenario, C should not be entitled to restitution from D because the work was performed by C for X.

The reason it matters whether the act C performed was for D is that if C has performed for X, as opposed to for D, it cannot be said that D's entitlement to C's performance of that act remained conditional. As discussed in chapter 3, what entitlement refers to in this context is D's deservingness of what C has done (or, in the case of a payment or transfer of a right, what has occurred between C and D). If an act is performed by C for X on an agreed condition with D, one would not refer to D's deservingness of what C has done as subject to the condition. Thus, in the example where C performed work for X on its farm, it would be odd to regard C and D as having agreed that D's entitlement to C's performance of the work was conditional. One cannot be entitled or not entitled to something that someone has done for someone else.

It is important to be clear how the claim that for C to be entitled to restitution of a performance of an act for a failure of condition works in cases involving subcontractors. Suppose that D, a subcontractor, enters into an unenforceable contract with C that requires C to perform certain building work on X's land in exchange for payment by D following substantial completion. C substantially performs the work, but D wrongly fails to pay the price. It might be thought that if C's services must have been performed for D, then C should not be entitled to restitution from D because C's services were performed for X. But this is an incorrect interpretation of who, on an objective analysis, C's services were performed for. Where the reason for C's performance of services on X's land is D's obligation to pay for the services upon completion, objectively considered, those services will have been performed for D and not X.[96]

V. Implications

A. Different Results

If D does not need to have been enriched at C's expense for restitution for a failure of condition to be awarded, there are cases where C may be entitled to restitution where it otherwise would not be. One such case, exemplified by *Planché v Colburn*,[97] is where C performs work towards the production of an end product that D receives no part of. So, suppose that C undertakes an entire obligation to manufacture and deliver five lorries in exchange for payment by D following delivery. The contract states that a title to the lorries is to pass via delivery. C performs part of the manufacturing work before the contract is terminated for D's repudiation. At the time of termination, none of the lorries have been delivered. In this scenario, it is implausible to regard D as having received something of value to it and therefore as having been enriched. However, if D does not need to be enriched for restitution for a failure of condition to be awarded, C should still be entitled to restitution because C's performance of the work will have been undertaken for D and on the condition that D does not wrongly deprive it of an opportunity of earning the price.[98]

Another situation where there may be a failure of condition where D has not been enriched is where C performs work at D's request on C's own land in anticipation of a right in relation to the land being conferred upon D, which is not in the end conferred. An example discussed above is *Brewer Street*.[99] Another example is

[96] This is consistent with the result in cases such as *Lumbers v W Cook Builders Pty Ltd (in liq)* (2008) 232 CLR 635 and *Costello v MacDonald* [2012] QB 244.

[97] *Planché v Colburn* (n 28).

[98] *Mann v Paterson Constructions Pty Ltd* (2019) 267 CLR 560.

[99] *Brewer Street Investments Ltd v Barclays Woollen Co Ltd* (n 42).

Waltons Stores (Interstate) Ltd v Maher.[100] During negotiations for a lease of land belonging to Mr and Mrs Maher, Waltons Stores (Interstate) Ltd asked the Mahers to demolish a building on their land and erect a new one. Following this request, the Mahers' solicitors sent the documents that needed to be signed to form a contract for lease. Before Waltons Stores had signed, the Mahers, to Waltons Stores' knowledge, began the requested work. The documents were later returned to the Mahers unsigned along with a letter stating that Waltons Stores did not want to proceed with the lease. By this time, the Mahers had demolished the building and performed part of the work of erecting the new building on their land.

Although *Waltons Stores* was dubiously[101] decided by reference to 'promissory estoppel',[102] it is strongly arguable that there was a failure of condition in respect of the work the Mahers had undertaken that would have justified an award of restitution.[103] The demolition work and part of the work erecting the new building were undertaken by the Mahers at Waltons Stores' request. Waltons Stores had also caused the Mahers to reasonably believe that a contract for lease would be formed between them as a matter of course. In those circumstances, the work that the Mahers performed can plausibly be regarded as having been undertaken on an agreed condition that a lease would subsequently be formed between them. When Waltons Stores refused to proceed, an agreed condition upon which the Mahers had performed the work therefore failed.

Significantly for present purposes, Waltons Stores cannot be regarded as having been enriched at the Mahers' expense. Although the Mahers performed part of the work that Waltons Stores had requested, the demolition of the building and partial erection of a new building were of no value to Waltons Stores in circumstances where Waltons Stores never acquired an interest in or use of the land. If, as has been argued, D does not need to have been enriched at C's expense for C to be entitled to restitution for a failure of condition, the Mahers should have been entitled to restitution because the work they undertook would have been performed on a condition that failed. But if D does need to have been enriched at C's expense for C to be entitled to restitution for a failure of condition, restitution would not have been available to the Mahers.

B. Measure of Restitution

Another implication of the account put forward relates to the measure of the sum awarded as restitution. The leading case to consider the valuation of restitutionary awards for a failure of condition is *Benedetti v Sawiris.*[104] As discussed, in that case a majority of the Supreme Court held that in a claim for restitution for a failure of

[100] *Waltons Stores (Interstate) Ltd v Maher* (1988) 164 CLR 387.
[101] Dubiously because 'estoppel' was being used as a cause of action.
[102] Deane and Gaudron JJ decided the case based upon evidential estoppel by representation.
[103] See also Stevens, *The Laws of Restitution* (n 3) 286–87.
[104] *Benedetti v Sawiris* (n 12).

condition, the sum that C is generally entitled to is the market value to D of the benefit it received, but that the sum C is entitled to will be reduced if D can prove that it valued the benefit at less than market value.[105] In unjust enrichment jargon, 'subjective devaluation' is possible.

The justification that is generally provided for reducing the sum that C is entitled to as restitution below market value based upon subjective devaluation is the same as the justification for D needing to be enriched in the first place. That is, D's 'freedom of choice' would be compromised if D were forced to make restitution of the market value of a benefit it valued at less than market value.[106]

It was argued above that protecting D's freedom of choice is not a convincing rationale for D having to be enriched. Instead, it was suggested that the most plausible explanation of the enrichment requirement is that an award of restitution should not leave D 'worse off', in the sense that D should not be required to give up something of greater value to it than what it directly received from C. This is also the best explanation for reducing the sum that D is entitled to as restitution below market value based upon subjective devaluation. That is, if D had to make restitution to C in an amount exceeding the value to D of the benefit it directly received from C, D would be left 'worse off' if it was required to make restitution of the market value.

Once it is appreciated that restitutionary awards for a failure of condition do not require D to make restitution of an enrichment it received, subjective devaluation becomes implausible. As discussed, what informs subjective devaluation is the idea that what restitutionary awards reverse is an enrichment D received at the expense of C, and that whether and to what extent D was enriched depends upon the value D subjectively placed on what it received. If restitutionary awards for a failure of condition are understood as reversing a performance between C and D, or a performance of an act by C for D, the foundation upon which subjective devaluation rests falls away.[107]

In addition, as argued above, not leaving D 'worse off' provides an unconvincing reason for refusing to award restitution for a failure of condition. The same is true regarding reducing the sum C is entitled to as restitution based upon the value D subjectively placed on the performance or act performed. Imagine that C performs a service for D on a condition that has now failed. Here, the sum that would, as far as money can, reverse C's performance of the service will be the service's market value. If the sum that C was entitled to as restitution could be reduced because D valued the service at less than the market value, the parties' agreement that D's entitlement to the performance of the service remained subject to a condition that has now failed would not be given full effect. This is because D would remain entitled to part of C's performance of the service.

[105] ibid [15]-[18] (Lord Clarke).
[106] ibid [13], [26], [29]; Mitchell, Mitchell and Watterson, *Goff & Jones* (n 1) [4-19].
[107] See also Stevens, *The Laws of Restitution* (n 3) 67–70.

C. Counter-Restitution

One of the most difficult – and, among common lawyers, underexplored[108] – areas of the law of restitution is counter-restitution.[109] Where C brings a claim for restitution against D, C may be required to make counter-restitution even if D has not brought (and, on one view, does not have)[110] a counterclaim against C.[111] Call this the counter-restitution principle.

In the Court of Appeal's decision in *School Facility Management Ltd v Governing Body of Christ the King College*,[112] Popplewell LJ observed that one possible justification for the counter-restitution principle is that 'benefits received by a claimant may prevent, or pro tanto reduce, the enrichment of the defendant, because the latter has paid or provided value to the claimant, in whole or in part, for the benefit he has received in exchange'.[113] If an award of restitution for a failure of condition does not reverse D's enrichment at C's expense, this cannot be the justification for the counter-restitution principle in cases involving a failure of condition.

The central feature of the counter-restitution principle that needs to be explained is why D may be entitled to counter-restitution despite D not having brought a counterclaim.[114] In the failure of condition context,[115] a justification for counter-restitution that accounts for this feature is that D's compliance with a court order to make restitution would cause there to be a failure of condition in respect of a performance that D rendered to C.[116] To clarify, consider the following: C and D enter into an unenforceable contract whereby C undertakes to perform services for D marketing a concert in exchange for payment of £10,000. After the services have been performed, D pays £6,000 to C but refuses to pay the remaining £4,000. Consequently, C terminates the contract and brings a claim for restitution of its performance of the services. The market value of the services performed is £9,000. If D was ordered to make restitution of £9,000 to C, following D's payment of the £9,000, there would be a failure of condition in respect of the £6,000 D previously paid. This is because D will be in a position where it has paid £6,000 to C but the services D paid for have been reversed via the restitutionary award, meaning it is as if D never received the services. To

[108] Counter-restitution has often been discussed by German lawyers: see, eg, R Zimmermann and J du Plessis, 'Basic Features of the German Law of Unjustified Enrichment' [1994] 2 *Restitution Law Review* 14, 41–42; P Hellwege, 'Unwinding Mutual Contracts: *Restitutio in Integrum* v the Defence of Change of Position' in D Johnston and R Zimmermann (eds), *Unjustified Enrichment: Key Issues in Comparative Perspective* (Cambridge, Cambridge University Press, 2002) 258–60; B Häcker, *Consequences of Impaired Consent Transfers* (Oxford, Hart Publishing, 2009) 71–77.

[109] I consider the defence at length in T Pilkington, 'The Counter-Restitution Defence' (forthcoming).

[110] cf *Vodafone Ltd v Office of Communications* [2020] QB 200.

[111] *Kleinwort Benson Ltd v Sandwell Borough Council* [1994] 4 All ER 890, 941 (Hobhouse J). See also Burrows, *The Law of Restitution* (n 2) 569–71.

[112] *School Facility Management Ltd v Governing Body of Christ the King College* [2021] 1 WLR 6129.

[113] ibid [34]. His Lordship did not endorse this justification.

[114] It is likely that the justification for the counter-restitution principle differs depending on the ground for restitution.

[115] In other contexts, the defence is likely a form of statutory set-off: see Pilkington, 'The Counter-Restitution Defence' (n 109).

[116] T Pilkington and D Winterton, 'Void Contracts, Counter-Restitution, and Change of Position' (2022) 138 *LQR* 21.

avoid this result, C should therefore be required to make counter-restitution of D's £6,000 payment. Practically, what this will mean is that the £9,000 C is entitled to as restitution will be netted off against the £6,000 D paid.

D. Subrogation to Discharged Rights[117]

Subrogation to discharged rights refers to a situation where C acquires, independently of an agreement[118] or court order,[119] new rights that are equivalent to the rights that X previously had against D but which have now been discharged.[120] Although the exact circumstances in which subrogation to discharged rights may occur is controversial, in most cases, C will either have: (1) made a payment to X, who is a creditor of D, that discharges a security interest X held against rights belonging D;[121] or (2) made a payment to D, the traceable substitute of which is used by D to discharge a security interest X held against rights belonging to D.[122]

An implication of the arguments of this and the previous chapter is that subrogation to discharged rights is not a restitutionary response to a failure of condition.[123] To re-state, under the account put forward, these restitutionary awards give effect to an agreement between C and D by reversing a payment made by C to D, a performance of service by C for D, or a transfer of a right from C to D. Subrogation reverses none of these things. Instead, where C is subrogated to X's discharged rights, C acquires new rights that are equivalent to the rights X previously had against D, but which have now been discharged. It should also be noted that for C to be subrogated to X's discharged rights against D, it is not necessary for there to be an agreement between C and D or C and X.[124] Accordingly, subrogation to discharged rights is also not a response to the failure of an *agreed* condition but is based on a different principle.[125]

E. Unjust Enrichment and Quasi-Contract

Another, more theoretical, implication of rejecting enrichment and at the expense of as elements of restitutionary claims for a failure of condition is that restitutionary

[117] The principal reason for discussing subrogation to discharge rights here is Lord Sumption's comments (at [30]) in *Swynson Ltd v Lowick Rose LLP* (n 74).

[118] *Banque Financière de la Cité v Parc (Battersea) Ltd* (n 11) 231 (Lord Hoffmann).

[119] *Halifax PLC v Omar* [2002] EWCA Civ 121, [84] (Jonathan Parker LJ).

[120] *Day v Tiuta International Ltd* [2014] EWCA Civ 1246, [42]–[43] (Gloster LJ).

[121] *Butler v Rice* [1910] 2 Ch 277.

[122] *Banque Financière de la Cité v Parc (Battersea) Ltd* (n 11).

[123] For support for the view that subrogation may be a 'restitutionary remedy for unjust enrichment', see Mitchell, Mitchell and Watterson, *Goff & Jones on Unjust Enrichment* (n 1) 1014–23, [39-05]–[39-24]. cf R Gregson, 'Is Subrogation a Remedy for Unjust Enrichment?' (n 74); Stevens, *The Laws of Restitution* (n 3) 153–54, 252–56.

[124] *Banque Financière de la Cité v Parc (Battersea) Ltd* (n 11); *Menelaou v Bank of Cyprus UK Ltd* (n 12).

[125] For a justification of this principle that does not invoke unjust enrichment, see R Gregson, *Subrogation and Marshalling* (London, Hart Publishing, 2024) ch 10; Stevens, *The Laws of Restitution* (n 3) ch 9.

awards for a failure of condition cannot be regarded as forming part of a law of unjust enrichment. If D does not need to have been enriched before restitution may be awarded to C, and if restitutionary awards for a failure of condition do not reverse D's enrichment at C's expense, these awards cannot plausibly be understood as having anything to do with enrichments that are unjust.

Under the agreement theory, restitutionary awards for a failure of condition form part of the law of agreements, of which the law of contract is a part. Such awards are an example of legal significance being given to agreements that are not necessarily contracts, and in a manner that does not involve the enforcement of an agreement. The relevant cause of action is failure of condition: what one pleads is the facts that would establish that a payment was made, service was performed, or transfer of a right was made on an agreed condition, and that condition has now failed.

The label 'quasi-contract' is apt to describe the kind of agreement that may justify restitution in certain cases. 'Quasi' means partly or almost. As discussed in the previous chapter, restitutionary awards for a failure of condition give effect to an agreement, which is not necessarily but may be a contract, that was intended to have certain legal effects. In cases where the agreement in which the now failed condition is found is not a contract, the agreement that an award of restitution gives effect to is capable of being described as a quasi-contract. It would, however, be dangerous to resort to this language as it is so bound up with the implied promise theory of restitution, which maintains that these awards enforce an implied promise. As discussed in chapter 3, under the agreement theory, although restitutionary awards for a failure of condition give effect to an agreement, such awards do not enforce an implied promise.

VI. Conclusion

This chapter began by arguing that for C to be entitled to restitution for a failure of condition, D should not need to be enriched at C's expense. Rather, it was argued that it should suffice that there has been a payment made by C to D, a performance of a service by C for D, or a transfer of a right from C to D on an agreed condition that has now failed. The chapter then demonstrated that if D does not need to be enriched at C's expense for C to be entitled to restitution for a failure of condition, this has important implications. These implications include that there are cases where C should be entitled to restitution where it otherwise would not be; that the sum awarded as restitution should not be reduced if D subjectively valued the performance or act performed at less than market value; that the justification for the counter-restitution principle in the failure of condition context is not related to enrichment; that subrogation to discharged rights is not a restitutionary response to a failure of condition; and that restitutionary awards for a failure of condition do not form part of a law of unjust enrichment but rather the law of agreements.

5

Total Failure of Consideration

I. Introduction

One of the most mysterious features of the law of restitution for a failure of condition is that restitution will not be awarded unless there has been a 'total failure of consideration' (the 'total failure rule').[1] The objective of this chapter is to examine the implications of the agreement theory of failure of condition for the total failure rule.

The chapter defends the following claims. First, the historical basis for the total failure rule is that in an action for money had and received, the consideration for a payment was originally understood as the payment obligation performed by C. For the consideration for a payment to fail, the payment obligation C performed had to be rescinded ab initio. If D had partly performed its side of the contract, restitutio in integrum was generally regarded as impossible, with the result that rescission was barred.

Secondly, under the current law, the total failure rule provides that restitution for a failure of condition will be denied if D's entitlement against C to a performance that C has rendered remained conditional upon D's provision of a counter-performance, which D has partly provided, and counter-restitution of D's partial counter-performance cannot be made by C in the same form.

Thirdly, from the standpoint of the agreement theory, the justifications for the total failure rule that have been provided are unconvincing and the rule should be abolished.[2]

Finally, a consequence of abolishing the total failure rule is that certain cases would be decided differently.

[1] *Whincup v Hughes* (1871) LR 6 CP 78; *Giedo van der Garde BV v Force India Formula One Team Ltd* [2010] EWHC 2373 (QB).

[2] This is not to suggest that the rule is defensible from the perspective of other theories of failure of condition. For scepticism of the total failure rule from the standpoint of the qualified intention theory, see K Barker, 'Restitution of Passenger Fare: *The Mikhail Lermontov*' (1993) *LMCLQ* 291, 293–94; A Burrows, 'Conditional Intention as an Unjust Factor' in E Bant, K Barker and S Degeling (eds), *Research Handbook on Unjust Enrichment and Restitution* (UK, Edward Elgar Publishing, 2020) 347–48; C Mitchell, P Mitchell and S Watterson, *Goff & Jones on Unjust Enrichment*, 10th edn (UK, Sweet & Maxwell, 2022) 467–75, [12-16]–[12-32].

II. Historical Foundation

The case that is generally regarded as having established the total failure rule is *Hunt v Silk*.[3] The parties formed an agreement whereby the defendant undertook to make certain alterations and repairs to a house and execute a formal lease within 10 days in exchange for the claimant paying £10 following the lease's execution. The claimant took immediate possession and, despite not being required to, paid the £10 in advance of the defendant's provision of the work or execution of the lease. The defendant performed none of the work and failed to execute the lease. The claimant continued to occupy the house for a short period before purporting to rescind the agreement. Subsequently, the claimant brought an action for money had and received to recover the £10 payment that it had made, alleging that the consideration for the payment (ie, the payment obligation that it had performed) had failed.

Lord Ellenborough CJ dismissed the action on the basis that the claimant's occupation of the house for a period after the 10 days had elapsed meant that there had been 'a part execution of the agreement', which had the consequence that the contract was 'incapable of being rescinded'.[4] Lawrence J considered that due to the occupation of the house beyond the period of 10 days, the agreement could not be rescinded as restitutio in integrum was impossible. His Lordship therefore held that the £10 payment could not be recovered.[5] Le Blanc J dismissed the action as the parties could not 'be put in the same situation they were in' before the agreement because the claimant 'had an occupation of the premises'.[6]

A similar case, decided not long after *Hunt v Silk*, is *Beed v Blandford*.[7] The claimant agreed to purchase the defendant's interest in a vessel. After the price had been paid, the claimant applied for a bill of sale, which the defendant refused to execute. The claimant's action for money had and received failed because he had occupied the vessel for a period. Vaughan B said:

> The decision in *Hunt v Silk* lays down a very clear and just rule in these cases: if the circumstances be such that, by rescinding the contract, the rights of neither party are injured, in that case, if one contracting party will not fulfil his part of the engagement, the other may rescind the contract, and maintain his action for money had and received.[8]

[3] *Hunt v Silk* (1804) 5 East 449; 102 ER 1142. For references by 19th century treatise writers to *Hunt v Silk* for a principle resembling the total failure rule, see J Chitty and J Russell, *A Practical Treatise on the Law of Contracts*, 5th edn (London, S Sweet, 1853) 543–44; C Addison and L Cave, *Addison on Contracts: Being a Treatise on the Law of Contracts*, 7th edn (London, Stevens & Sons, 1875) 233–34. For more modern reference to *Hunt v Silk* as the foundation of the total failure rule, see R Goff, 'Reform of the Law of Restitution' (1961) 24 *Michigan Law Review* 85, 89.

[4] *Hunt v Silk* (n 3) 452–53; 1143.

[5] ibid 453; 1144.

[6] ibid.

[7] *Beed v Blandford* (1828) 2 Y & J 278; 148 ER 924.

[8] ibid 286; 926.

The key to understanding *Hunt v Silk* and *Beed v Blandford* is to appreciate that when these cases were decided, in an action for money had and received, the consideration for a payment was generally understood as the juristic reason for the payment. In most cases, the juristic reason for the payment was C's payment obligation. If C was obliged to make the payment, for the consideration of the payment to fail, the payment obligation that C had performed needed to be rescinded ab initio.[9] This was because unless C's payment obligation was rescinded, there was still a juristic reason for the payment C had made.[10] The availability of an action for money had and received upon a consideration that failed in circumstances where D failed to perform the contract is explicable on the basis that, in this period, a failure of counter-performance was often regarded as justifying rescission ab initio.[11] The significance of *Hunt v Silk* and *Beed v Blandford* was to make clear that if restitutio in integrum was impossible, the consideration (in the sense of the juristic reason) for a payment did not fail as rescission was barred.

The reason that this rule came to be understood as a requirement for a total failure of consideration is that, as discussed in chapter 1, from about the mid-eighteenth century, courts, in the context of actions for money had and received, began using the concept of failure of consideration not to refer to a failure of the juristic reason for a performance but a substantial failure of counter-performance. But despite this development, it remained the case that an action for money had and received upon a consideration that failed generally would not lie if D had provided part of the counter-performance for C's payment.[12] What started as a consequence of the principle that rescission ab initio was barred if restitutio in integrum was impossible therefore took on life as an independent requirement for a 'total failure of consideration'.

III. Content Of The Total Failure Rule

Before considering whether the total failure rule can be justified, it is important to define the rule with some precision. This section argues that under the current law the total failure rule provides that restitution for a failure of condition will be denied if D's entitlement against C to a performance C rendered remained conditional upon a counter-performance by D, which D has partly provided, and counter-restitution of D's partial counter-performance cannot be made by C in the same form.

[9] *Dutch v Warren* (1721) 1 Str 406, 406; 93 ER 598, 599 (Pratt CJ); *Moses v Macferlan* (1760) 2 Bur 1005, 1011; 97 ER 676, 680 (Lord Mansfield); *Towers v Barrett* (1786) 1 Term Rep 133, 136; 99 ER 1014, 1016 (Buller J).

[10] cf P Mitchell, 'Artificiality in Failure of Consideration' (2010) 29 *University of Queensland Law Journal* 191, 194.

[11] S Lurie, 'Towards a Unified Theory of Breach: Tracing the History of the Rule that Rescission Ab Initio Is Not a Remedy for Breach of Contract' (2003) 19 *Journal of Contract Law* 250, 264–66, 271–72.

[12] *Whincup v Hughes* (n 1). See also Addison and Cave, *Addison on Contracts: Being a Treatise on the Law of Contracts* (n 3) 233–34.

A. Provision of Part of the Bargained-For Benefit

In *Rover International Ltd v Cannon Film Sales Ltd (No 3)*,[13] Kerr LJ said that if C has 'received any part of the benefit bargained for under the contract or purported contract', there is not a total failure of consideration.[14] One interpretation of this statement is that the total failure rule provides:

> **TFR1:** where D has conferred a benefit upon C in the performance of a contract or a 'purported contract', C is not entitled to restitution of the benefit for a failure of condition.

TFR1 is not an accurate statement of the total failure rule because there are cases where restitution for a failure of condition has been awarded where D has conferred a benefit upon C in the performance of a contract. In *Stevenson v Snow*,[15] the claimant paid an insurance premium in advance for a voyage from London to Halifax. The insurance was conditional upon the vessel being accompanied by a convoy. The vessel sailed from London to Portsmouth with the convoy. Before setting off to Halifax from Portsmouth, the convoy abandoned the vessel and the insured sought to recover the premium. It was held that the premium could be apportioned and that the insured was entitled to restitution of the part of the premium that was apportionable to the voyage from Portsmouth to Halifax.[16] It was further held that had the ship been lost in the journey between London and Portsmouth, the insurer would have been liable, meaning that the insured received part of the benefit that it bargained for in exchange for the premium.

A more plausible interpretation of Kerr LJ's statement in *Rover International* is that the total failure rule provides:

> **TFR2:** where D has conferred any part of the benefit bargained for in exchange for a benefit C conferred, C will not be entitled to restitution of the benefit for a failure of condition.

However, this interpretation is also problematic. There is no case where it has formed part of the ratio that for the total failure rule to apply it is necessary for the partial counter-performance that D has undertaken to have conferred a benefit upon C, in the sense of something of value to C. Further, the authorities suggest that the total failure rule is irrelevant where C can make counter-restitution of D's partial counter-performance in the same form that the counter-performance was provided.[17] A counter-performance will be reversible in the same form if C can make counter-restitution via a performance of the same kind as the counter-performance undertaken by D. Thus, for example, if C performs a service for

[13] *Rover International Ltd v Cannon Film Sales Ltd (No 3)* [1989] 1 WLR 912.
[14] ibid 923.
[15] *Stevenson v Snow* (1761) 3 Burr 1237; 97 ER 808.
[16] ibid 1240; 811.
[17] *Pavey & Matthews Pty Ltd v Paul* (1987) 162 CLR 221; *Lusty v Finsbury Securities Ltd* (1991) 58 BLR 66. See also J Edelman, 'The New Doctrine of Partial Failure of Consideration' (1996) 15 *Australian Bar Review* 229, 241; A Burrows, *The Law of Restitution*, 3rd edn (Oxford, Oxford University Press, 2011) 333.

D under an unenforceable contract in exchange for payment following substantial completion, and D pays part of the agreed sum, C can make counter-restitution of D's counter-performance in the same form: that is, C can make counter-restitution of the payment by also making a payment.

A case that supports the proposition that restitution may be awarded where C can make counter-restitution of D's partial counter-performance in the same form is *Pavey & Matthews Pty Ltd v Paul*,[18] the facts of which were set out in chapter 1.[19] For present purposes, it should be recalled that in that case, after the claimant builder had substantially completed the work, the defendant landowner paid the builder $36,000. Restitution for a failure of condition was nevertheless awarded to the builder. In other words, despite the landowner having partly performed her payment obligation, and therefore having partly provided the agreed counter-performance for the builder's work, restitution was still awarded.

Another case where restitution for a failure of condition was awarded, where C was able to make counter-restitution of D's partial counter-performance in the same form, is *Lusty v Finsbury Securities Ltd*.[20] There, an architect was awarded restitution of a performance of services undertaken for a project that the defendants ultimately decided not to pursue, despite the architect having been paid an interim fee of £10,000.

B. Provision of Part of a Counter-Performance the Defendant was Obliged to Undertake

In *Stocznia Gdanska SA v Latvian Shipping Co*,[21] Lord Goff said that there will not be a total failure of consideration if 'the [defendant] has performed any part of the contractual duties in respect of which the payment is due'.[22] One interpretation of this statement is that the total failure rule provides:

> **TFR3:** where D's entitlement against C to a performance C rendered remains conditional upon D's performance of a certain obligation, and D has partly performed that obligation, C is not entitled to restitution for a failure of condition.

Under TFR3, D must have partly performed *an obligation* before the total failure rule applies. This interpretation of the total failure rule has been criticised on the basis that the rule may prevent restitution from being awarded where there is a failure of a contingent condition.[23] As discussed in chapter 1, a contingent condition is a condition that neither party is under an obligation to ensure is fulfilled.

[18] *Pavey & Matthews Pty Ltd v Paul* (n 17).
[19] Text to n 85.
[20] *Lusty v Finsbury Securities Ltd* (n 17).
[21] *Stocznia Gdanska SA v Latvian Shipping Co* [1998] 1 WLR 574.
[22] ibid 588.
[23] F Wilmot-Smith, 'Reconsidering "Total" Failure' (2013) 72 *CLJ* 414, 417.

Although there does not appear to be any case where the total failure rule has precluded an award of restitution following the failure of a contingent condition, it would be strange if the rule did not apply where a contingent condition failed due to a failure of counter-performance by D. Compare:

(1) C and D enter into an agreement whereby D's entitlement against C to an advance payment remains conditional upon D's performance of a dependent obligation to cut and deliver five tons of wood. After one ton of the wood has been cut, the agreement is terminated for D's repudiation.

(2) C and D enter into an agreement whereby D's entitlement against C to an advance payment remains conditional upon D cutting and delivering five tons of wood, but D is not under an obligation to cut and deliver any of the wood.[24] After one ton of the wood has been cut, the agreement is terminated for D's repudiation.

In scenario (1), restitution for a failure of condition will be denied on the basis that there is not a total failure of consideration in respect of C's advance payment, as counter-restitution of D's part performance cannot be made by C in the same form. Although there does not appear to be any case resembling scenario (2), it is very difficult to see why it should make a difference that D was not obliged to perform the services that it provided.

Where, however, D's entitlement to a performance that C has rendered remains subject to a condition (including a contingent condition) that does not involve the provision of a counter-performance by D, it is less clear that the total failure rule should apply. As discussed below, the leading justification for the total failure rule in the cases is that the rule ensures that restitution is not available in circumstances where it is too difficult to determine what would constitute adequate counter-restitution. This rationale for the rule is not applicable where D has not undertaken a counter-performance because there will be nothing for C to make counter-restitution of. Thus, suppose that C makes a payment of £10,000 to D and it is agreed that D's entitlement against C to the payment remains conditional upon D staying married to X for at least three years. After two years of marriage, D and X divorce. Given that D has not undertaken a performance for C, there is nothing for C to make counter-restitution of, meaning the most prominent justification for the total failure rule barring restitution does not apply.

C. Fulfilment of any Part of a Condition

Professor Virgo's interpretation of the total failure rule is:

> **TFR4:** where any part of a condition that D's entitlement against C to a benefit C conferred remained subject to has been fulfilled, C is not entitled to restitution for a failure of condition.[25]

[24] This would be an unusual agreement, but it helps to illustrate the present point.
[25] G Virgo, *The Principles of the Law of Restitution*, 4th edn (Oxford, Oxford University Press, 2024) 213.

TFR4 has been criticised on the basis that 'the language of total and partial failure is inapt as applied to conditions' since a 'condition either fails or it does not'.[26] While it is true that a condition can only fail or not fail, it is meaningful to refer to the state of affairs that D's entitlement to a performance rendered remained subject to as having partly materialised or sustained itself. This is presumably what Virgo means when he says that restitution will be denied if any part of the condition has been fulfilled. The language of a condition having partly failed, or no part of a condition having been fulfilled, will occasionally be used here for ease of expression despite its conceptual imperfections.

With this clarification, the interpretation of the total failure rule favoured by Virgo can be re-stated as:

> **TFR5:** where D's entitlement against C to a benefit conferred remains conditional upon a certain state of affairs materialising or sustaining itself, and that state of affairs has partly materialised or sustained itself, restitution for a failure of condition will be denied.

TFR5 also appears to be the interpretation of the total failure rule favoured by the authors of *Goff & Jones on Unjust Enrichment*,[27] who claim that the rule provides that if 'part of the benefit which formed the basis for the [transfer] has been conferred, no action [for restitution for a failure of condition] will lie'.[28]

Dr Wilmot-Smith has objected to TFR5 on the basis that it 'cannot explain a key distinction the total failure rule draws', which is that '[w]here an enrichment is transferred on the condition that the defendant render performance, the satisfaction of a "collateral" obligation … will not bar restitution'.[29] An obligation is 'collateral' where D's entitlement to a performance C rendered does not remain conditional upon D's performance of the obligation (ie, the collateral obligation) but the performance of a different obligation. In *Baltic Shipping Co v Dillon*,[30] to explain the concept of a collateral obligation, Deane and Dawson JJ gave the example of an airfare. Their Honours observed that generally the consideration for an airfare will totally fail if 'the aircraft were forced to turn back due to negligent maintenance on the part of the carrier' and no alternative transport could be found.[31] However, Deane and Dawson JJ suggested that if the airline merely fails to perform its obligations to provide an in-flight film and meal, there will generally not be a total failure of consideration because these are collateral obligations.[32]

It is unclear why Wilmot-Smith regards TFR5 as inconsistent with the proposition that D's part performance of a collateral obligation will not prevent an award of restitution for a failure of condition. Where D has performed a collateral

[26] Burrows, 'Conditional Intention as an Unjust Factor' (n 2) 348.
[27] Mitchell, Mitchell and Watterson, *Goff & Jones* (n 2).
[28] ibid 467, [12-16].
[29] Wilmot-Smith, 'Reconsidering "Total" Failure' (n 23) 418–20.
[30] *Baltic Shipping Company v Dillon* (1993) 176 CLR 344.
[31] ibid 378.
[32] ibid.

obligation, no part of the condition that D's entitlement to a performance C rendered remained subject to will have been fulfilled. So, imagine that D's entitlement to an advance payment of £10,000 C made remains conditional upon D's substantial performance of an obligation to install a new kitchen in C's house. Suppose that D is also under an obligation to tile C's bathroom and that D's entitlement to an advance payment of £5,000 made by C remains conditional upon D's substantial performance of this obligation. The total failure rule will not prevent C from being entitled to restitution of the £5,000 payment if D performs its obligation to install the kitchen but performs no part of its obligation to tile the bathroom. Contrary to what Wilmot-Smith appears to claim, this is consistent with TFR5 because no part of the condition that D's entitlement to the £5,000 payment made remained subject to will have been fulfilled.

The real problem with TFR5 is that it is inconsistent with the observation that where D's entitlement against C to a performance rendered remains conditional upon D's performance of a certain obligation, and counter-restitution of D's part performance of that obligation can be made by C in the same form, restitution may still be awarded. TFR5 also suggests that where D's entitlement against C to a performance rendered remains subject to a condition that does not take the form of the provision of a counter-performance by D, and that condition has been partly fulfilled, restitution will be denied on the basis that there is not a total failure of consideration. Although there is no authority on the point, it was suggested above that this is seriously doubtful.

D. A Substantial Failure of Condition

Wilmot-Smith has argued that the best interpretation of the total failure rule is that if 'a claimant transfers an enrichment to a defendant subject to a condition, the claimant can recover only if a substantial part of the condition fails'.[33] This suggests that the total failure rule provides:

> **TFR6:** where D's entitlement against C to a benefit conferred remains conditional upon a certain state of affairs materialising or sustaining itself, C will only be entitled to restitution if that state of affairs substantially fails to materialise or sustain itself.

In cases where C undertakes a performance in exchange for a counter-performance by D, Wilmot-Smith appears to regard there as being an insubstantial failure of condition if a substantial part of the agreed counter-performance is provided.[34] However, it is suggested below that the better view is that where C undertakes a performance in exchange for D's counter-performance, D's entitlement to the performance rendered is generally agreed to remain conditional upon D's

[33] Wilmot-Smith, 'Reconsidering "Total" Failure' (n 23) 414, 422.
[34] ibid 430.

counter-performance having substantially been provided. If no substantial part of D's counter-performance remains unperformed, there will therefore not be a failure of condition. TFR6 also again incorrectly suggests that the total failure rule applies where C can make counter-restitution of D's part performance in the same form.

E. Total Failure Rule Defined

The definition of the total failure rule that is most consistent with the positive law is:

> **TFR7:** where D's entitlement against C to a performance rendered remains conditional upon D's provision of a counter-performance, which D partly provides, and counter-restitution of D's counter-performance cannot be made by C in the same form, restitution for a failure of condition will be denied.

To clarify when the total failure rule applies according to TFR7, consider the following example. C and D enter into a contract whereby C is obliged to pay £10,000 in advance in exchange for D's performance of a dependent obligation to provide certain improvements to C's land. Assume that the advance payment is not a deposit. On the contract's proper construction, D's entitlement to the £10,000 advance payment C made remains conditional upon D's substantial performance of its dependent obligation to provide the improvements. Under TFR7, if D performs half of the work before the contract is terminated for D's repudiation, C will not be entitled to restitution. D's entitlement to the advance payment remained conditional upon D's substantial performance of its obligation to perform the work, which D has partly performed, and counter-restitution of D's performance of the work cannot be made by C in the same form.

By contrast, under TFR7, restitution should be available in the following scenario. C and D enter into an unenforceable contract whereby C agrees to repair D's roof in exchange for payment of £5,000 following substantial completion. C completes the work, but D, in breach of the agreement, only pays £2,000. Here, C should be entitled to restitution for a failure of condition because counter-restitution of D's performance can be made by C in the same form.

TFR7 should be preferred as an interpretation of the total failure rule for the following reasons. First, TFR7 is consistent with cases such as *Pavey*, which suggest that where C can make counter-restitution of D's part performance in the same form, restitution will not be denied because the consideration did not totally fail. Secondly, TFR7 recognises that where D has performed a collateral obligation, this will not prevent restitution from being awarded. Finally, TFR7 is consistent with the suggestion above that where D's entitlement to a performance C rendered remains subject to a condition, but this condition does not involve the provision of a counter-performance by D, the total failure rule will not prevent restitution from being awarded.

IV. Evaluating the Total Failure Rule

From the perspective of the agreement theory of failure of condition, the effect of the total failure rule is to potentially deny C a claim for restitution that would give effect to an agreement between C and D that D's entitlement to a performance C rendered remained subject to a condition that has now failed. This is because where C undertakes a performance in exchange for a counter-performance by D, as argued below, generally D's entitlement against C to the performance rendered will have been agreed to remain conditional upon D's substantial provision of the counter-performance as opposed to D's provision of any part of the counter-performance. Whether the total failure rule can be justified therefore depends upon whether it is defensible to refuse to give effect to an agreement via a restitutionary award where D has partly provided a counter-performance that is not reversible in the same form. This section evaluates the most prominent justifications for the total failure rule. It argues that none of them is persuasive.

A. Justifications

i. Determining Adequate Counter-Restitution

The leading justification for the total failure rule in the cases is that the rule prevents restitution from being awarded where it is too difficult to determine what constitutes adequate counter-restitution.[35] In *Whincup v Hughes*,[36] Montague Smith J said that 'the action for money received cannot lie where the contract has been partly performed on both sides', because to ascertain the amount the claimant would have to make as counter-restitution 'it would be necessary to go into a great variety of considerations, the relative weight of which it would be almost impossible correctly to estimate'. This justification for the rule also finds support in *David Securities v Commonwealth Bank*.[37] In that case, it was suggested that 'where consideration can be apportioned *or where counter-restitution is relatively simple*, insistence on total failure of consideration can be misleading or confusing'.[38]

This justification for the total failure rule is unconvincing. As discussed in chapter 3, C should often not be required to make counter-restitution to D in a claim for restitution for a failure of condition because an award of counter-restitution would undermine the parties' agreement.

It is also incoherent, in the sense of treating materially alike cases differently, to deny restitution on the basis that it is too difficult to determine the

[35] Note that this justification has a strong fit with TFR7.
[36] *Whincup v Hughes* (n 1) 85–86.
[37] *David Securities v Commonwealth Bank* (1992) 175 CLR 353.
[38] ibid [55] (Mason CJ, Deane, Toohey, Gaudron and McHugh JJ) (emphasis added).

counter-restitution that C should potentially be required to make to D following a failure of condition.[39] Compare these examples:

(1) C and D enter into an unenforceable contract whereby C is under an entire obligation to thatch D's roof in exchange for payment following substantial completion. When C has performed half of the work, the agreement is terminated for D's repudiation.

(2) C and D enter into an unenforceable contract whereby C is required to make an advance payment in exchange for D's performance of an entire obligation to thatch C's roof. After C has made the advance payment and D has performed half of the work, the agreement is terminated for D's repudiation.

Assume for the sake of argument that in the latter scenario, D is entitled to counter-restitution of its part performance of the work. In scenario (1), where C's work is performed in advance of payment, the law does not regard it as too difficult to determine the sum that C is entitled to as restitution. It cannot be that in scenario (2), where all that has changed is the order of performance, it somehow becomes too difficult to determine the sum that C should be required to make as counter-restitution. Further, as explained immediately below, in scenario (2), assuming counter-restitution is required, when determining the sum that D should be entitled to as counter-restitution, the task is not to ascertain the proportion of the contract price that D has earned. Given that D's dependent service obligation is entire, no part of the contract price is apportionable to a part performance of this obligation. Rather, where D is entitled to counter-restitution from C, the measure of the sum that D is entitled to should generally be the market value of the counter-performance D has undertaken.

ii. Difficulty of Apportionment

Another, similar, justification for the total failure rule is that the rule ensures that C is not entitled to restitution where it is too difficult to apportion the price that C has paid to the counter-performance that D has undertaken. In Professor Treitel's words:

> If [C] employs [D] for a lump sum, paid in advance, to paint [C]'s house, and [D] abandons the job before it is finished, [C] cannot recover back any part of the payment: his only remedy is in damages. The reason for the rule appears to be that the law cannot easily apportion the contract price to the amount of work actually done by [D].[40]

This justification for the total failure rule is also flawed. To explain why, it is helpful to first clarify the difference between dependent obligations that are entire, divisible into entire parts, and infinitely divisible. A party, D, will owe a dependent

[39] See also Burrows, *The Law of Restitution* (n 17) 331.
[40] G Treitel, *The Law of Contract*, 8th edn (London, Sweet & Maxwell, 1991) 927.

obligation to C where its obligation to do (or refrain from doing) something is conditional upon C first strictly or substantially performing an obligation C owed. So, in the example provided by Treitel, D's obligation to paint C's house will be dependent if this obligation was, as is almost certainly the case, agreed to be conditional upon C's performance of its obligation to pay the lump sum in advance.

In distinguishing between the different kinds of dependent obligations, it is helpful to assume that in Treitel's example the sum that C paid to D was £10,000. If D's dependent obligation to paint the house is entire, D's entitlement to the lump sum payment made will have been agreed to remain conditional upon D's substantial performance of its obligation to paint C's house. If D's dependent obligation is divisible into several entire parts, D's entitlement to certain parts of the lump sum payment made will remain conditional upon D's substantial performance of certain parts of the work. For example, D's entitlement to £2,000 out of the £10,000 payment made might be conditional upon D having painted the garage, and the remaining £8,000 conditional upon D painting the rest of the house. Finally, if D's dependent obligation is infinitely divisible, D will become unconditionally entitled to the payment in proportion to every infinitely divisible part of the work performed. Thus, the parties might agree that D is entitled to the payment in proportion to the extent of the work completed, meaning that if D performs 40% of the work, D will have unconditionally earned 40% of the advance payment (ie, £4,000).

When Treitel suggests that the reason for the total failure rule appears to be that the contract price cannot easily be apportioned to the amount of work done by D, it is not entirely clear what this means. After it has been determined whether, on the agreement's proper construction, D's dependent obligation was entire, divisible into entire parts, or infinitely divisible, it is a question of fact whether D has unconditionally earned any part of the lump sum payment made and, if so, what amount. Of course, this factual question will not always be straightforward to answer, but it is hard to believe that it is generally so difficult that it justifies refusing to recognise a claim for restitution for a failure of condition if any part of the work is performed. It is also not easy to accept that where a question of fact may be difficult to answer in certain circumstances, this provides a good reason for refusing to recognise a particular claim in those circumstances.

iii. Escaping a Bad Bargain

A further justification for the total failure rule that is often suggested, although rarely endorsed, is that the rule prevents a claimant from escaping a bad bargain. In *Ali v Dinc*,[41] Professor Worthington, sitting as a Deputy High Court Judge, observed that the total failure rule's 'one obvious benefit is that it prevents claimants

[41] *Ali v Dinc* [2020] EWHC 3055 (Ch).

resorting to unjust enrichment remedies when it is advantageous to unravel a bad bargain and return to the pre-contractual position'.[42]

A problem with this escaping a bad bargain justification is that if the law were concerned with preventing claimants from escaping bad bargains, it would be strange to adopt the total failure rule as opposed to a rule that C is not entitled to restitution if it would allow C to escape a bad bargain. Restitution for a failure of condition has also been awarded in cases where C made a bad bargain, which suggests that the escaping a bad bargain justification has a poor fit with the positive law. An example is *Wilkinson v Lloyd*,[43] where the claimant entered into a contract with the defendant to purchase the defendant's shares in a mining company, but the defendant wrongly failed to transfer the shares to the claimant. The claimant successfully recovered the price even though the value of the shares had fallen below the agreed price.

iv. Restitution is not Justified where the Total Failure Rule Applies

A final noteworthy justification for the total failure rule is that the rule prevents restitution from being awarded in circumstances where the justification for restitution is, despite there being a failure of condition, absent. This is the argument made by Wilmot-Smith in support of his preferred interpretation of the total failure rule (ie, TFR6). Specifically, Wilmot-Smith claims:

> restitution only makes sense when there is a dissonance between the position that the claimant anticipated and the position that she is actually in. The closer the claimant's position is to the one that she anticipated, the weaker the reasons for restitution. This point demonstrates the value of the total failure rule. It prevents restitution where the failure of the condition is insubstantial. In so doing, it seeks to ensure that restitution is granted only when its award is justified.[44]

However, where an agreed condition has failed, even insubstantially, D's entitlement against C to the performance rendered will still have been subject to a condition that has now failed, meaning that the justification for restitution is established. Even if it is accepted that the closer that C's 'position is to the one that [C] anticipated, the weaker the reasons for restitution', this does not mean that the justification for restitution is completely eroded where a condition has insubstantially failed: an insubstantial failure of condition is still a failure of condition. In addition, and as foreshadowed, it is argued below that where C undertakes a performance in exchange for a counter-performance by D, generally the most plausible interpretation of the parties' agreement is that D's entitlement to the

[42] ibid [282].

[43] *Wilkinson v Lloyd* (1845) 7 QB 27; 115 ER 398. See also *Taylor v Motability Finance Ltd* [2004] EWHC 2619 (Comm), [25] (Cooke J).

[44] Wilmot-Smith, 'Reconsidering "Total" Failure' (n 23) 430.

performance remains conditional upon D's substantial provision of the counter-performance. Consequently, independently of the total failure rule, there will generally only be a failure of condition potentially justifying restitution where there is a substantial dissonance between the position C anticipated and the position that C is actually in.

B. Against the Total Failure Rule

The following reasons positively support the abolition of the total failure rule. First, the effect of the rule is to potentially deny C a claim that would give effect to the parties' agreement that D's entitlement against C to a performance rendered remained subject to a condition that has now failed.

Secondly, the rule produces results that are difficult to accept. Suppose that C makes a payment in advance in exchange for D's performance of certain services. The agreement is unenforceable. After C has made the payment, D performs a small part of the services. In this example, C will not be entitled to damages or specific performance because the agreement is unenforceable. If C is not entitled to restitution, C will therefore be left without a remedy, which, provided such an award would not undermine the policy of the statute rendering the agreement unenforceable, seems the wrong result.

Finally, what historically provided the doctrinal basis for the total failure rule is irrelevant in the failure of condition context. As discussed above, the historical foundation for the total failure rule was that in an action for money had and received, the consideration for a payment only failed if the juristic reason for the payment was rescinded ab initio. Where restitutio in integrum was impossible, rescission was denied, which meant that the consideration (ie, juristic reason) for the payment did not fail. As discussed in chapter 1, in the mid-nineteenth century, the meaning of consideration in this context shifted and came to be understood as the jointly understood reason for the payment, with this reason generally being the provision of the agreed counter-performance. With this shift, the idea that an action for money had and received would not lie where restitutio in integrum was impossible was recast as the total failure rule. Given that a failure of condition does not denote a failure of the juristic reason for a performance, what originally provided the basis for the total failure rule is irrelevant to restitutionary claims for a failure of condition.

It might be objected that the total failure rule is too well-established to be judicially abolished. But arguments along these lines often do not make clear why a rule is too well-ingrained to be abolished judicially. This is not to deny that there are such rules. The point is that such a claim is, without more, a conclusion without an argument. It is difficult to identify anything that would make it inappropriate for the total failure rule to be judicially abolished. If parties widely contracted on the basis that the total failure rule applied, this would be an important factor to be weighed in the balance, but there is no evidence to suggest this is the case. There also does not appear to be any legislation that would be undermined if the rule were abolished.

V. Implications of Abolishing the Total Failure Rule

If the total failure rule were abolished, in circumstances where the rule presently applies, whether C is entitled to restitution for a failure of condition will depend principally upon whether, as a matter of construction of the parties' agreement, D's entitlement against C to a performance rendered remained subject to a condition that has now failed. This section outlines how this constructional question ought, at a general level, to be approached in cases where the total failure rule presently precludes a claim for restitution. The section then demonstrates that certain notable cases would be decided differently in the absence of the rule.

A. Determining whether there is a Failure of Condition

If the total failure rule were abolished, the most prominent situation where a claim for restitution for a failure of condition would become available to C is where D has partly performed a dependent obligation, the performance of which is not reversible in the same form, before the contract is terminated for D's breach or repudiation. In this scenario, in considering whether there has been a failure of condition in respect of the performance that C has undertaken, one of the first questions that will need to be answered is whether D's obligation was entire, divisible into entire parts, or infinitely divisible. As explained, if D's obligation is entire, generally D will need to have substantially performed the obligation to become unconditionally entitled to the performance C rendered. If D's obligation is divisible into entire parts, D will need to substantially perform each entire part of the obligation to become unconditionally entitled to a part of the performance C has rendered. If D's obligation is infinitely divisible, every infinitely divisible part of D's performance of the obligation will unconditionally entitle D to part of the performance C rendered.

In examining whether D's entitlement to a performance rendered remained subject to a condition, a useful cross-check is to consider whether the condition would have been a condition precedent to D becoming unconditionally entitled to C undertaking the performance if the order for performance were the reverse.[45] Compare:

(1) C and D enter into a contract whereby D undertakes an entire obligation to construct a barn on C's land. C is required to pay £50,000 for the work following substantial completion. D completes half of the work before the contract is terminated for D's repudiation.

[45] R Stevens, 'Is there a Law of Unjust Enrichment?' in S Degeling and J Edelman (eds), *Unjust Enrichment and Commercial Law* (NSW, Lawbook Co, 2008) 28–29.

(2) C and D enter into a contract whereby D undertakes an entire obligation to construct a barn on C's land. C is required to pay £50,000 in advance. The payment is not a deposit. After the payment is made, D completes half of the work before the contract is terminated for D's repudiation.

In scenario (1), it will generally have been agreed that for D to become unconditionally entitled to payment of the £50,000, D must substantially perform the work. As D has only performed half of the work, D's obligation will not have substantially been performed, meaning a condition precedent to D becoming unconditionally entitled to C's performance of its payment obligation will not have been fulfilled.

In scenario (2), where the order for performance is reversed, this should usually not make a difference to the condition that D's entitlement to the payment, which this time has been made in advance, is subject to. It cannot be, other things being equal, that a change in the order for performance affects what the parties agreed D must do to become unconditionally entitled to the payment. Consequently, in scenario (2), D's entitlement to the £50,000 payment made by C will generally have been agreed to remain conditional upon D's substantial performance of its obligation to provide the work. As D has only performed half of the work, there will be a failure of condition justifying restitution.

Where, for example, C and D enter into a contract whereby C undertakes an entire obligation to provide services in advance in exchange for payment of an agreed sum by D, to become unconditionally entitled to payment C must generally substantially (as opposed to strictly or partly) perform its entire service obligation.[46] If C does not substantially perform, C will not be entitled to be paid anything by D. Applying the above mirror-image approach, where C makes an advance payment in exchange for D's performance of an entire service obligation, D's entitlement to the payment made should therefore generally be regarded as remaining conditional upon D's substantial performance of its entire service obligation. Further, if D's entitlement to the performance C rendered was agreed to remain conditional upon D's strict performance of its entire obligation, it would implausibly mean that the parties agreed that any defect or delay however minor in D's counter-performance was to have the consequence that D is undeserving of the performance.

The concept of substantial performance of an obligation is, however, a potentially misleading label for what it denotes. The most familiar circumstance where this concept appears is in actions for the agreed sum. Where D has agreed to pay a specific sum and this payment obligation is conditional upon C's prior performance of an independent service obligation, generally the condition precedent to D's obligation to make the payment is that C substantially, as opposed to strictly or partly, performs its service obligation.[47] In other words, the reason that C is generally entitled to payment of the agreed sum from D where it has substantially

[46] *Dakin v Lee* [1916] 1 KB 566, 579–80 (Lord Cozens-Hardy MR), 580–82 (Pickford LJ).
[47] ibid.

performed an entire obligation is that, following substantial performance, D's obligation to pay the agreed sum will have fallen unconditionally due for performance. There is no independent 'doctrine of substantial performance'.

An obligation will have been substantially performed if no substantial part of the obligation remains unperformed.[48] Every obligation has both a substantive and a temporal component: that is, the party who owes the obligation will be obliged to perform before, at, or for a specific time. Where a party fails to substantially perform, what this generally means is that they have failed to perform a substantial part of the substantive component of the obligation substantially before, at, or for a certain time. Thus, if D is obliged to construct a garage for C before 6 April, that obligation will have been substantially performed if D substantially constructs the garage not substantially later than 6 April.

The substantive and temporal components of a condition may require different standards of performance for a condition precedent to a dependent obligation to be fulfilled.[49] Imagine that C and D enter into a contract whereby D undertakes to build a shed for C before 27 May in exchange for payment of £5,000 following completion. On the contract's proper construction, the time for completion is of the essence. In this example, C's £5,000 payment obligation will be conditional upon D substantially building the shed strictly before 27 May.

Different standards of performance of the substantive and temporal components of an obligation may also be required for D to become unconditionally entitled to a performance C has rendered. Suppose, for example, that C agrees to pay D £5,000 in advance in exchange for D repairing its shed before 14 May. On the contract's proper construction, the time for completion is of the essence. In this example, D's entitlement against C to the £5,000 payment made will be conditional upon D substantially constructing the barn strictly before 14 May.

B. Cases that would be Decided Differently

In *Whincup v Hughes*,[50] the claimant paid a £25 premium in advance for his son to be apprenticed to the defendant watchmaker for six years. The claimant paid the premium, but the defendant died after one year, frustrating the defendant's obligations under the contract. The claimant brought an action for money had and received upon a consideration that failed to recover all or part of the premium. The action was dismissed on the basis that 'where a contract has been in part performed no part of the money paid under such contract can be recovered back'.[51]

[48] *Bolton v Mahadeva* [1972] 2 All ER 1322, 1325–26 (Cairns LJ); *Hoenig v Isaacs* [1952] 2 All ER 176, 182–83 (Romer LJ).

[49] A case where the time at which a condition failed was relevant is *Nu Line Construction Group Pty Ltd v Fowler* [2014] NSWCA 51.

[50] *Whincup v Hughes* (n 1). See also *Ferns v Carr* (1885) 28 Ch D 409.

[51] *Whincup v Hughes* (n 1) 81 (Bovill CJ).

If, as the court held, the defendant's obligation to mentor the claimant's son was entire, the £25 premium should have been recoverable absent the total failure rule. The defendant's entitlement to the £25 advance payment made would, on the contract's proper construction, have been agreed to remain conditional upon the defendant's substantial performance of his obligation to mentor the son for six years. When the defendant died after one year, that condition failed. Restitution should have followed.

More difficult is whether the defendant should have been entitled to counter-restitution. In the previous chapter, it was suggested that in the failure of condition context, counter-restitution should be required where D's compliance with an order to make restitution to C would result in the failure of a condition in respect of a performance D rendered. If the defendant had made restitution of the £25 premium to the claimant, would there have been a failure of condition in respect of the services he had provided? In the next chapter, it is argued that entire service obligations are generally performed on the condition that the service provider is not prevented from unconditionally earning the agreed counter-performance other than through the 'fault'[52] of the service provider's own. On this interpretation, there would have been a failure of condition in respect of the defendant's services as he was prevented from unconditionally earning the premium due to his death. The sum that the claimant would have been entitled to absent the total failure rule would therefore have been £25 minus the sum the defendant was entitled to as counter-restitution, which would have been the market value of the services the defendant had performed.

Another example of a case that would be decided differently without the total failure rule is *Giedo van der Garde BV v Force India Formula One Team Ltd*.[53] The claimant made an advance payment of approximately $3 million to the defendant. The defendant's entitlement to the payment was agreed to remain conditional upon the defendant allowing the claimant to drive a racing car in testing, practice, or racing for at least 6,000 kilometres, and allowing the claimant to participate in Friday morning testing. The claimant was allowed to participate in testing but was wrongly only allowed to drive 2,004 kilometres.

Stadlen J refused to award restitution because the consideration for the $3 million payment did not totally fail. If the total failure rule did not exist, the claimant would have been entitled to restitution of the whole of the $3 million payment because the defendant's entitlement to the $3 million payment remained conditional upon the claimant being allowed to drive at least 6,000 kilometres. Counter-restitution also should not have been required. If counter-restitution had been ordered, the defendant would, in practice, have been entitled to part of the $3 million payment in circumstances where the parties agreed the defendant

[52] 'Fault' here is used in the same sense as 'fault' in the context of frustration. As to the meaning of fault in the frustration context, see E Peel, *Frustration and Force Majeure*, 4th edn (London, Sweet & Maxwell, 2022) ch 14.

[53] *Giedo van der Garde BV v Force India Formula One Team Ltd* (n 1).

was not so entitled. Such an award would therefore have undermined the parties' agreement.

VI. Conclusion

This chapter has considered whether it should be necessary for there to have been a total failure of consideration before restitution for a failure of condition may be awarded. The chapter began by explaining that the historical basis for the total failure rule was that, where restitutio in integrum was impossible, rescission ab initio was denied, which had the further consequence that the consideration (ie, juristic reason) for the payment did not fail. Next, it was argued that the best interpretation of the total failure rule under the current law is that where D's entitlement against C to a performance C rendered remains conditional upon D's provision of a counter-performance, which D has partly provided, and counter-restitution of D's part performance cannot be made by C in the same form, restitution will be denied. Finally, it was argued that the most prominent justifications for the total failure rule are unconvincing and that the rule should be abolished, which would result in certain cases being decided differently.

6

Failure of Condition and Contract

I. Introduction

In certain circumstances, a party may be entitled to restitution of a performance of a valid contractual obligation for a failure of condition.[1] The purpose of this chapter is to consider how restitutionary awards for a failure of condition interact with the law of contract. The chapter begins by examining the relationship between failure of condition and contract in general. It is explained that, under the agreement theory, restitutionary awards for a failure of condition are not 'complementary' or 'subsidiary' to contract. Rather, in the view of this theory, the justification for awarding restitution of a contractual performance relates to the content of the contract itself. The chapter then considers when, in the light of the interpretation of the relationship between failure of condition and contract put forward, restitution of a contractual performance should be available and how the agreed price should, if at all, affect the sum awarded.

II. Contract and Restitution for a Failure of Condition in General

A. The Prevailing View

The prevailing academic view, which is based upon the qualified intention theory discussed in chapter 2, is that restitution of a contractual performance may be awarded for a failure of condition where: (1) C intended for D's entitlement to retain a benefit C conferred in the performance of the contract to be subject to a condition; (2) D knew, or a reasonable person in D's position would have known, of the intended condition when the benefit was conferred; and (3) the intended condition has now failed.[2] A qualification that is then usually added is

[1] *Fibrosa Spolka Akcyjna v Fairbairn Lawson Combe Barbour Ltd* [1943] AC 32.

[2] A Burrows, 'Conditional Intention as an Unjust Factor' in E Bant, K Barker and S Degeling (eds), *Research Handbook on Unjust Enrichment and Restitution* (UK, Edward Elgar Publishing, 2020) 346–47.

that restitution should be denied if it would be inconsistent with the contract.[3] On this view, it is not the content of the parties' contract that justifies restitution of a contractual performance for a failure of condition but rather an independent unjust enrichment principle.[4]

This interpretation of the relationship between restitution for a failure of condition and contract recently found support in *Dargamo Holdings Ltd v Avonwick Holdings Ltd*.[5] In that case, Carr LJ said that 'the law of unjust enrichment can be seen as complementary, though not subsidiary, to the law of contract'.[6] Her Ladyship later added that 'whilst failure of [condition] ranks alongside the unjust factors of mistake, duress and undue influence as a factor negativing consent, it differs in that it is concerned with qualification of consent, as opposed to impaired or vitiated consent'.[7] Together, these statements suggest that the justification for awarding restitution of a benefit conferred in the performance of a contract for a failure of condition is linked to C's qualified intention to benefit D via the performance.

A difficulty the orthodox account confronts is why C may be entitled to restitution of a contractual performance it was obliged to undertake on the grounds of failure of condition, but not mistake.[8] Compare:

(1) C mistakenly performs a £1,000 contractual payment obligation that it owed to D.

(2) C makes an advance payment of £1,000 in the performance of a contractual payment obligation that it owed to D in exchange for D's performance of certain services. When D has performed none of the services, the contract is terminated for D's repudiation.

In scenario (1), consistently with the authorities,[9] proponents of the qualified intention theory generally maintain that C should not be entitled to restitution because C's payment discharged an obligation that it owed to D.[10] In other words, restitution should be denied because there was a juristic reason (in the form of C's now discharged payment obligation) for the payment. But in cases exemplified by scenario (2), where C's payment has also discharged an obligation that it owed to D, again consistently with the authorities,[11] C is generally regarded as entitled to

[3] P Birks, *An Introduction to the Law of Restitution*, rev edn (Oxford, Oxford University Press, 1989) 46–47; A Burrows, *The Law of Restitution*, 3rd edn (Oxford, Oxford University Press, 2011) 327–29.

[4] Burrows, 'Conditional Intention as an Unjust Factor' (n 2) 346–47.

[5] *Dargamo Holdings Ltd v Avonwick Holdings Ltd* [2022] 1 All ER (Comm) 1244.

[6] ibid [76].

[7] ibid [79].

[8] This difficulty is acknowledged in Burrows, 'Conditional Intention as an Unjust Factor' (n 2) 348–49.

[9] *Kleinwort Benson Ltd v Lincoln City Council* [1999] 1 AC 349, 407–08 (Lord Hope); *Fairfield Sentry Ltd (in liq) v Migani* [2014] 1 CLC 611, [18] (Lord Sumption); *DD Growth Premium 2X Fund v RMF Market Neutral Strategies (Master) Ltd* [2018] Bus LR 1595, [62] (Lord Sumption).

[10] Burrows, 'Conditional Intention as an Unjust Factor' (n 2) 348.

[11] *Giles v Edwards* (1797) 7 TR 181; 101 ER 920; *Fibrosa Spolka Akcyjna v Fairbairn Lawson Combe Barbour Ltd* (n 1); *Prinwalla Holdings Pty Ltd v Stanton (WA) Pty Ltd* [2016] NSWSC 963.

restitution for a failure of condition.[12] If the justification for restitution for a failure of condition is analogous to the justification for restitution in the core case of mistake as the qualified intention theory maintains, it would seem that by denying a claim for restitution in scenario (1), but allowing a claim in scenario (2), the law is treating alike cases differently.

In response to this difficulty, Justice Edelman and Professor Bant have suggested that 'the contract may have provided a juristic reason to receive the benefit but it does not provide a juristic reason to retain the enrichment after the failure of [condition]'.[13] A different way of putting this is that the failure of condition removes the juristic reason for the contractual performance. But this argument does not explain why the contractual obligation performed does not provide a juristic reason for the performance following a failure of condition. Edelman and Bant's suggestion also does not identify a normative reason why, in the view of the qualified intention theory, the existence of a juristic reason for a performance should prevent a claim for restitution for mistake but should not prevent a claim for restitution for a failure of condition.

To expand upon the first objection to Edelman and Bant's suggestion, the juristic reason for a contractual performance is the contractual obligation to undertake the performance. Whether there is a juristic reason for a contractual performance depends upon whether there *was* an obligation to undertake the performance when the performance occurred. This is because, following the performance of a contractual obligation, the obligation (and hence the juristic reason for the performance) does not exist because the obligation is discharged. Thus, if C is under a contractual obligation to pay £1,000 to D and makes the payment, C's payment obligation is no longer owed and therefore ceases to exist. But there was a juristic reason for the £1,000 payment as C was under a now discharged obligation to pay this sum to D. Unless one is prepared to accept that a failure of condition rescinds the contractual obligation C performed ab initio, a failure of condition cannot be regarded as removing the juristic reason for a contractual performance.

It is also worth reiterating that it is incorrect to treat termination as having the effect that a contract's obligations cease to provide a juristic reason for a performance. Termination does not rescind ab initio contractual obligations that have been discharged through performance. Rather, termination discharges unperformed obligations that have not unconditionally accrued but leaves unaffected obligations that have previously been discharged through performance or which have unconditionally accrued.[14] The claim that termination has the effect that

[12] Burrows, 'Conditional Intention as an Unjust Factor' (n 2) 345–46, 348–49.

[13] J Edelman and E Bant, *Unjust Enrichment*, 2nd edn (Sydney, Hart Publishing, 2016) 252.

[14] *McDonald v Dennys Lascelles Ltd* (1933) 48 CLR 457, 475–78 (Dixon J); *Holland v Wiltshire* (1954) 90 CLR 409, 416 (Dixon CJ); *Johnson v Agnew* [1980] AC 367, 396–98 (Lord Wilberforce). The fact that an obligation has accrued (ie, fallen due for performance) does not necessarily mean that the obligation has unconditionally accrued. Suppose that C agrees to pay £1,000 in advance on 16 August in exchange for D's performance of a dependent service obligation. On 17 August, after C's payment obligation has fallen due but before the £1,000 payment was made, the contract is terminated for D's repudiation. In this example, on 16 August, C's payment obligation accrued. However, that obligation did not accrue

there ceases to be a juristic reason for a contractual performance is a version of the rescission fallacy. It was also explained in chapter 3 that where a contract is unenforceable, there will still be a juristic reason for a performance of the unenforceable contract because such agreements create legally recognised obligations.

The principal difficulty with the qualified intention theory in the context of contractual performances is therefore that it fails to convincingly explain why a contractual obligation to undertake a performance prevents restitution from being awarded on the grounds of mistake but not a failure of condition. This difficulty arises because, in the view of the qualified intention theory, the justification for restitution for mistake is analogous to the justification for restitution for a failure of condition. As discussed in chapter 1, this analogy is that, as in cases of mistake, where there is a failure of condition C did not intend for D to be enriched at its expense in the circumstances.

B. The Position under the Agreement Theory

Under the agreement theory, what justifies restitution of a contractual performance for a failure of condition is the parties' contractual agreement itself. Consider again the example provided above, where C makes an advance payment of £1,000 to D in the performance of a contractual payment obligation in exchange for D's performance of a dependent service obligation, which D wrongly performs no part of. For the agreement theory, the reason that C may be entitled to restitution of the payment is that, on the contract's proper construction, D's entitlement against C to the £1,000 payment remained conditional upon D's substantial performance of its service obligation. If that condition fails, the justification for awarding restitution is to ensure that D is not entitled against C to the £1,000 payment in circumstances where it was agreed that D was not so entitled. On this view, restitutionary awards for a failure of condition are not 'complementary' or 'subsidiary' to contract because the justification for restitution relates to the content of the contract itself. As McHugh J said in *Baltic Shipping Co v Dillon*,[15] '[w]hether or not a payment is the subject of a condition at the time a contract is discharged depends upon the express and implied terms of the contract.' The sense in which the justification for restitution relates to the content of the contract is not that the contract contains a promissory obligation to make restitution in the circumstances, but rather that the agreed condition which has failed formed part of the contract.

To treat D's entitlement to a contractual performance rendered by C as subject to a condition that was not incorporated into the parties' contract will also almost always be inconsistent with that contract. This is because, in nearly every case,

unconditionally because it remained conditional upon it not becoming impossible for C to earn the agreed counter-performance. Consequently, following termination, D will be unable to recover the £1,000 in an action for the agreed sum.

[15] *Baltic Shipping Co v Dillon (The Mikhail Lermontov)* (1993) 176 CLR 344, 390.

where the conditions incorporated into the contract have been fulfilled, the proper interpretation of the contract will be that D is unconditionally entitled to the performance rendered. The only exception is where the contract is silent on whether D is unconditionally entitled to C's performance in the circumstances.[16] Furthermore, there is no conceptual space for an agreed condition existing outside of the contract that may justify restitution. If the condition is agreed upon and intended to have legal effect, which, as explained in chapter 3, is sufficient to render D's entitlement against C to a performance conditional, the condition will be a term of the contract. This is because a contractual term is a proposition of law regarding the relations between the parties to an enforceable agreement that is made true by that agreement (express terms or terms implied in fact) or because the parties have entered into an agreement of a certain kind (terms implied by law).[17]

A conceptual point that is worth emphasising at this juncture is that, as discussed in chapter 1, a contract is a certain kind of agreement. More specifically, a contract is an agreement that contains one or more enforceable promissory obligations or undertakings between the parties to the agreement. Where parties have formed a contract, it is therefore a mistake to think of the contract and the agreement as distinct. Rather, where a contract is formed, an agreement of a certain kind is formed. If the agreement in which a condition is found is a contract, the condition therefore forms part of (ie, has been incorporated into) the contract.

Cases holding that restitution of a performance that was mistakenly rendered will not be awarded where there was a juristic reason for the performance do not present a difficulty for this account. The justification for restitution for a failure of condition is, according to the agreement theory, not analogous to the justification for restitution for mistake, meaning that these cases are not alike. Moreover, as observed in chapter 3, the fact that there was a juristic reason for a performance does not necessarily mean that D should be treated as unconditionally entitled to the performance after it has been rendered. To refuse to award restitution of a contractual performance for a failure of condition because C was contractually obliged to undertake the performance would be to fail to give effect to the parties' agreement that D's entitlement against C to the performance rendered remained subject to a now failed condition.

C. The Evidence Admissible when Determining Conditions

A consequence of the difference between what the qualified intention and the agreement theories regard as potentially justifying restitution of a contractual performance concerns the evidence that should be admissible in establishing that D's entitlement

[16] For an excellent discussion of contractual silence, see R Gregson, 'The Limits of Implication' (2025) 141 *LQR* 413.

[17] For a similar definition, see F Wilmot-Smith, 'Term Limits: What is a Term?' (2019) 39 *OJLS* 705.

to a contractual performance undertaken by C remained subject to a condition. In *Dargamo*, Carr LJ said that 'in unjust enrichment, the practical policy reasons for excluding previous negotiations in the interpretative exercise do not arise'.[18] In support, Carr LJ referred to an article by Dr Wilmot-Smith, where it was said:

> in the interpretation of contracts and trust documents, 'previous negotiations' are excluded from the court's construction of the meaning of documents. These exclusions are justified for reasons of 'practical policy', the view being that the certainty and predictability of litigation is increased and third parties are better protected by the rule. The exclusion is not needed for the construction of conditions: the policy concerns are entirely different.[19]

If the existence of a condition depends upon whether C held an intention, which D knew of, for D's entitlement to a benefit conferred to remain subject to the condition, there is a respectable argument that different evidence should be admissible to the evidence that is admissible when construing a contract. This is because, on this view, the fact that one is trying to determine in a failure of condition claim is different from the fact that one is trying to determine when construing a contract. As just observed, the former fact is whether C intended the condition and D knew of this intention. By contrast, when construing a contract, one is trying to determine the meaning the contract would convey to a reasonable bystander familiar with the relevant context.[20]

From the perspective of the agreement theory, when examining the conditions that D's entitlement against C to a contractual performance rendered remained subject to, the same evidence should be admissible as the evidence that is admissible when construing a contract, and only that evidence.[21] As observed, for this theory, what renders D's entitlement against C to a contractual performance subject to a condition is the contract itself. The existence of such a condition is therefore a matter of contractual interpretation. Consequently, if, for example, evidence of prior negotiations and subsequent conduct is inadmissible when construing a contract, such evidence should also be inadmissible when determining whether D's entitlement to a contractual performance rendered remained subject to a condition.

III. Restitution of Contractual Performances

The remainder of this chapter examines, through the lens of the agreement theory, the availability and measure of restitution of contractual performances for a failure

[18] *Dargamo Holdings Ltd v Avonwick Holdings Ltd* (n 5) [133].

[19] F Wilmot-Smith, 'Replacing Risk-Taking Reasoning' (2011) 127 *LQR* 610, 622.

[20] *Investors Compensation Scheme v West Bromwich Building Society* [1998] 1 WLR 896, 912–13 (Lord Hoffmann).

[21] See also C Mitchell, P Mitchell and S Watterson, *Goff & Jones on Unjust Enrichment*, 10th edn (UK, Sweet & Maxwell, 2022) 479–80, [13-04]–[13-05].

of condition in various scenarios. As just explained, under this theory, the availability of restitution of a contractual performance for a failure of condition depends upon the construction of the parties' contract. The section begins by considering when restitution for a failure of condition should be awarded following a contractual breach or repudiation. Next, consideration is given to how, if at all, the agreed price should affect the sum awarded as restitution. Finally, the availability of restitution for a failure of condition following frustration is discussed.

A. Restitution for a Failure of Condition following a Breach or Repudiation

i. Partly Performed Service Obligation by an Innocent Party

Scenario 1:

> C and D enter into a contract whereby C undertakes an entire obligation to construct a stable on D's land in exchange for payment following substantial completion. After C has completed half of the work, D wrongly refuses C access to its land, thereby depriving C of an opportunity to substantially perform the work. C accepts D's repudiation and has an enforceable right to damages.

The leading case to consider whether C can claim restitution for a failure of condition in this scenario, where D's repudiation has prevented C from substantially performing an entire service obligation and C has an enforceable right to damages, is *Mann v Paterson Constructions Pty Ltd.*[22] In that case, a bare majority of the High Court of Australia held that the claimant builder could claim non-contractual quantum meruit despite having an enforceable right to damages. Of that majority, Nettle, Gordon and Edelman JJ considered that the doctrinal basis for this non-contractual quantum meruit award, which their Honours regarded as a restitutionary quantum meruit, was a failure of condition.[23] The other member of the majority, Gageler J, held that the basis for awarding non-contractual quantum meruit was an obligation imposed by law to pay reasonable remuneration for the executed consideration in the circumstances.[24]

The difficulty with Gageler J's analysis is that there is no good reason for treating the claim that is potentially available where an innocent party has partly performed an entire payment obligation as different from the claim that is available where an innocent party has partly performed an entire service obligation.[25] As *Fibrosa Spolka Akcyjna v Fairbairn Lawson Combe Barbour Ltd*,[26] which is discussed

[22] *Mann v Paterson Constructions Pty Ltd* (2019) 267 CLR 560.
[23] ibid [175]–[176].
[24] ibid [73].
[25] D Winterton and T Pilkington, '*Mann v Paterson Constructions Pty Ltd*: The Intersection of Debt, Damages and Quantum Meruit' (2021) 44 *Melbourne University Law Review* 679, 711–12
[26] *Fibrosa Spolka Akcyjna v Fairbairn Lawson Combe Barbour Ltd* (n 1).

further below, illustrates, where a contract is terminated when an innocent party has partly performed an entire advance payment obligation, the innocent party can generally bring a claim for restitution for a failure of condition. By analogy, where a contract is terminated when an innocent party has partly performed an entire service obligation, the innocent party should have a claim for restitution for a failure of condition.

Nettle, Gordon and Edelman JJ's view that C may have concurrent claims against D for restitution for a failure of condition and damages subject to the rule against double recovery should be endorsed. In explaining why, it is helpful to first consider the arguments against C having a claim for restitution for a failure of condition where C has an enforceable right to damages, before setting out the positive reasons that support the possibility of concurrent claims.

A first argument against C having a claim for restitution where D's breach or repudiation has resulted in a failure of condition and C has an enforceable right to damages is that it may allow C to escape a bad bargain. However, there are cases where restitution for a failure of condition has been awarded where it has enabled C to escape a bad bargain,[27] which suggests that the law does not regard this as a good reason for denying restitution.

A second argument is that to allow a claim for restitution for a failure of condition where there is an enforceable right to damages would subvert the 'contractual allocation of risk' and 'quantification of liabilities'. In *Mann*, Kiefel CJ, Bell and Keane JJ said:

> [t]he extent of the obligation to pay damages for loss of bargain, governed as it is by the terms of the terminated contract, reflects the parties' allocation of risk and rights as between each other under the contract. To allow a restitutionary remedy by way of a claim for the reasonable value of work performed unconstrained by the terms of the applicable contract would undermine the parties' bargain as to the allocation of risks and quantification of liabilities, and so undermine the abiding values of individual autonomy and freedom of contract.[28]

It is difficult to understand why, as Kiefel CJ, Bell and Keane JJ claimed, the existence of an enforceable right to damages for loss of bargain would mean that an award of restitution would subvert the contractual risk allocation and quantification of liabilities unless one regards C as having contracted for either D's performance or damages in substitution thereof, so that what is agreed covers the remedies available to C in the event of D's breach or repudiation.[29] This idea, commonly referred to

[27] *Wilkinson v Lloyd* (1845) 7 QB 27; 115 ER 398.

[28] ibid [19]–[20]. See also *Taylor v Motability Finance Ltd* [2004] EWHC 2619 (Comm); *Howes Percival LLP v Page* [2013] EWHC 4104 (Ch).

[29] F Wilmot-Smith, 'Contract and Unjust Enrichment in the High Court of Australia' (2020) 136 *LQR* 196, 198; Winterton and Pilkington, '*Mann v Paterson Constructions Pty Ltd*: The Intersection of Debt, Damages and Quantum Meruit' (n 25) 698–99; R Stevens, *The Laws of Restitution* (Oxford, Oxford University Press, 2023) 134.

as the 'Holmesian fallacy',[30] has been rejected by the High Court itself[31] and thoroughly discredited by commentators.[32] The essential problem with this view is that the obligation to pay damages is a secondary obligation imposed by law.[33] Although the contract is necessary for the existence of a secondary obligation to pay damages for loss of bargain, such an obligation is not agreed upon.[34]

A final argument against C having a claim for restitution where D's breach or repudiation has resulted in a failure of condition and C has an enforceable right to damages is that the damages award will place C, so far as money can, in a position where the condition that has failed has been fulfilled. Any justification for awarding restitution, proceeds the argument, is therefore absent. However, even if an award of damages would fully cure the injustice that exists following a failure of condition, it is unclear why this should rule out the possibility of an alternative claim for restitution. The fact that C may be entitled to a remedy against D that would fully cure an injustice that has arisen does not, on its own, provide a good reason against C having a different claim. Further, damages are often an imperfect substitute for the lost performance. As Professor Williston observed, 'when a buyer buys a horse, warranted sound, the real thing [they are] after is a sound horse ... [they do] not want an unsound horse, worth half the money, and the difference in damages.'[35] An award of damages may therefore not place C in a position where the condition that has failed due to D's breach or repudiation has been fulfilled.[36]

In addition to there being no compelling reason against there being a claim for restitution for a failure of condition where there is an enforceable right to damages, the following reasons positively support recognising the possibility of concurrent claims subject to the rule against double recovery. First, as Wilmot-Smith has observed, '[i]t is incoherent for the law to permit a claim [for restitution for a failure of condition] where the contract is unenforceable but deny it where the claim can be enforced: the law should not provide extra rewards to those whose instruments are unenforceable.'[37]

To expand upon Wilmot-Smith's point, where an agreement is unenforceable, this does not mean that the agreement cannot be breached or repudiated, nor that

[30] See OW Holmes Jr, *The Common Law* (New Jersey, Lawbook Exchange, 2005) 301. It is arguable that Holmes did not actually endorse this fallacy: see JM Perillo, 'Misreading Oliver Wendell Holmes on Efficient Breach and Tortious Interference' (2000) 68 *Fordham Law Review* 1085.

[31] *Tabcorp Holdings Ltd v Bowen Investments Pty Ltd* (2009) 236 CLR 272, [13] (French CJ, Gummow, Heydon, Crennan and Kiefel JJ).

[32] See, eg, L Smith, 'Understanding Specific Performance' in N Cohen and E McKendrick (eds), *Comparative Remedies for Breach of Contract* (Oxford, Hart Publishing, 2005) 221; D Winterton, *Money Awards in Contract Law* (Oxford, Hart Publishing, 2015) ch 4; R Stevens, 'Rights Restricting Remedies' in A Robertson and M Tilbury (eds), *Divergences in Private Law* (Oxford, Hart Publishing, 2016) 159, 165.

[33] *Moschi v Lep Air Services Ltd* [1973] AC 331, 345 (Lord Reid), 350 (Lord Diplock).

[34] F Wilmot-Smith, 'Termination after Breach' (2018) 134 *LQR* 307, 321–22.

[35] S Williston, 'Rescission for Breach of Warranty' (1903) 16 *Harvard Law Review* 465, 472.

[36] F Wilmot-Smith, 'Reconsidering "Total" Failure' (2013) 72 *CLJ* 414, 430–31.

[37] Wilmot-Smith, 'Contract and Unjust Enrichment in the High Court of Australia' (n 29) 197–98. See also Stevens, *The Laws of Restitution* (n 29) 134.

the breach or repudiation cannot give rise to an unenforceable secondary right to damages. As discussed in chapter 1, where an agreement is unenforceable, what this means is that neither party to the agreement has a right against the court to an order enforcing any of the obligations the agreement created. The reason that a secondary obligation to pay damages is also unenforceable where an agreement is unenforceable is that awarding damages would involve indirectly enforcing the unenforceable contract via a monetary award. To recognise a claim for restitution for a failure of condition where there is an unenforceable right to damages, but not where there is an enforceable right to damages, would mean that the unenforceability of an obligation to pay damages is either conferring an extra entitlement in the form of a claim for restitution or removing a barrier to a claim for restitution. But it is mysterious why the unenforceability of a right to damages should confer such a claim.

Secondly, there are cases where restitution for a failure of condition has been awarded where there would have been an enforceable right to damages. An example is *Barber v NWS Bank Plc*.[38] A motorcar dealer transferred a title to a motorcar to the defendant finance company, which entered into a conditional sale agreement with the claimant. The claimant later discovered that the motorcar was subject to a prior finance agreement. This constituted a breach by the defendant of an implied 'condition'. The claimant terminated the contract and was held to be entitled to recover the instalment payments that he had made. Restitution of the instalments was therefore awarded even though the claimant would have had an enforceable right to damages.

Finally, the existence of a claim for restitution for a failure of condition where there is an enforceable right to damages is of practical utility. As Gageler J observed in *Mann*:

> The availability of the action allows the innocent party to choose to adopt the course of quickly and cheaply obtaining judgment for an easily quantifiable liquidated amount instead of embarking on a long and more expensive and more uncertain pursuit of a potentially larger judgment for unliquidated damages. Choice by the innocent party to adopt that course has the flow-on systemic advantage of shortening trial and pre-trial processes.[39]

An issue that arises regarding *Mann* is how it is to be reconciled with the decision in *Sumpter v Hedges*,[40] which it is argued below is correctly decided. In *Sumpter*, the claimant builder undertook an entire obligation to build two houses and stables on the defendant's land, but only did part of the work before the contract was terminated for the builder's repudiation. The builder's action for non-contractual quantum meruit failed. The only material difference between *Sumpter* and *Mann* is that in

[38] *Barber v NWS Bank Plc* [1996] 1 WLR 641. See also *Holmes v Hall* (1704) 6 Mod 161; 87 ER 918; *Butterworth v Kingsway Motors Ltd* [1954] 1 WLR 1286.

[39] *Mann v Paterson Constructions Pty Ltd* (n 22) [87].

[40] *Sumpter v Hedges* [1898] 1 QB 673. See further *Ellis v Hamlen* (1810) 3 Taunt 52; 128 ER 21; *Oliver v Lakeside Property Trust Pty Ltd* [2005] NSWSC 1040.

Sumpter, the contract was terminated for the claimant builder's repudiation, whereas in *Mann*, the contract was terminated for the defendant landowner's repudiation.

The most plausible way of reconciling *Sumpter* and *Mann* is to regard the performance of an entire service obligation by C as generally undertaken on the condition that D does not wrongly deprive C of an opportunity to substantially perform its entire service obligation.[41] On this view, the condition that failed and which grounded the builder's restitutionary claim in *Mann* was that the Manns deprived the builder of an opportunity to substantially perform certain entire stages of the work by wrongly excluding the builder from their land. In *Sumpter*, by contrast, because the landowner did not deprive the builder of an opportunity to substantially perform the work, there was not a failure of condition.

An implication of this interpretation of the condition that failed in *Mann* is that there will only be a failure of condition in respect of a part performance of an entire service obligation by an innocent party where the repudiation must be accepted.[42] If the innocent party can affirm the contract and earn the agreed counter-performance because the repudiating party's co-operation is not required for the innocent party to perform, as for example in *White & Carter (Councils) Ltd v McGregor*,[43] a claim for restitution for a failure of condition should generally fail.

ii. Strictly or Substantially Performed Service Obligation

Scenario 2:

> C and D enter into a contract whereby C undertakes an entire obligation to construct a stable on D's land in exchange for payment following substantial completion. C substantially performs the work, but D, in breach of contract, refuses to pay.

The leading case to address the availability of restitution for a failure of condition in this scenario is also *Mann*. There it was held that where C has an enforceable right to be paid for work it has performed, C will not have a claim for restitution of its performance of the work for a failure of condition in the alternative to an action for the agreed sum.[44] The justification provided by Nettle, Gordon and Edelman JJ for that conclusion was that in such circumstances there is not a failure of condition.[45] This holding suggests that their Honours regarded the Manns' entitlement to the builder's performance of each entire stage of the work as conditional upon the

[41] Winterton and Pilkington, '*Mann v Paterson Constructions Pty Ltd*: The Intersection of Debt, Damages and Quantum Meruit' (n 25) 704–06. See also Mitchell, Mitchell and Watterson, *Goff & Jones* (n 21) 64, [3-38]; Stevens, *The Laws of Restitution* (n 29) 132.

[42] Winterton and Pilkington, '*Mann v Paterson Constructions Pty Ltd*: The Intersection of Debt, Damages and Quantum Meruit' (n 25) 706.

[43] *White & Carter (Councils) Ltd v McGregor* [1962] AC 413.

[44] *Mann v Paterson Constructions Pty Ltd* (n 22) [19] (Kiefel CJ, Bell and Keane JJ), [62]–[63] (Gageler J), [176] (Nettle, Gordon and Edelman JJ).

[45] ibid [176] (Nettle, Gordon and Edelman JJ). See also *GEC Marconi Systems Pty Ltd v BHP Information Technology Pty Ltd* (2003) 128 FCR 1, [656] (Finn J).

builder earning an *enforceable* right to payment following substantial completion. The reason the enforceability of the right to payment must have been part of the condition is that it is otherwise difficult to reconcile *Mann* with *Pavey & Matthews Pty Ltd v Paul*,[46] where restitution was awarded despite the builder having earned an *unenforceable* right to be paid for the work it had performed.

Despite certain statements in first instance decisions to the contrary,[47] there is a strong argument that in England it is possible to claim restitution for a failure of condition in the alternative to an action for the agreed sum. First, the authorities suggest that C may be entitled to restitution for a failure of condition where C has earned an unenforceable right to payment of the agreed sum.[48] Secondly, the authorities suggest that D's entitlement against C to a contractual performance C has rendered is generally *not* conditional upon the enforceability of the parties' agreement. This latter proposition is supported by *Thomas v Brown*,[49] where Quain J rejected an argument that a payment was recoverable due to the mere fact that the parties' agreement was unenforceable. The same conclusion was reached in *Monnickendam v Leanse*,[50] where Horridge J held:

> there being … a good contract between the parties, but one which could not be enforced under the Statute of Frauds, and the deposit having been paid in pursuance of that contract and the defendant being entitled to hold it as security against the purchaser's not going on with the transaction, *there had been no total failure of consideration*.[51]

What *Thomas v Brown* and *Monnickendam v Leanse* suggest is that in cases exemplified by *Pavey*, where restitution is awarded where C has earned an unenforceable right to be paid for work performed but payment has not been made, the condition that fails is not that C's right to be paid is unenforceable but rather that D has failed to pay the agreed sum (within a certain time). This in turn suggests that in England, contrary to what appears to be the position in Australia following *Mann*, if C has an enforceable right to payment for work it has performed but D has not made the payment by a certain time, there may be a failure of condition in respect of C's performance of the work.

iii. Partly Performed Service Obligation by a Repudiating Party

Scenario 3:

> C and D enter into a contract whereby C undertakes to provide consulting services for D in relation to a corporate takeover. C's obligation is entire. C performs half of the services before repudiating the contract. D accepts the repudiation.

[46] *Pavey & Matthews Pty Ltd v Paul* (1987) 162 CLR 221.
[47] cf *Taylor v Motability Finance Ltd* (n 28) [23]–[27] (Cooke J); *Elek v Bar-Tur* [2013] EWHC 207 (Ch), [13] (David Donaldson QC).
[48] *Scarisbrick v Parkinson* (1869) 20 LT 175; *Pavey & Matthews Pty Ltd v Paul* (n 46).
[49] *Thomas v Brown* (1876) 1 QBD 714, 723.
[50] *Monnickendam v Leanse* (1923) 39 TLR 445.
[51] ibid 447 (emphasis added).

The leading case concerning the availability of restitution for a failure of condition in cases exemplified by this example is *Sumpter*.[52] As observed above, in that case it was held that a repudiating party is not entitled to restitution of a part performance of an entire service obligation.

Before explaining why *Sumpter* is correctly decided, it is worth clarifying that an entire obligation is an obligation that must be strictly or substantially performed for the performing party to unconditionally earn any part of the agreed counter-performance.[53] Although the concept of an entire obligation is generally used to refer to a particular kind of service obligation, payment obligations and other obligations may also be entire. Suppose, for example, that C undertakes an obligation to make three instalment payments of £10,000 to D in advance in exchange for D transferring a title to certain goods via delivery after the third payment has been made. In this scenario, each of the £10,000 instalment payments made by C can be regarded as a part performance of an entire payment obligation because it is only if all of the instalments are paid that C will be unconditionally entitled to any part of the agreed counter-performance from D.

The most comprehensive discussion of why restitution for a failure of condition should not be awarded in cases exemplified by *Sumpter* is by Professors McFarlane and Stevens.[54] Those authors argue that in *Sumpter* restitution was correctly denied because '[w]here a contract imposes an entire obligation, work is done in the expectation that it will be paid for *when complete*. There is no shared expectation that part performance is to be rewarded.'[55] One interpretation of McFarlane and Stevens' argument is that *Sumpter* is correctly decided because the claimant builder was not entitled under the contract to be paid for a part performance of the work. This explanation should be rejected. It would mean that restitution should also be denied in cases such as *Mann*, where *an innocent* party has partly performed an entire service obligation before wrongly being deprived by the repudiating party of an opportunity to substantially perform, because here the innocent party is also not entitled under the contract to payment.

A preferable interpretation of McFarlane and Stevens' argument is that if restitution was awarded to a party who has partly performed an entire service obligation before the contract is terminated for this party's repudiation, it would undermine the purpose of the service obligation being entire. This suggests that there is not a failure of an agreed condition in such circumstances. The purpose of an obligation being entire is to give the performing party an additional incentive not to fail to perform by providing that they are not entitled to any part of the agreed counter-performance unless the obligation is substantially performed. Although an award of restitution does not strictly require an innocent party to pay for the repudiating party's part performance of an entire service obligation, there is practically little difference between the two. Consequently, to award restitution of a part performance of an entire service obligation to a repudiating party would

[52] See also *Sinclair v Bowles* (1829) 9 B & C 92; 109 ER 35.
[53] *Steele v Tardiani* (1946) 72 CLR 386, 401 (Dixon J).
[54] B McFarlane and R Stevens, 'In Defence of *Sumpter v Hedges*' (2002) 118 *LQR* 567.
[55] ibid 577 (emphasis in original).

undermine the purpose of the service obligation being entire as the repudiating party would effectively be entitled to part of the agreed counter-performance.

iv. Partly Performed Payment Obligations by a Repudiating Party

Scenario 4:

> C and D enter into a contract for the sale of a title to goods for £100,000. It is agreed that a title to the goods is to be transferred to C via delivery. It is a condition precedent to D's obligation to deliver the goods that the entire price is paid by C in advance. C pays a deposit of £10,000 and an instalment of £30,000 before repudiating the contract. D accepts the repudiation.

The authorities suggest that C is generally entitled to restitution for a failure of condition against D in this scenario, where C has partly performed an entire payment obligation before it became impossible for C to earn the agreed counter-performance. This is illustrated by *Mayson v Clouet*,[56] where a repudiating purchaser was held to be entitled to recover two instalment payments it had made under a contract for the sale of a fee simple title to land. *Mayson v Clouet* suggests that a part performance of an advance payment obligation is generally undertaken on the condition that the payor is not prevented from earning the agreed counter-performance for the payment. The reason the repudiating purchaser was prevented from earning the agreed counter-performance on the facts is that, following termination, the purchaser's payment obligation was discharged. The repudiating purchaser could therefore no longer earn the agreed counter-performance because the vendor's duty to convey a title to the land was conditional upon the purchaser's performance of its now discharged payment obligation.

If a part performance of a payment obligation was not recoverable by a repudiating payor, the concept of a deposit would be redundant because the innocent payee would be entitled to retain any part payment made by a repudiating payor in advance. A part performance of a payment obligation, unlike a part performance of an entire service obligation, can also be reversed in the same form. The significance of this is that requiring the innocent payee to make restitution of a part performance of an entire payment obligation does not in practice entitle the repudiating party to part of the agreed counter-performance for its part performance of the entire obligation.[57] Consequently, awarding restitution will not undermine the purpose of the payment obligation being entire, which suggests that it is plausible to regard there as having been a failure of an agreed condition.

[56] *Mayson v Clouet* [1924] AC 980. See also *Dies v British and International Mining and Finance Corp* [1939] 1 KB 724; *Baltic Shipping Co v Dillon (The Mikhail Lermontov)* (n 15) 390 (McHugh J).

[57] See also McFarlane and Stevens, 'In Defence of *Sumpter v Hedges*' (n 54) 584–85.

B. *Barton v Morris*

In *Barton v Morris*,[58] Mr Barton formed an oral contract with Foxpace Ltd, which had a title to land known as Nash House that it wanted to sell. The only express term of the contract was that if Barton introduced a purchaser to Foxpace, who then concluded a sale of Nash House for £6.5 million to the purchaser, Foxpace would pay Barton £1.2 million. Barton introduced Western UK (Acton) Ltd to Foxpace, who initially agreed to purchase Nash House for £6.5 million. However, upon learning that Nash House was situated on land that might be acquired for the High Speed 2 rail project, the price was reduced to £6 million. There was no suggestion that the price was reduced so that Foxpace could avoid paying Barton £1.2 million. As the sale price was lower than £6.5 million, Foxpace refused to pay Barton the £1.2 million. When the case reached the Supreme Court, the question was whether Barton was entitled to the market value of the services he had performed (£450,000) based upon a term implied in fact or law, or to restitution of his performance of the services for a failure of condition. The issue that is presently relevant is whether Barton should have been entitled to restitution.

There was a disagreement between the members of the Supreme Court concerning the proper construction of the contract between Barton and Foxpace. The first construction, favoured by Lady Rose, with whom Lord Briggs and Lord Stephens agreed, was that Barton was entitled to payment if, and only if, Nash House sold for £6.5 million.[59] Lady Rose did, however, appear to accept that there was a term implied in fact, providing that the price would not be reduced by Foxpace below £6.5 million to avoid having to pay Barton £1.2 million.[60]

Assuming Lady Rose's construction of the contract was correct, should Barton have been entitled to restitution for a failure of condition? Where a contract provides that C is entitled to be paid by D for services that C has performed if, and only if, a certain state of affairs materialises, to award restitution if that state of affairs does not materialise would be inconsistent with the contract. This is because an award of restitution to C would, in practice, require D to pay for C's services in circumstances where the contract stated that C was not entitled to payment.

The second construction of the contract, favoured by Lord Leggatt and Lord Burrows in separate judgments, was that the parties did not agree on whether Barton was entitled to be paid if Nash House sold for less than £6.5 million to a purchaser Barton had introduced. In other words, the contract was silent regarding what was to occur in the event of a sub-£6.5 million sale. But Lord Leggatt and Lord Burrows held that there was a term implied in law entitling Barton to reasonable remuneration for his services, which the parties had not excluded by their contract.

[58] *Barton v Morris* [2023] AC 684.
[59] ibid [96]-[98] (Lady Rose).
[60] ibid [31] (Lady Rose).

Under Lord Leggatt and Lord Burrows' preferred construction, should Barton have been entitled to restitution for a failure of condition? For Lord Leggatt, the answer was 'no' because 'there is no room for an unjust enrichment claim where there is a subsisting contract between the parties'.[61] If what Lord Leggatt meant by a 'subsisting contract' is a contract that has not been terminated, this reasoning is unpersuasive for reasons that have been elaborated: if there is 'no room' for a claim for restitution for a failure of condition while the contract is on foot, there should be no room for a claim for restitution if the contract has been terminated. The contrary view is the rescission fallacy under another guise.

Unlike Lord Leggatt, Lord Burrows was prepared to accept that if there was not a term implied in law entitling Barton to reasonable remuneration for the services he had performed, Barton would have had a claim for restitution for a failure of condition. In Lord Burrows' words:[62]

> there has been a relevant failure of basis. Mr Barton rendered the beneficial services to Foxpace on the basis, objectively shared with Foxpace, that he would be paid £1.2m for those services if Nash House was sold to Western for £6.5m. That basis failed (in Birks' words, the basis failed to materialise) when the sale to Western was for a price lower than £6.5m so that Mr Barton was not entitled to, and was not paid, the promised £1.2m. It is this failure of basis that supplies the unjust factor that Asplin LJ left unclear having (correctly) put to one side free acceptance.

In this passage, Lord Burrows suggests that Foxpace's entitlement to Barton's performance of the services remained conditional upon Nash House in fact selling for £6.5 million and Barton being paid £1.2 million following the sale. In considering the plausibility of this condition, it should be reiterated that for Lord Burrows the parties had not agreed that Barton was entitled to payment if, and only if, Nash House sold for £6.5 million. Rather, it had only been agreed that Barton was entitled to be paid £1.2 million if, and only if, Nash House sold for £6.5 million.

It is not contradictory to say that there was not an express term or a term implied in fact stipulating whether Barton was entitled to be paid if Nash House sold for less than £6.5 million, but that the parties had nevertheless agreed that Barton's services were performed on the condition that Nash House would sell for £6.5 million and Barton would be paid £1.2 million. That being said, it is difficult to conclude that the parties reached an agreement concerning whether Foxpace was entitled to Barton's performance of the services in the circumstances that occurred if they had not agreed upon whether Barton was entitled to be paid for his services in the circumstances. If the parties did not agree on whether Barton was entitled to be paid or not, it is more likely that the agreement was also silent on whether Foxpace was unconditionally entitled to Barton's performance of the services in the circumstances. Consequently, restitution should have been denied because no agreed condition failed.

[61] ibid [189].
[62] ibid [234].

C. Relevance of the Agreed Price

A difficult question that has arisen is how the agreed price should, if at all, affect the sum awarded as restitution of a contractual performance for a failure of condition. It is now argued that the sum awarded should sometimes be less than the agreed price, but that the agreed price should almost always provide an overall cap.

i. Agreed Price Exceeds the Market Value

Scenario 5:

> C and D enter into an unenforceable contract whereby C undertakes to construct a garage on D's land in exchange for payment following substantial completion. C's obligation to perform the work is entire. The price is £10,000. The market value of the work is £8,000. C substantially performs the work, but D, in breach of the agreement, refuses to pay.

In this scenario, is C entitled to restitution of more than the market value of its work because the agreed price exceeded the market value? *Benedetti v Sawiris*[63] strongly suggests that C is not. Recall that in that case it was held that C is not entitled to restitution in an amount exceeding the market value of services performed on a condition that has now failed based upon a principle of 'subjective revaluation'. It would be surprising if C was not entitled to recover more than the market value of services performed where D values the services above market value, but was entitled to recover more than the market value where the agreed price exceeds the market value.

In addition, in chapters 3 and 4 it was explained that the purpose of an award of restitution of a performance of services undertaken on a condition that has now failed is to reverse, so far as possible, the performance of the services, thereby giving effect to the parties' agreement. A performance of services cannot ever truly be reversed. The closest the law can come to doing so is to order the party for whom the services were performed to pay the market value of the services at the time they were undertaken to the service provider. On this view, if the services were priced above market value, this should be irrelevant to the sum that is awarded as restitution.

ii. Market Value Exceeds the Agreed Price

Scenario 6:

> C and D enter into an unenforceable contract whereby C undertakes to construct a garage on D's land in exchange for payment following substantial completion. C's obligation to perform the work is entire. The price is £10,000. C partly performs the work, but D, in breach of the agreement, refuses to pay. The market value of the work performed is £11,000.

[63] *Benedetti v Sawiris* [2014] AC 938.

In this scenario, does the agreed price impose an overall cap on the sum that C is entitled to as restitution? The leading case to examine this issue is once again *Mann*. As observed, in that case a majority of the High Court held that C may be entitled to an award of non-contractual quantum meruit where C has an enforceable right to damages. Of that majority, Nettle, Gordon and Edelman JJ held that the sum awarded should generally not exceed the overall price. But their Honours suggested that there may be exceptional cases where it would be unconscionable to limit the sum recoverable to the agreed price.[64] Gageler J, by contrast, considered that the sum recoverable should never exceed the overall price.[65] Kiefel CJ, Bell and Keane JJ did not address the point. There was therefore no majority.

Nettle, Gordon and Edelman JJ suggested that an example where it would be unconscionable to limit the sum awarded to the agreed price was arguably afforded by the famous American case of *Boomer v Muir*.[66] The preferable interpretation, however, is that a restitutionary award exceeding the agreed price was not made in *Boomer* itself. The relevant facts were that RC Storrie & Co entered into a contract with the Feather River Power Co for a major construction project. Storrie subcontracted with HH Boomer for the construction of a dam for a price of $300,000. Boomer later terminated the contract due to Storrie having persistently prevented it from performing, which caused significant delays and increased performance costs to Boomer.

At trial, the jury awarded Boomer $258,000 as 'quantum meruit'. Importantly, this award sought to compensate Boomer for additional costs that it had incurred performing its side of the contract due to Storrie's breaches, thereby constituting an award that would now typically be characterised as damages for consequential loss. Put another way, the 'quantum meruit' awarded to Boomer was not measured only by having regard to the market value of the services Boomer had performed. That this award included compensation for additional costs Boomer had incurred has been appreciated in the United States. Professor Feldman, for example, has observed:

> the trial court granted Boomer a judgment in rescission and restitution for an additional $258,000 for the market value of his extra labor and materials, which was the difference between Boomer's costs attributable to Storrie's delays and other interferences and what Storrie had already paid this subcontractor.[67]

Professor Stevens has argued that the agreed price should always provide an overall cap on the sum awarded as restitution for a failure of condition.[68] According to Stevens, where C performs a service in exchange for payment following substantial completion, generally D's entitlement to the performance of the

[64] *Mann v Paterson Constructions Pty Ltd* (n 22) [216].

[65] ibid [91].

[66] *Boomer v Muir* 24 P 2d 570 (Cal Ct App, 1933).

[67] S Feldman, 'Rescission, Restitution, and the Principle of Fair Redress: A Response to Professors Brooks and Stremitzer' (2013) 47 *Valparaiso University Law Review* 399, 449.

[68] Stevens, *The Laws of Restitution* (n 29) 134. This is supported by *Taylor v Motability Finance Ltd* (n 28) [26] (Cooke J).

service rendered is agreed to remain conditional upon payment of the agreed sum. Once C has been paid this sum, Stevens claims that the condition attaching to the performance of the service is fulfilled and an award of any further sum as restitution therefore unjustified. Wilmot-Smith has made essentially the same argument:

> Where the anticipated counter-performance is the payment of money, any claim based on the failure of [condition] should not exceed the price set out in the contract: any restitutionary award above the debt due under the contract would cure no injustice. … The injustice of a failure of [condition] claim arises only if the condition of the performance is unsatisfied. Where the builder is owed a contractual debt, therefore, the condition will be satisfied and the injustice cured by payment of the contractual debt.[69]

A problem with this argument, when applied to scenario 6, is that in such cases there is not a failure of condition due to D having failed to pay for the services. Rather, there is a failure of condition because D wrongly deprived C of an opportunity to substantially perform the services. It cannot be that there is a failure of condition in respect of C's performance of services due to a failure by D to pay for the services if D's obligation to pay for the services did not accrue. It is therefore wrong to say that in scenario 6 if D was paid £10,000 there would not be a failure of condition.

A further difficulty is that Stevens and Wilmot-Smith appear to be claiming that there will not be a failure of condition no matter how late the agreed sum is paid. This is implied by their argument because if the condition attaching to C's performance of the services is payment of the agreed sum within a certain time, Stevens and Wilmot-Smith's suggestion that after the agreed sum has been paid there is *not* a failure of condition is not necessarily true. Imagine that C and D enter into a contract whereby C agrees to perform certain services for D in exchange for payment of £10,000 no later than one week after the services have been substantially performed. If the condition attaching to D's entitlement to the services rendered is payment of £10,000 not substantially later than one week after the services have been performed, there will still be a failure of condition if one year after the services were performed D pays £10,000. This is because the temporal component of the condition will still remain unfulfilled after the payment has been made.

The agreed price should nevertheless almost always provide an overall cap on the sum that is awarded as restitution for a failure of condition. At this point, a distinction needs to be drawn between cases where the price has been earned and those where it has not. Consider:

(1) C and D enter into an unenforceable contract whereby C is under an entire obligation to erect a fence on D's farm in exchange for payment following substantial completion. The price is £10,000. After C has substantially performed the work, D refuses to pay. The market value of the work is £11,000.

[69] Wilmot-Smith, 'Contract and Unjust Enrichment in the High Court of Australia' (n 29) 200.

(2) C and D enter into an unenforceable contract whereby C is under an entire obligation to erect a fence on D's farm in exchange for payment following substantial completion. The price is £10,000. Before C has substantially performed the work, the agreement is terminated for D's repudiation. The market value of the work performed is £11,000.

In scenario (1), where C has earned the agreed sum, the price should always cap the sum recoverable. To require D to make restitution of an amount exceeding this sum would in practice require D to pay more for C's performance than it agreed to pay. Such an award would therefore undermine the parties' agreement.

More difficult is scenario (2), where C has not earned the agreed sum. Here, it cannot be said that to require D to make restitution in an amount exceeding the agreed sum would in practice be to require D to pay more for the services than it agreed to pay because D never undertook to pay for a part performance. That said, once C has received a sum as restitution equivalent to that which it would have been entitled to following substantial performance plus interest and, where appropriate, damages, it will be as if the condition that D's entitlement to a *complete* performance of the services was subject to has been fulfilled. C will therefore have consented to the position that it now finds itself in, in the sense that C is in the position that it expected to and agreed to end up in, making C undeserving of an award of any further sum as restitution.[70]

If the justification for the agreed price providing an overall cap on the sum awarded as restitution in cases exemplified by scenario (2) is that, following C's receipt of a sum as restitution equivalent to the price, C will be in a position that it consented to ending up in, there will, as Nettle, Gordon and Edelman JJ held in *Mann*, be exceptional cases where the agreed price should not provide an overall cap. An example is where C agrees to perform certain work for less than market value to use the completed work to generate future business.[71] In this example, where a substantial part of C's reason for performing the work is not payment of the agreed sum but using the completed work to generate future business, C cannot be regarded as having consented to the position it will find itself in after it has received an amount as restitution equivalent to the price. The agreed price should therefore not provide an overall cap.

Another example where Justice Edelman, writing extra-judicially, has suggested that the agreed price should not provide an overall cap is as follows.[72] A landowner contracts for work to be done on their land with a date of completion of 1 July 2024, time being of the essence. The owner and the contractor agree on a price of £200,000. The contractor thinks that they might need more time, and renegotiates a price of £180,000 with a date for completion of 1 December 2024. In June

[70] This idea of consenting to the position one finds itself in comes from Stevens, *The Laws of Restitution* (n 29) 76–78.

[71] A case that bears some resemblance to this example is *Vivian Fraser & Associates Pty Ltd v Shipton* [1999] FCA 60.

[72] J Edelman, 'The Laws of Restitution by Robert Stevens' (2024) 140 *LQR* 321, 325–26.

2024, the owner repudiates. The work, with a market value of £200,000, can be completed without much additional cost before 1 July 2024. Edelman suggests that the agreed price should not operate as a ceiling here because it would mean that an award of restitution was capped at £180,000 based on a premise (completion by 1 December 2024) that does not apply and despite a known market value of the work of £200,000, which was recognised by both parties as the value of the work if the work was completed by 1 July 2024.

This is not a convincing example. The driver of the argument appears to be that it is unfair to limit the contractor to £180,000 in restitution because: (1) the work was known to both parties to have a market value of £200,000; and (2) the additional time that the contractor thought they required to complete the work was not in fact needed. But suppose that in the example the landowner never repudiated the contract: that is, despite the contractor having negotiated an extension until 1 December 2024, the contractor finished the work before 1 July 2024, as originally contemplated. In this scenario, the contractor would not be entitled under the contract to an additional £20,000 to the £180,000. It is very difficult to see why the fact that the landowner repudiated the contract (and thus deprived the contractor of completing the work) means that it becomes unfair for the contractor to only recover £180,000 as restitution.

iii. No Rateable Cap

Although the agreed price should almost always provide an overall cap on the sum awarded as restitution for a failure of condition, it should not provide a rateable cap. Suppose that C contracts with D to construct a swimming pool on D's land in exchange for payment of £10,000 following substantial completion. C's service obligation is entire. When the work is half complete, the contract is abandoned and C brings a claim for restitution for a failure of condition. The market value of the work is £6,000. In this scenario, a rateable cap should not be imposed on the sum awarded, such that the restitutionary award made to C is limited to £5,000.

The argument made above for the agreed price almost always providing an overall cap on the sum recoverable does not justify a rateable cap. If £5,000 was awarded as restitution, it would not mean that it is as if the condition that D's entitlement to a complete performance of C's work remained subject to has been fulfilled. Further, to award only £5,000 as restitution will fail to give full effect to the parties' agreement because D will, in effect, still be entitled to a part of the performance of the services that C has undertaken.

For completeness, it is worth observing that although the agreed price may provide some evidence of the market value of a part performance of an entire service obligation,[73] it will usually be of limited evidentiary value. This is because

[73] *BP Exploration Co (Libya) Ltd v Hunt (No 2)* [1979] 1 WLR 783, 825 (Robert Goff J); *Vedatech Corpn v Crystal Decisions* [2002] EWHC 818 (Ch), [76] (Jacob J).

the price is generally impacted by the total amount of services contracted for,[74] as well as the date for completion.

D. Frustration

The availability of restitution for a failure of condition following the frustration of a contract's obligations[75] is now governed principally by the Law Reform (Frustrated Contracts) Act 1943 ('Frustrated Contracts Act'),[76] which significantly alters the circumstances in which restitution may be awarded following frustration. It is argued that whether the powers conferred upon courts by the Frustrated Contracts Act are justified depends principally upon what the basis for the doctrine of frustration is.

i. Nature of Frustration

Before considering the availability of restitution for a failure of condition following frustration, it is helpful to briefly set out the two leading explanations for why frustration occurs.[77]

The first is that, on an objective analysis, the parties formed a contract based upon certain presuppositions that have, due to a change in circumstances following contract formation for which neither of them is legally responsible, been undermined.[78] As these presuppositions have been undermined, to hold the parties to contractual obligations that have not unconditionally accrued would be to hold them to obligations they cannot be regarded as having agreed to. In Lord Reid's words in *Davis Contractors v Fareham Urban DC*, the contract is not 'wide enough to apply to the new situation'.[79]

Another justification is that a frustrating event results in the failure of an agreed condition that certain of the contract's obligations were subject to.[80] The condition that fails may be a condition precedent to an obligation accruing, or a

[74] G Palmer, 'The Contract Price as a Limit on Restitution for Defendant's Breach' (1959) 20 *Ohio State Law Journal* 264, 276.

[75] Frustration does not affect obligations that have previously been discharged or which have unconditionally accrued but have not yet been performed: *Stubbs v Holywell Railway Co* [1867] LR 2 Exch 311; *Joseph Constantine SS Line v Imperial Smelting Corp* [1942] AC 154, 187 (Lord Wright); E Peel, *Frustration and Force Majeure*, 4th edn (London, Sweet & Maxwell, 2022) [15-014].

[76] For contracts to which the Act does not apply, see the Law Reform (Frustrated Contracts) Act 1943 ('Frustrated Contracts Act'), s 2(5).

[77] For other possible justifications, see Peel, *Frustration and Force Majeure* (n 75) ch 16.

[78] In support for a justification resembling this one, see F Wilmot-Smith, 'Termination after Breach' (n 34) 314; R Stevens, 'Objectivity, Mistake and the Parol Evidence Rule' in A Burrows and E Peel (eds), *Contract Terms* (Oxford, Oxford University Press, 2007) 105–06.

[79] *Davis Contractors v Fareham Urban DC* [1956] AC 696, 720–21 (Lord Reid). See also *Denny, Mott and Dickson Ltd v James B Fraser & Co Ltd* [1944] AC 265, 274 (Lord Wright).

[80] For support, see J English, *Discharge of Contractual Obligations* (Oxford, Oxford University Press, 2025) ch 5; Stevens, *The Laws of Restitution* (n 29) 137–39.

condition subsequent in the sense of a condition the obligation remained subject to after it accrued but before it has been performed. According to this justification, in the example provided above where D was obliged to repair C's roof, the reason D's obligation was discharged is that the parties agreed that D's obligation to repair the roof was conditional upon it not becoming impossible for D to perform the obligation in circumstances where neither C nor D was legally responsible for this impossibility. On this view, the justification for frustration is to give effect to the parties' agreement that one or more of the contract's obligations was subject to a condition that has now failed. Frustration is therefore arguably another example of the law giving effect to but not enforcing an agreement.

It is beyond this chapter's scope to consider which of these accounts provides a better interpretation of frustration.[81] However, one reason that might be given in support of frustration occurring due to the failure of an agreed condition is that there are cases suggesting that a contract's obligations may be frustrated despite the frustrating event being reasonably foreseeable as a real possibility.[82] If a contract's obligations can still be frustrated where the frustrating event was foreseeable as a real possibility at the time of contract formation, this does not sit comfortably with the justification for frustration being that the contract is not wide enough to apply to the new circumstances. It is difficult to regard a contract as not wide enough to apply to circumstances that the parties, objectively considered, foresaw as a real possibility when they formed their contract.

ii. Payments made before Frustration

a. Common Law Position

Before the introduction of the Frustrated Contracts Act, there were cases involving successful claims for restitution of payments made before the frustration of a contract's obligations. In *Fibrosa*,[83] the claimant, a Polish company, contracted with the defendant English company for the manufacture and supply of machines. The machines were to be shipped CIF by the defendant to Gdynia in Poland. The price was £4,800, with £1,600 payable with the order and the balance against shipping documents. £1,000 was paid by the claimant on account of the initial £1,600 owing. The defendant's obligation to manufacture and ship the machines was then frustrated due to the occupation of Poland by Nazi Germany. The claimant successfully recovered its £1,000 payment for a 'total failure of consideration'.

[81] It may be that these justifications are not mutually exclusive in the sense that certain frustration cases are best explained by the failure of an agreed condition and others by the contract not having been wide enough to apply to the new situation. If this is correct, then frustration may occur in response to two different events.

[82] *WJ Tatem Ltd v Gamboa* [1939] 1 KB 132, 135 (Goddard J); *Ocean Tramp Tankers Corp v V/O Sovfracht (The Eugenia)* [1964] 2 QB 226, 239 (Lord Denning MR). See further Peel, *Frustration and Force Majeure* (n 75) 489–92.

[83] *Fibrosa Spolka Akcyjna v Fairbairn Lawson Combe Barbour Ltd* (n 1).

Although *Fibrosa* is widely cited for the proposition that, in the restitutionary context, the 'consideration' for an advance payment is generally the provision of the agreed counter-performance,[84] it is doubtful that on the facts there was a failure of condition due to a failure of counter-performance. There is no indication that the £1,000 the claimant paid was apportionable to any part of the defendant's performance of the contract. In other words, there was no agreed counter-performance for the £1,000 that had been paid.[85] It also appears that it was a condition precedent to the defendant's obligation to begin manufacturing the machines that the claimant had paid £1,600. If the claimant never earned the defendant's counter-performance, it would be unusual if there was a failure of condition due to a failure of counter-performance. A better explanation is that the condition that failed was that the claimant was deprived of an opportunity to unconditionally earn a right to the defendant's performance. The reason the claimant was deprived of this opportunity was that the defendant's obligation to manufacture and supply the machines was conditional upon the location for delivery not becoming enemy territory.[86]

The results of certain cases involving common law claims for restitution of payments made before the frustration of a contract's obligations cannot be defended. In *Chandler v Webster*,[87] the claimant, Mr Chandler, agreed to hire a room from the defendant, Mr Webster, to view King Edward VII's coronation procession in exchange for payment of £141 in advance. The claimant paid £100 to the defendant. The procession was then cancelled, which was regarded as frustrating the contract's obligations. The claimant sought restitution of the £100 for a total failure of consideration. The defendant counterclaimed for the agreed sum, arguing that the £41 balance remained due. The claimant's action failed and the defendant's succeeded. The result suggests that the court regarded the defendant's obligation to allow the claimant to use the room as having been discharged, but not the claimant's payment obligation. If the claimant's payment obligation had been discharged, there would have been no basis for ordering the claimant to pay the £41.

The reason given for rejecting the claim for restitution was that frustration does not rescind a contract's obligation ab initio. Collins MR said:

> If the effect [of frustration] were that the contract were wiped out altogether, no doubt the result would be that money paid under it would have to be repaid as on a failure of consideration. But that is not the effect of the doctrine; it only releases the parties from further performance of the contract. Therefore the doctrine of failure of consideration does not apply.[88]

[84] P Birks, *Unjust Enrichment*, 2nd edn (Oxford, Oxford University Press, 2005) 140; Mitchell, Mitchell and Watterson, *Goff & Jones* (n 21) 465, [12-12].

[85] *Fibrosa Spolka Akcyjna v Fairbairn Lawson Combe Barbour Ltd* (n 1) 37–38.

[86] ibid 38.

[87] *Chandler v Webster* [1904] 1 KB 493.

[88] ibid 499. See also 501 (Romer LJ).

As discussed in chapter 1, historically, in an action or money had and received, a failure of consideration was understood as a failure of the juristic reason for a payment, with this juristic reason generally being the payment obligation performed. Unless the contract was rescinded ab initio, there was still a juristic reason for the payment and therefore not a failure of consideration. However, as also discussed in chapter 1, by the time *Chandler v Webster* was decided there was authority for the proposition that in an action for money had and received a failure of consideration did not refer to a failure of the juristic reason for a payment, but generally a substantial failure of counter-performance. This suggests that while *Chandler v Webster* is not as heretical as is sometimes believed, it was still probably incorrect when it was decided.

The preferable analysis of *Chandler v Webster* is that although the claimant's advance payment obligation had fallen due, the obligation (until it had been performed) remained conditional upon the procession not being cancelled. The defendant's entitlement to the £100 payment made would also have been agreed to remain conditional upon the procession not being cancelled. This construction is supported by the observation that the defendant had agreed to let the room specifically for the viewing of the procession. When the procession was cancelled, both conditions failed. Restitution of the £100 payment should have followed, and the defendant's counterclaim for the agreed sum ought to have failed. Instead, the result was that the defendant was treated as entitled to the £100 payment made and to the remaining £41 in circumstances where, on the contract's proper construction, the defendant was not so entitled.

b. Frustrated Contracts Act

Section 1(2) of the Frustrated Contracts Act provides:

> All sums paid or payable to any party in pursuance of the contract before the time when the parties were so discharged (in this Act referred to as 'the time of discharge') shall, in the case of sums so paid, be recoverable from him as money received by him for the use of the party by whom the sums were paid, and, in the case of sums so payable, cease to be so payable:
>
> Provided that, if the party to whom the sums were so paid or payable incurred expenses before the time of discharge in, or for the purpose of, the performance of the contract, the court may, if it considers it just to do so having regard to all the circumstances of the case, allow him to retain or, as the case may be, recover the whole or any part of the sums so paid or payable, not being an amount in excess of the expenses so incurred.

One of the effects of section 1(2) is to confer a power on the court to allow a payee to 'retain' the whole or part of a payment in circumstances where this would be inconsistent with the parties' contract.[89] So, suppose that C and D enter into a

[89] See also Stevens, *The Laws of Restitution* (n 29) 141; R Stevens, 'Repeal the Law Reform (Frustrated Contracts) Act 1943' in E Peel and R Probert (eds), *Shaping the Law of Obligations* (Oxford, Oxford University Press, 2023).

contract whereby D undertakes an entire obligation to build C a boat. C is required to pay £25,000 to D in advance. D's entitlement against C to the £25,000 payment is agreed to remain conditional upon delivery of the substantially completed boat. When the boat is half built, D dies. At the time of frustration, D has spent £10,000 from the advance payment on materials required to build the boat but has not commenced the work. On its face, section 1(2) suggests that D may be entitled to retain up to £10,000 of the £25,000, which would be inconsistent with the contract. Under the contract, D's entitlement against C to any part of the £25,000 payment remained conditional upon delivery of the substantially completed boat. If D could 'retain' any part of the £25,000, D would therefore be entitled to part of the payment in circumstances where it was agreed that D was not.

There does not, however, appear to be any English case where following a failure of condition restitution has been denied, or a lesser or greater sum than that which would be awarded at common law has been ordered, under section 1(2).[90] The leading case involving a claim under section 1(2) is *Gamerco SA v ICM/Fair Warning (Agency) Ltd*.[91] The claimants, who were concert promoters, entered into a contract with the defendant to promote a concert at a stadium in Madrid, Spain. Shortly before the concert, the use of the stadium was banned and no suitable alternative venue could be found, which was regarded as frustrating the contract's obligations.

Before frustration, the claimants had paid the defendant $412,500 and owed a further $362,500. This payment appears to have been made on account of a sum guaranteed to the defendant for the concert. The claimants had incurred $450,000 in expenses and the defendant $50,000. Garland J held that the claimants were entitled to restitution of the $412,500 paid under section 1(2) and that no deduction should be made for expenses the defendant had incurred. The same result would probably have followed at common law. On the contract's proper construction, the defendant's entitlement to the $412,500 payment made, as well as the claimants' obligation to pay the remaining $362,500, would likely have been conditional upon neither party being legally responsible for the concert being cancelled. The claimant would therefore have been entitled to restitution of the $412,500 payment for a failure of condition and its obligation to pay the $362,500 would have been discharged.

The justification that is generally provided for the power in section 1(2) to allow D to retain all or part of a payment is that D's 'reliance interest' may merit protection in circumstances where it is not possible for D, who is legally innocent, to vindicate its 'expectation interest'. Professor McKendrick writes:

> The expenditure was incurred justifiably in the pursuance of what was at the time a valid and subsisting contract. Justice and reasonableness surely demand that such ex-

[90] I am also not aware of any Australian case where such an order has been made under the equivalent statutory provisions.

[91] *Gamerco SA v ICM/Fair Warning (Agency) Ltd* [1995] 1 WLR 1226. See also *Lobb v Vasey Housing Auxiliary (War Widows Guild)* [1963] VR 239.

> penditure be brought into account so that, on the frustration of a contract, the position is reached whereby both parties are discharged from their obligations to perform in the future (the expectation interest of neither party being protected), benefits conferred must be paid for (thus protecting the restitution interest), and losses suffered as a result of wasted expenditure be apportioned between the parties (thus taking account of the reliance interest).[92]

Whether this argument is persuasive, and the power conferred by section 1(2) justified, depends principally upon what the basis for the doctrine of frustration is.[93] If frustration occurs because certain of a contract's obligations were subject to an agreed condition that has now failed, refusing to award restitution or allowing D to retain part of the payment where this would be inconsistent with the contract cannot be justified. On this view, frustration does not deprive the contract of its normative force but occurs because of the contract. It is mysterious why harm to D's 'reliance interest', for which C is not legally responsible, is of concern to C and provides a reason for potentially requiring C to in practice pay for something that it did not agree to pay for.

If, however, the justification for frustration is that the contract was formed based on certain presuppositions that have been undermined, section 1(2) is more defensible. If a contract is not 'wide enough' to apply to the new circumstances, the most equitable result will usually be to share (at least to some degree) the loss caused by the frustrating event.[94] The defect in the common law position from this perspective, and which section 1(2) attempts to remedy, is that frustration may lead to a distributively unjust result between the parties because, although neither of them was legally responsible for the frustrating event, one of them may be left significantly worse off than the other. In carrying out this loss-sharing exercise, proceeds the argument, it is unobjectionable to allow D to retain all or part of the payment even though this would be inconsistent with the contract because the contract is not 'wide enough' to apply to the new circumstances and has therefore been deprived of its normative force.

iii. Services Performed Before Frustration

a. Common Law Position

Where an entire service obligation has not substantially been performed before frustration, the common law position is that the service provider is generally not entitled to restitution of its performance of the services for a failure of condition. In *Cutter v Powell*,[95] Mr Cutter was a sailor who was to be paid for his services on a voyage no later than 10 days after the ship arrived. On the voyage, Cutter died.

[92] E McKendrick, 'Frustration, Restitution and Loss Apportionment' in A Burrows (ed), *Essays on the Law of Restitution* (Oxford, Clarendon Press, 1991) 169.
[93] This argument is also made in Stevens, *The Laws of Restitution* (n 29) 142.
[94] ibid.
[95] *Cutter v Powell* (1795) 6 Term Rep 320; 101 ER 573.

Cutter's administratrix failed in an action for non-contractual quantum meruit for services Cutter had performed on the voyage because his service obligation was, on the contract's proper construction, entire. This construction was supported by the especially high wages to which Cutter would have been entitled following the completion of the voyage.

A similar case is *Appleby v Myers*.[96] The claimants entered into a contract with the defendant to erect machinery on the defendant's land in exchange for payment following substantial completion. Before the work had been completed, the premises and machinery that the claimants had erected were destroyed in a fire, which frustrated the claimants' obligations. The claimants failed in an action for non-contractual quantum meruit. Blackburn J held that because the claimants' service obligation was entire, the claimants were not entitled to an award of quantum meruit.

Cutter v Powell and *Appleby v Myers* support the proposition that D's entitlement against C to a part performance of an entire service obligation generally does not remain conditional upon C not being deprived, through no fault of C's own, of an opportunity to substantially perform the service obligation. This construction is questionable. As discussed above, the purpose of an obligation being entire is to provide the performing party with an additional incentive to perform by depriving this party of a right to any part of the agreed counter-performance unless the obligation is substantially performed. That purpose is not undermined if D's entitlement to a part performance of the service obligation is treated as remaining conditional upon C not being deprived through no fault of its own of an opportunity of substantially performing.

It is unlikely that parties generally agree that D is unconditionally entitled to a part performance of an entire service obligation in circumstances where it has become impossible, through no fault of C's own, for C to earn the agreed counter-performance. The difficulty with this construction is that it would have the consequence that, following frustration, D will often be left in a better position, and C in a worse position, than each of them would have been in if the contract had been performed. Suppose again that a contract is entered into whereby C undertakes an entire obligation to repair D's roof in exchange for payment following substantial completion. After C has performed half of the work, C dies. If D was unconditionally entitled to C's part performance in this circumstance, D is likely to be left in a better position than it would have been in if the contract had been performed as D will have received half of the work without having to pay.

It is true that where C has partly performed an entire service obligation, D may also be left worse off following frustration than if the contract had been performed. But where this is the case, C will also usually be left worse off. Thus, suppose that in the example just given, instead of C's service obligation having been frustrated due to C having died, the obligation is frustrated because of D's house burning down.

[96] *Appleby v Myers* (1867) LR 2 CP 651.

In this variation, both C and D are likely to be left worse off than they would have been if the contract had been performed.

The preferable view is that parties generally structure their relationship so that a deprivation of performance of the contract, for which neither of them is legally responsible, is more likely to result in both of them being left worse off than if the contract had been performed than just one of them being left better off. If this is accepted, D's entitlement against C to a part performance of an entire service obligation should generally be treated as having been agreed to remain conditional upon C not being deprived of an opportunity of substantially performing through no fault of C's own. This is because such a construction will usually prevent D from being left better off following frustration than it would have been if the contract had been performed.

It does not follow that *Cutter v Powell* is incorrectly decided. Due to the especially high wages that Cutter would have been entitled to following completion of the voyage, the most plausible construction is that the defendant's entitlement to any services rendered by Cutter only remained conditional upon Cutter not being wrongly deprived *by the defendant* of an opportunity of performing his service obligation and payment following substantial completion. The result in *Appleby v Myers*, on the other hand, is more questionable. In that case, the only reason given for refusing to award non-contractual quantum meruit was that the claimant's service obligation was entire. If the argument just made is accepted, this should not necessarily be fatal to a claim for restitution of a part performance of an entire service obligation.

b. Frustrated Contracts Act

The availability of a monetary award in respect of services performed before frustration has again been affected by the Frustrated Contracts Act. Section 1(3) provides:

> Where any party to the contract has, by reason of anything done by any other party thereto in, or for the purpose of, the performance of the contract, obtained a valuable benefit (other than a payment of money to which the last foregoing subsection applies) before the time of discharge, there shall be recoverable from him by the said other party such sum (if any), not exceeding the value of the said benefit to the party obtaining it, as the court considers just, having regard to all the circumstances of the case and, in particular,—
>
> (a) the amount of any expenses incurred before the time of discharge by the benefited party in, or for the purpose of, the performance of the contract, including any sums paid or payable by him to any other party in pursuance of the contract and retained or recoverable by that party under the last foregoing subsection, and
>
> (b) the effect, in relation to the said benefit, of the circumstances giving rise to the frustration of the contract.

Section 1(3) has been treated as conferring a power on the court to make a monetary award that is inconsistent with the parties' contract. This is illustrated by the complicated case of *BP Exploration (Libya) Ltd v Hunt (No 2)*,[97] which is the leading decision involving a claim under section 1(3). Mr Hunt, an American oil tycoon, obtained an oil concession from the Libyan government in 1957. To exploit the concession, in 1960 Hunt entered into a joint-venture agreement with BP Exploration (Libya) Ltd. The contract was structured so that BP would bear the risk of no oil being discovered, but if oil was discovered, it would initially acquire most of the profit. More specifically, under the contract:[98]

(1) Hunt was to assign half of his interest in the concession to BP.
(2) BP was to make certain 'farm-in contributions' to Hunt in cash and oil.
(3) BP was to explore the concession and, if oil was discovered, develop the field; create the necessary facilities to bring the field on stream; and thereafter produce the oil and further develop the field and facilities.
(4) BP was to bear the costs necessary to bring oil on stream.
(5) After oil came on stream, the cost of producing the oil and developing the field was to be borne equally.
(6) BP and Hunt were to have an equal share in the oil produced.
(7) BP was entitled to three-eighths of Hunt's half share in the oil initially produced as reimbursement oil until 125% of the farm-in contributions Hunt received were repaid and half of the expenditure BP incurred exploring the field and developing the facilities to bring oil on stream was recovered.

Stated simply, the parties' 1960 agreement was therefore that BP would provide the services exploring and developing the concession, be paid for that work from oil produced from the field, and, following that payment, share equally in the further oil produced.

A major oil field was discovered, and oil came on stream in 1967. The parties' contract was amended in 1967 so that BP would receive 50,000,000 barrels from the oil field as payment in kind for the services it had performed. The value of the 50,000,000 barrels at the date they were delivered or to be delivered was about (£25,573,908 + £56,287,621 =) £81,861,529.[99] This was a bad bargain for Hunt because a subsequent increase in the oil price meant that BP would be paid significantly more than the costs it had incurred. In 1971, the Libyan government expropriated BP's interest in the concession and then, in 1973, Hunt's. As a result, the parties' obligations were frustrated. At the time of frustration, BP had not yet received 16,899,189 barrels out of the 50,000,000 barrels and £550,032 in reimbursement oil as repayment of the farm-in contributions.[100] BP brought a

[97] *BP Exploration Co (Libya) Ltd v Hunt (No 2)* (n 73).
[98] ibid 789–90.
[99] ibid 824, 845.
[100] ibid 824.

successful claim against Hunt under section 1(3) and was awarded £5,666,399 plus interest and a further US$10,801,534 plus interest.[101]

The question of whether there was a failure of condition turns upon what one regards the parties as having agreed in 1967, when they amended their agreement. Two possibilities arise. One is that Hunt agreed to pay BP 50,000,000 barrels for its services from the oil field. The other is that Hunt agreed to pay BP 50,000,000 barrels for its services from the oil field if, and only if, more than 50,000,000 barrels were produced. If the correct interpretation is the former, there was a failure of condition because BP did not receive 50,000,000 barrels from the oil field. But if the correct interpretation is the latter, there was not a failure of condition, because Hunt's obligation to provide those barrels depended on more than 50,000,000 barrels being produced.

Robert Goff J said:

> if BP had received the whole of the reimbursement oil, as well as their half share of the concession, then I am satisfied that no sum should have been awarded to BP under the Act . .. However, in point of fact there remained a balance of 16,899,189 barrels of oil of the first oil debt, and the equivalent in oil of £550,032 of the second oil debt (i.e. 125 per cent. X £420,026), outstanding by way of reimbursement oil at the date of frustration.[102]

This suggests that Robert Goff J regarded Hunt as having agreed to pay BP 50,000,000 barrels for its services from the oil field. If the agreement was that Hunt agreed to pay BP 50,000,000 barrels for its services from the oil field if, and only if, they were produced, it would be wrong to say that there was a balance 'of 16,899,189 barrels of oil of the first oil debt' because this payment obligation would have been conditional upon the oil barrels being produced from the field. It is, however, unclear why Robert Goff J thought there remained an 'oil debt' following frustration (ie, why BP had an unconditional right to payment of 50,000,000 barrels from the field, with the consequence that 16,899,189 barrels remained outstanding).

Under the original 1960 agreement, BP was entitled to three-eighths of Hunt's half share in the oil initially produced as reimbursement oil until 125% of the farm-in contributions were repaid, and half of the expenditure BP incurred exploring the field and developing the facilities to bring oil on stream was recovered. BP therefore did not have an unconditional right to payment in kind for its services: its entitlement to payment depended upon oil in fact being produced. But it is less clear that under the 1967 amended agreement (which was formed after the oil field had been discovered) the parties agreed that Hunt's obligation to pay 50,000,000 barrels was conditional upon that amount actually being produced.

It is difficult to determine which interpretation of the 1967 agreement is correct because the judgments provide limited detail beyond the fact that the

[101] ibid 845.
[102] ibid 824.

50,000,000 barrels were 'fixed on a compromise basis'. As observed, Robert Goff J appears to have regarded the 1967 agreement as providing that BP was entitled to 50,000,000 barrels from the oil field, regardless of whether that number was produced. In support, it could be said that in circumstances where the parties in 1967 knew that the oil field was almost certainly capable of producing 50,000,000 barrels, BP had incurred significant costs to-date and had agreed to payment in the form of 50,000,000 barrels as a 'fixed compromise', under the 1967 agreement they agreed to shift the risk of non-payment from oil field production from BP onto Hunt. However, under their previous 1960 arrangement, it was clearly contemplated that BP would be compensated from oil production that actually took place (ie, BP bore the risk of non-payment from oil field production), and there was nothing that clearly pointed to the parties having agreed to overhaul that risk allocation.

If there was a failure of condition, then, at common law, BP would have been entitled to restitution of the market value of the services it had performed exploring the field and bringing oil on stream at the time the services were performed. The market value of BP's services was not determined. But it is unlikely that the value substantially exceeded £30,800,281, being the expenditure BP incurred exploring the concession and bringing oil on stream. This sum would, most likely, have been netted off against a sum Hunt would have been entitled to as counter-restitution of payments in kind he had made for BP's services before frustration (ie, the value of the 33,101,811 barrels Hunt previously paid to BP, which was £25,573,908). As observed, BP was awarded £5,666,399 plus interest[103] and US$10,801,534 plus interest[104] under section 1(3). Given that BP's costs were £30,800,281 and BP had already been paid £25,573,908, the sum awarded was likely different (although not significantly) to what would have been awarded at common law if there was a failure of condition.

Whether the power conferred under section 1(3) to make a monetary award that is inconsistent with the contract can be justified depends, as with section 1(2), principally upon what the basis for frustration is.[105] If frustration occurs because of a failure of an agreed condition that certain of the contract's obligations were subject to, then section 1(3), and the result in *BP Exploration (Libya) Ltd v Hunt (No 2)*,[106] are difficult to justify because the section confers a power to make an award that is inconsistent with the contract. But if frustration occurs because the contract is not 'wide enough to apply to the new situation', an award under section 1(3) that is inconsistent with the contract can be defended on the basis that the

[103] This sum was arrived at by taking the cost to BP of bringing oil on stream (£30,800,281), deducting the value of the reimbursement oil BP had received (£25,573,908), and then adding the cost to BP of the services it provided after oil came on stream (£440,026): *BP Exploration Co (Libya) Ltd v Hunt (No 2)* (n 73) 845.

[104] This sum was arrived at by adding the farm-in payment ($2,000,000) BP had made to Hunt and the value of the title to the farm-in oil ($8,801,534) transferred to Hunt.

[105] This argument is also made in Stevens, *The Laws of Restitution* (n 29) 142.

[106] *BP Exploration Co (Libya) Ltd v Hunt (No 2)* (n 73).

frustrating event deprived the contract of its normative force. On this view, section 1(3) can be understood as an attempt to ensure that frustration does not result in an inequitable distribution of the loss caused.

IV. Conclusion

This chapter has examined the relationship between the law of contract and restitutionary awards for a failure of condition. It began by explaining that the justification for restitution of a contractual performance for a failure of condition relates to the content of the contract performed. More specifically, restitution of a contractual performance is justified where the contract provided that D's entitlement against C to a performance of the contract undertaken remained subject to a condition that has now failed. The chapter then examined the availability and measure of restitution for a failure of condition in the context of contractual performances. In this regard, the following principal claims were made. First, restitution for a failure of condition should potentially be available where there is an enforceable right to damages. Secondly, *Sumpter v Hedges* and *Mayson v Clouet* are correctly decided. Thirdly, a claim for restitution for a failure of condition should potentially be available in the alternative to an action for the agreed sum. Fourthly, the agreed price should almost always provide an overall cap on the sum awarded as restitution, but not a rateable cap. Finally, whether sections 1(2) and 1(3) of the Frustrated Contracts Act are defensible depends principally upon what the justification for frustration is.

7

Failure of Condition, Rights, and Trusts

I. Introduction

This chapter addresses two questions. The first is when D should come under a restitutionary duty, which a court will specifically enforce, to transfer a right to C on the grounds of a failure of condition. The second is when a trust should arise following a failure of condition. In addressing these questions, it is helpful to distinguish at the outset between cases exemplified by the following examples:

(1) C transfers a title to Picasso's *Bouquet of Peace* to D. The parties agreed that D's entitlement to the transfer of a title remained subject to a condition and that condition has now failed.

(2) C transfers a title to 1,000 footballs of a certain kind to D. The parties agreed that D's entitlement to the transfer of a title to 1,000 footballs of this kind remained subject to a condition and that condition has now failed.

(3) C pays £10,000 to D via bank transfer. The parties agreed that D's entitlement to the £10,000 payment made remained subject to a condition and that condition has now failed.

In scenario (1), D's entitlement against C to the transfer of a specific (ie, particular identifiable) right remained subject to a condition that has now failed. In scenario (2), D's entitlement against C to the transfer of rights of a certain kind remained subject to a condition that has now failed. In scenario (3), no right was transferred.

To answer the questions posed by this chapter, it is necessary to consider in relation to each of these scenarios: (i) when D should come under a restitutionary duty to transfer the specific right it received back to C; (ii) when D should come under a restitutionary duty to transfer a right of the same kind as the right it received to C; (iii) when a court should specifically enforce D's restitutionary duty to transfer a right to C; and (iv) when D will hold the right transferred on trust for C. The structure of this chapter is to examine these issues in turn.

From the standpoint of authority, the answer to the above questions is largely unclear, making it necessary to consider these issues by reference to first principles. The chapter defends the following claims. First, where C and D agreed that D's entitlement against C to the transfer of a specific right remained subject to a condition that has now failed, D should generally come under a restitutionary duty to re-transfer the right that it received back to C.

Secondly, where C and D agreed that D's entitlement against C to the transfer of a right of a certain kind remained subject to a condition that has now failed, D should generally come under a restitutionary duty to transfer a right of the same kind as the right it received from C.

Thirdly, the considerations that justify refusing to order a party to specifically perform a contractual duty to transfer a right apply to orders to perform a restitutionary duty to transfer a right.

Finally, where D has come under a restitutionary duty to transfer a specific right to C following a failure of condition, which a court will specifically enforce, a trust should arise.

The implications of these claims for the above examples are that in scenarios (1) and (2), but not in scenario (3), D should generally come under a restitutionary duty to transfer a right to C. In scenario (1), D should come under a restitutionary duty to transfer the specific right that it received back to C, whereas in scenario (2), D should come under a restitutionary duty to transfer rights of the same kind as those it received to C. In scenario (1), although not in scenario (2), D's restitutionary duty to transfer a right to C should prima facie be specifically enforceable because the right D is under a restitutionary duty to transfer is unique. In scenario (1), but not in scenarios (2) and (3), D should be regarded as holding the right that it is under a restitutionary duty to transfer to C on trust.

II. Concepts

A. 'Proprietary' Restitution

A distinction is often drawn between personal and proprietary rights to restitution[1] and personal and proprietary restitutionary remedies.[2] A personal right to restitution is a restitutionary right C has that is exigible against D personally. A proprietary restitutionary right, on the other hand, is said to be a restitutionary right that is exigible against D, as well as certain third parties, in relation to 'property' that is 'effected or realised by proprietary remedies'.[3] Examples that are typically given of 'proprietary remedies' that 'effect or realise' a proprietary restitutionary right include a constructive trust, equitable charge and subrogation to discharged rights.[4]

In discussions of proprietary restitution, there is often a failure to clearly distinguish between two different legal responses. One is an order requiring D to transfer a right to C as restitution. The other is a declaration that a right is held

[1] See, eg, A Burrows, *The Law of Restitution*, 3rd edn (Oxford, Oxford University Press, 2011) 14–15.

[2] See, eg, C Mitchell, P Mitchell and S Watterson, *Goff & Jones on Unjust Enrichment*, 10th edn (UK, Sweet & Maxwell, 2022) Pt 7.

[3] Burrows, *The Law of Restitution* (n 1) 168.

[4] W Swadling, 'Policy Arguments for Proprietary Restitution' (2008) 28 *Legal Studies* 506, 511; Burrows, *The Law of Restitution* (n 1) 168–73.

on trust. A trust is not a remedy. As discussed below, a trust is an indefeasible duty not to use a specific patrimonial right for one's own benefit other than to the extent authorised by an instrument governing the trust. A court-ordered remedy is a court order that seeks to cure an injustice.[5] A duty not to use a specific right for one's own benefit is not, on its own, a cure for an injustice. Further, in England, where remedial constructive trusts are not recognised, courts do not order a party to hold a right on constructive trust but declare that a trust has arisen. A declaration that a certain state of affairs exists is not, on the definition above, a remedy; on its own, it does not cure an injustice.

Where C is entitled to restitution of a transfer of a right against D, this does not necessarily mean that C has a 'proprietary' right. A proprietary right, as it is used here, is a right to exclude others from a physical thing. C can have a restitutionary right to have D transfer a right to it without having a proprietary right. This is because it is possible to have personal rights in relation to physical things.[6] For example, if D is under a contractual duty to transfer a title to a specific Apple MacBook to C via delivery, this does not necessarily mean that C has a proprietary right before a title to the laptop has been transferred to it.

The fact that C has a right to restitution of a transfer of a right against D also does not necessarily mean that C has a restitutionary right in relation to property. The most useful definition of property, and the one adopted here, is a thing with a location in space-time that a legal person has a right to exclude other legal persons from.[7] In other words, property is a thing that is the object of a certain kind of right. Where, for example, C has a right to recover an equitable right that it transferred to D, on the above definition, C does not have a restitutionary right in relation to property. Equitable rights are rights in relation to other rights and therefore not rights in relation to things.[8]

Instead of referring to proprietary restitution, this chapter uses the language of a restitutionary duty to transfer a right. One reason for preferring this terminology is that it is consistent with the possibility of C having a right to have D transfer a right to it as restitution, despite C not having a property right. This language is also consistent with the possibility that D may come under a restitutionary duty to transfer a right to C even though the right D is under a duty to transfer is not a property right. A further advantage of the language of a restitutionary duty to transfer a right is that it makes clear that the question of whether D has come under a restitutionary duty to transfer a right is separate from whether a trust has

[5] P Birks, 'Rights, Wrongs, and Remedies' (2000) 20 *OJLS* 1, 9.

[6] *Hill v Tupper* (1863) 2 H & C 121; 159 ER 51.

[7] For a similar understanding, see B McFarlane, *The Structure of Property Law* (Oxford, Hart Publishing, 2008) 4–5, 12–13; W Swadling, 'Property' in A Burrows (ed), *English Private Law*, 3rd edn (Oxford, Oxford University Press, 2013) 173.

[8] B McFarlane and R Stevens, 'The Nature of Equitable Property' (2010) 4 *The Journal of Equity* 1; B McFarlane and R Stevens, 'What's Special About Equity?: Rights about Rights' in D Klimchuk, I Samet and H Smith (eds), *Philosophical Foundations of the Law of Equity* (Oxford, Oxford University Press, 2020) ch 9.

arisen.[9] As explained below, there are situations where D should come under a restitutionary duty to transfer a right where a trust should not arise.

B. Specific, Non-Specific and Unique Rights

The most helpful way of clarifying the concepts of specific and non-specific rights is through some examples. To begin, consider:

> C owes a duty to transfer a title to Turner's *Dido Building Carthage* to D.

In this example, C's duty is to transfer a specific right to D. The sense in which C's duty is to transfer a specific right is that C owes a duty to transfer a particular identifiable right to D and not merely a right of a certain kind.

A duty to transfer a unique right, as 'unique' is understood in the specific performance context,[10] is however not necessarily a duty to transfer a specific right. For example:

> C owes a duty to transfer a title to any Rembrandt to D.

All Rembrandts are unique, which means that C is under a duty to transfer a unique right to D. But because C is under a duty to transfer a right of a certain kind (ie, a title to any Rembrandt) and not a particular identifiable right (ie, a title to a particular Rembrandt), C is not under a duty to transfer a specific right to D.

On the other hand, C may owe a duty to transfer a specific right to D even though the right is not unique. For example:

> C owes a duty to transfer a title to the only mountain bike currently sitting in its garage to D.

Here, C is under a duty to transfer a particular identifiable right to D, and therefore a specific right, but the right is not unique.

Parties may agree that D's entitlement against C to a transfer of a specific right was to remain conditional after the right is transferred. For example:

> C transfers a title to Picasso's *The Old Guitarist* to D. It was agreed that D's entitlement against C to the transfer of title was to remain conditional upon payment of £10,000,000 by a certain date.

In this example, it was agreed that D's entitlement against C to the transfer of a specific right remained conditional after the transfer was made. This is because it

[9] The idea that these things should be uncoupled is also advocated in E Bant and M Bryan, 'Specific Restitution without Trusts' (2012) 6 *The Journal of Equity* 181.

[10] This is how 'unique' is used throughout this chapter.

was agreed that D's entitlement to the transfer of a particular identifiable right was to remain subject to a condition.

By contrast:

> C transfers a title to 1,000 footballs of a certain kind to D. It was agreed that D's entitlement against C to the transfer of a title to 1,000 footballs of this kind was to remain conditional upon payment of the agreed sum within a reasonable time.

In this example, it was agreed that D's entitlement against C to the transfer of non-specific rights remained conditional. This is because it was agreed that D's entitlement against C to a transfer of rights of a certain kind remained conditional upon payment of the agreed sum by a certain time.

D's entitlement against C to a transfer of a specific right may remain conditional even if the transfer is not of a unique right. Consider:

> C and D agree that D's entitlement against C to the transfer of a title to the only table currently in C's living room is to remain conditional upon payment of the agreed sum within a reasonable time after the transfer is made.

There are also conceivably cases where C is not under a duty to transfer a specific right, but the parties agreed that D's entitlement against C to the transfer of the specific right in fact transferred was to remain conditional. For example:

> C and D enter into an unenforceable contract whereby C is under a duty to transfer a title to a Pollock in exchange for payment of the market value of the painting, but the agreement does not specify which Pollock C is under a duty to transfer a title to.

In this example, it is likely that although C was not obliged to transfer a specific right to D, but rather a right of a certain kind, on the proper construction of the agreement, D's entitlement against C to the transfer of the specific right in fact transferred was to remain conditional upon payment of the market value within a reasonable time.

III. Restitutionary Duties to Transfer a Right

This section considers whether, and if so when, D should come under a restitutionary duty to transfer a right to C following a failure of condition. It is argued that where C has transferred a right to D on a condition that has now failed, D may come under a restitutionary duty to: (i) transfer the specific right it received back to C; or (ii) transfer a right of the same kind as the right it received to C. Where, however, there is a performance on a condition that has now failed that does not involve the transfer of a right (eg, a payment via bank transfer), D should not come under a restitutionary duty to transfer a right to C. To restate, the question of whether D has come under a restitutionary duty to transfer a right is separate from whether this duty should be specifically enforced, which is discussed in the next section.

A. Transfers of Specific Rights

Where C and D agreed that D's entitlement against C to the transfer of a specific right remained subject to a condition that has now failed, D should generally come under a restitutionary duty to transfer the specific right it received back to C. Thus, suppose that C and D enter into an unenforceable contract whereby C undertakes to transfer a title to the *Macmillan Aryballos* to D via delivery in exchange for payment. C duly delivers the vase, but D, in breach of the agreement, fails to pay the agreed sum. In this scenario, D ought to transfer the title to the *Macmillan Aryballos* that it received back to C. On the agreement's proper construction, D's entitlement against C to the transfer of a title to the *Macmillan Aryballos* will have been conditional upon payment of the agreed sum following delivery. That condition failed. If D were to retain the title, D would be disregarding the parties' agreement that its entitlement to the transfer of a specific right remained subject to a condition that has now failed. D therefore ought to make restitution of the transfer. Given that it was agreed that D's entitlement against C to the transfer of a specific right was subject to a now failed condition, the only way for D to give effect to the agreement is for D to transfer the very right it received back to C.

For D to come under a restitutionary duty to transfer back to C the specific right it received following a failure of condition, it should not be necessary for the right transferred to be unique. Imagine that C and D agree that D's entitlement against C to the transfer of a title via delivery to the only sofa currently in C's living room, which is not unique, is to remain subject to a condition. C transfers a title to the sofa. The condition then fails. In this scenario, D ought to come under a restitutionary duty to re-transfer to C the title to the sofa it received. The parties agreed that D's entitlement against C to the transfer of a specific (although not unique) right remained subject to a now failed condition. If D did not transfer the right back, D would be disregarding the parties' agreement that its entitlement against C to the transfer of a specific right, as opposed to a right of a certain kind, remained subject to a condition that has now failed.

Where C and D agreed that D's entitlement against C to the transfer of a specific right remained subject to a now failed condition, but D no longer has the right transferred, because, for example, D has sold the right, D should generally not come under a duty to transfer the right it received back to C. This is because it will generally be impossible for D to perform this duty. In this scenario, D's duty will be to do the next best thing to reversing the transfer, which is to pay the market value of the right transferred at the time of receipt. If the market value exceeds the overall price, for reasons discussed in the previous chapter, the sum that D should be required to pay as restitution should generally be capped at that price.

It might be objected that where D no longer has the right transferred, D's duty should be to pay the market value of the right it received at the time the relevant condition failed. This, claims the objection, is because in such circumstances what D should do is the next best thing to re-transferring the right that it received. But what the parties agreed was that D's entitlement against C to the transfer of a specific right remained subject to a now failed condition. To give effect to that agreement following the failure of condition, the transfer must be reversed. The best way of reversing the transfer will be for D to transfer back to C the specific right it received. If D cannot transfer back that right, the best way of reversing the transfer will be for D to pay the value of the right at the time of receipt and not at the time of the failure of condition.

B. Transfers of Non-Specific Rights

i. Non-Specific Rights

Where C and D agreed that D's entitlement to a transfer of a non-specific right remained subject to a condition that has now failed, D should generally come under a restitutionary duty to transfer a right to C of the same kind as the right that it received. Suppose, for example, that C and D enter into a contract whereby C undertakes to transfer a title to 1,000 footballs on the condition of D's substantial performance of a dependent service obligation. C duly delivers the footballs, but D, in breach of contract, performs none of the service. In this scenario, D should generally come under a restitutionary duty to transfer a title to 1,000 footballs of the same kind as those received. It was agreed that D's entitlement against C to the transfer of a title to 1,000 footballs of a certain kind remained conditional upon D's substantial performance of a service obligation. That condition failed. If D did not transfer a title to 1,000 footballs to C of the kind received, D would be disregarding the parties' agreement that its entitlement to the transfer of rights of a certain kind remained subject to a now failed condition. The reason that D should not come under a duty to re-transfer the title to the specific footballs it received is that where it was agreed that D's entitlement against C to a transfer of a right of a certain kind remained subject to a now failed condition, the agreement can be given full effect without D re-transferring the very right(s) it received.

More difficult is the position where rights of a certain kind are transferred on a condition that has now failed, but the transferee no longer has any or all of the rights. So, imagine that in the example just given, D no longer has a title to any of the 1,000 footballs or has a title to only some of the footballs transferred. One possibility is that in this scenario, D should go into the market and purchase a title to 1,000 footballs of the same kind as those received, or the shortfall, and then transfer a title to 1,000 footballs of this kind to C. But a problem with this suggestion is that the market price of the footballs may have increased, meaning that to acquire 1,000 footballs of the same kind D may have to spend more than it agreed to pay for the footballs, or more than the market value of the 1,000 footballs when they were received. Further, D will often incur expenses going into the market to acquire the footballs. Given that D's restitutionary duty does not respond to a breach of duty, it is difficult to justify imposing a restitutionary duty on D that may require D to incur substantial costs to perform. It is also not clear what good reason there is for D, as opposed to C, being the party that should have to go into the market. The preferable view is that, in these circumstances, D's restitutionary duty takes the form of a duty to pay the market value of the footballs it no longer has at the time of receipt, provided that the market value does not exceed the overall price. If the market value exceeds the overall price, the sum D should be required to pay as restitution should generally be capped at that price.

ii. Cash

When a payment is made in cash (ie, using coins, banknotes, or another negotiable instrument), title to the cash transfers from the payor to the payee. A transfer of title to cash is not synonymous with a payment but is a species of the genus payments.[11]

If a payment is made in cash on an agreed condition, what is ordinarily agreed to remain conditional is the payee's entitlement to the payment, rather than the transfer of title to cash of a certain value or the specific cash used to effect the payment.[12] This is supported by the observation that agreements typically impose only an obligation on C to pay a sum of money to D. If C is not obliged to make a payment in cash, or a payment using specific cash, it will generally be implausible to construe the agreement as implicitly providing that D's entitlement to the transfer of title to cash of a certain value, or to the specific cash used to make the payment, remained conditional. Consequently, where, for example, C makes a payment to D using banknotes on a condition that subsequently fails, D should generally not come under a restitutionary duty to transfer a title to banknotes of an equivalent value, or the specific banknotes used to make the payment, to C.

There may, however, be rare cases where it was agreed that D's entitlement against C to the transfer of a title to cash of a certain value was to remain conditional. In this circumstance, if the relevant condition fails, D's restitutionary duty should take the form of a duty to transfer a title to cash of an equivalent value to that which it received. In the still more exceptional case where it was agreed that D's entitlement against C to the transfer of title to the specific cash used to make the payment was subject to a now failed condition, provided D still has the cash, D should generally come under a restitutionary duty to transfer the very cash it received back to C.

[11] As evident from the fact that a payment can be made via bank transfer.

[12] See also R Stevens, 'When and Why Does Unjustified Enrichment Justify the Recognition of Proprietary Rights?' (2011) 92 *Boston University Law Review* 919, 927–28.

iii. No Right Transferred

If there is a performance on a condition that has now failed which does not involve the transfer of a right, as for example where there is a payment via bank transfer, D should not come under a duty to (or be ordered to) transfer a right to C as restitution. The reason is that if C's performance does not involve the transfer of a right, the parties' agreement that D's entitlement to the performance remained subject to a condition that has now failed can be given full effect without D transferring a right to C. This is not to deny that D can usually perform its duty to reverse the performance by transferring a right to C. For example, if C pays £1,000 to D via bank transfer on a condition that has now failed, D's duty to reverse the payment can generally be discharged by paying £1,000 to C in cash, which will involve the transfer of a right.

C. The Authorities

The claims advanced above have received limited support from the authorities to date. But they should not be regarded as radical because there is no case where proper consideration has been given to whether, and if so when, D may come under a restitutionary duty to transfer a right to C following a failure of condition. The line of cases that provides the strongest support for the proposition that D may come under a restitutionary duty to transfer a right following a failure of condition is those involving the recovery of engagement presents. At common law,[13] if the transferee breaks off the engagement, the transferor is generally entitled to recover the title to the engagement present.[14] If the engagement is mutually dissolved, the present can also usually be recovered.[15] However, if the transferor breaks off the engagement, the transferor generally cannot recover the present.[16]

One reason for regarding cases where engagement presents have been recovered at common law as involving an award of restitution for a failure of condition is that the circumstances in which an engagement present is recoverable reflect those in which a deposit is recoverable. This is not surprising because, historically,[17] engagement presents, like deposits, were earnests.[18] This is significant because the basis upon which a deposit is recoverable is a failure of condition,[19] which strongly suggests that, from a modern perspective, this is also the best interpretation of the

[13] The circumstances in which an engagement present may be recovered are now governed by s 3 of the Law Reform (Miscellaneous Provisions) Act 1970.

[14] *Cohen v Sellar* [1926] 1 KB 536, 547 (McCardie J).

[15] ibid 548.

[16] ibid 547–48.

[17] Section 3(2) of the Law Reform (Miscellaneous Provisions) Act 1970 makes it difficult to regard an engagement present as still being an earnest.

[18] *Jacobs v Davis* [1917] 2 KB 532, 533 (Shearman J); *Cohen v Sellar* (n 14) 548 (McCardie J).

[19] *Gribbon v Lutton* [2002] 2 WLR 842, [60] (Robert Walker LJ); *Unaoil Ltd v Leighton Offshore Pte Ltd* [2014] EWHC 2965 (Comm), [65] (Eder J).

ground for recovery of engagement presents. On this view, the reason an engagement present was recoverable at common law where the engagement was broken off by the donee or mutually dissolved and not where the engagement was broken off by the donor is that, in the former circumstances, there was a failure of condition, but in the latter circumstance, there was not.

There are statements in the authorities that might be regarded as casting doubt on the proposition that D may come under a restitutionary duty to transfer a right to C following a failure of condition. In *Re BA Peters Plc*,[20] Nicholas Strauss QC said:

> The ordinary position, where a seller transfers title to the goods in advance of receiving payment is that his only remedy is to sue for the price. He cannot recover the goods on the basis of a total failure of consideration, because it would be anomalous to enable him to prefer his position to that of the general creditors.[21]

However, if D's restitutionary duty is to transfer a unique right to C, it is difficult to understand why it would be anomalous to order D to re-transfer the right. Courts do not refuse to order the specific performance of a contractual duty to transfer a unique right on the basis that such an order would give C 'priority' over D's general creditors in D's insolvency.[22] If D may be ordered to specifically perform a contractual duty to transfer a unique right in such circumstances, like cases being treated alike, a court should not refuse to order D to perform a restitutionary duty to transfer a unique right on the basis that such an order may give C priority over D's general creditors. It is also unclear why priority in insolvency should be of relevance in cases where D is not insolvent.

In *Spaul v Spaul*,[23] which concerned a claim to recover shares, Rimer LJ asserted that 'even if [the claimant] is entitled to restitution on the basis that [the defendant] was unjustly enriched by the share transfer, a remedy for a failure of [condition] can only be a damage-based award for restitution of the value by which the share transfer unjustly enriched [the defendant], not a return of the shares themselves'.[24] Rimer LJ did not explain why, as a matter of principle, this was the case or cite any authority.

An interpretation of Rimer LJ's analysis that is consistent with the present argument is that shares are not recoverable following a failure of condition because they are not unique. As explained in the next section, although D may come under a restitutionary duty to transfer a right, generally this duty should not be

[20] *Re BA Peters Plc* [2008] EWHC 2205 (Ch).

[21] ibid [77].

[22] See, eg, *In re Bastable, Ex parte the Trustee* [1901] 2 KB 518; *Pearce v Bastable's Trustee in Bankruptcy* [1901] 2 Ch 122; *Francis v Cowcliffe* (1977) 33 P & CR 368; *Freevale Ltd v Metrostore (Holdings) Ltd* [1984] Ch 199. Strictly speaking, C is not being given 'priority' over D's general creditors. Rather, the effect of an order to specifically perform an obligation to transfer a right in such circumstances is that the right is not available for realisation and distribution among D's creditors in D's insolvency.

[23] *Spaul v Spaul* [2014] EWCA Civ 679.

[24] ibid [40].

specifically enforced, which will have the consequence that C is unable to recover the right it transferred or a right of the same kind as the right it transferred. It is also worth observing that shares are not transferred but novated.[25] The proposition that shares are not recoverable following a failure of condition therefore does not strictly stand in the way of the claim that where C transfers a right to D on a condition that has now failed, D may come under a restitutionary duty to transfer a right to C, which a court may specifically enforce.

IV. Ordering the Performance of a Restitutionary Duty to Transfer a Right

This section argues that the same reasons that justify refusing to order D to specifically perform a contractual duty to transfer a right to C are relevant to whether D should be ordered to perform a restitutionary duty to transfer a right following a failure of condition. A consequence of this argument is that D should only be ordered to perform a restitutionary duty to transfer a right where C has transferred a unique right to D on a condition that has now failed.

A. The Specific Performance Analogy

Compare:

(1) C and D enter into a contract whereby C agrees to perform certain services for D in exchange for D transferring a title to 100 cattle of a certain kind to C following the substantial performance of the services. The contract states that a title to the cattle is to be transferred via delivery. C substantially performs the services, but D, in breach of contract, delivers none of the cattle.

(2) C and D enter into a contract for the sale of a title to 100 cattle of a certain kind in exchange for D's performance of certain services. The contract states that a title to the cattle is to be transferred via delivery. C delivers the cattle, but D, in breach of contract, performs none of the services.

In cases exemplified by the first example, a court would not order D to perform its duty to transfer a title to 100 cattle because the cattle are not unique. As discussed above, in the second example, D should come under a restitutionary duty to transfer a title to 100 cattle of the same kind as those it received title to back to C. Given all that has changed in the second example is the order for performance, it would

[25] P Davies, S Worthington and C Hare, *Gower: Principles of Modern Company Law*, 11th edn (London, Sweet & Maxwell, 2021) [26-005], fn 19, citing *Ashby v Blackwell* (1765) 2 Eden 299, 302–03; 28 ER 913, 914 (Northington LC) and *Simm v Anglo-American Telegraph Co* (1879) 5 QBD 188, 204 (Bramwell LJ). See also E Micheler, 'Farewell to Quasi-negotiability? Legal Title and Transfer of Shares in a Paperless World' (2002) *Journal of Business Law* 358, 360–62.

also seem that an order requiring D to transfer a title to 100 cattle of the same kind to those received as restitution generally should not be made. As Lord Millett observed extra-judicially:

> the right to re-conveyance is a form of specific performance (or 'specific unperformance') which equity makes available because a money judgment is an inadequate remedy. If this is right, then the remedy should be confined to cases of land or other property of special value to the transferor.[26]

Millett's argument has subsequently been developed by Justice Edelman, also writing extra-judicially.[27] For Edelman, the justification for D coming under a restitutionary duty to transfer a right is that it 'may be the most perfect way of making restitution' where D's 'enrichment' is the receipt of a right.[28] An order to perform a restitutionary duty to transfer a right, Edelman argues, is sufficiently analogous to an order to perform a contractual duty to transfer a right, such that the same considerations should apply to whether a party is ordered to perform a restitutionary duty to transfer a right.[29] Edelman therefore claims that an order to perform a restitutionary duty to transfer a right should only be made where a monetary restitutionary award is 'inadequate', in the sense that concept is understood in the specific performance context.[30] For reasons that are now developed, Millett and Edelman's thesis should be endorsed.[31]

B. Reasons for Refusing to Order the Transfer of a Right

The order that is most commonly made following a contractual breach or repudiation is an order to perform a payment obligation that has accrued. As others have observed, an order requiring a party to pay an agreed sum is an order for specific performance.[32] Courts generally only order the performance of contractual obligations that do not take the form of a payment obligation if damages are 'inadequate'. Conventionally, damages are regarded as adequate where an award of a monetary substitute for the lost performance can be used in the market to acquire a

[26] P Millett, 'Restitution and Constructive Trusts' in W Cornish, R Nolan, J O'Sullivan and G Virgo (eds), *Restitution: Past, Present and Future* (Oxford, Hart Publishing, 1998) 216.

[27] J Edelman, 'Restitution of (Property) Rights' in E Bant and M Bryan (eds), *Principles of Proprietary Remedies* (Pyrmont, NSW, Lawbook Co, 2013) ch 3.

[28] ibid 50.

[29] ibid 51. See also W Swadling, 'Unjust Enrichment: Value, Rights, and Trusts' (2021) 137 *LQR* 56, 74–75, who prefers the analogy with orders for the delivery up of converted goods.

[30] Edelman, 'Restitution of (Property) Rights' (n 27) 51–52.

[31] This view receives some support from certain Canadian authorities: see *Kerr v Baranow* [2011] 1 SCR 269, [50]–[52] (Cromwell J).

[32] S Smith, *Rights, Wrongs, and Injustices: The Structure of Remedial Law* (Oxford, Oxford University Press, 2019) 140. Of course, orders to specifically perform an obligation to transfer a right are typically understood as a form of equitable relief whereas orders to perform a payment obligation are not, which has consequences for the available defences.

close substitute for the lost performance. If a close substitute cannot be acquired because, for example, the duty not performed was a duty to transfer a unique right, damages will be inadequate.

In considering why courts generally do not order the performance of contractual duties to transfer rights, it is helpful to compare two further examples:

(1) C and D enter into a contract for the sale of a title to 100kg of merino wool via delivery in exchange for payment of £10,000 following delivery. C performs its obligation to deliver the wool, but D, in breach of contract, fails to pay the agreed sum.

(2) C and D enter into a contract for the sale of a title to 100kg of merino wool via delivery in exchange for payment of £10,000 in advance. C pays the £10,000 in advance, but D, in breach of contract, fails to deliver the wool.

In the former scenario, C will generally be entitled to an order requiring D to pay the agreed sum. In the latter, D is unlikely to be ordered to perform its obligation to deliver the wool. What explains this difference? In other words, why will a party generally be ordered to perform a contractual payment obligation but not a contractual obligation to transfer a non-unique right?

One difference between the examples is the relative difficulty of complying with a court order to specifically perform the duty owed. Consider that if D was ordered to perform its duty to transfer a title to the wool, it is significantly more likely that D will fail to comply with the order despite a bona fide attempt. D may breach the order, among other ways, because of a defect in the quality of the wool delivered of which D was unaware; because D mistakenly delivered less wool than promised; because D mistakenly delivered wool of a different kind than the wool that it was required to deliver; or because D mistakenly delivered the wool late. By contrast, it will be an unusual situation where D fails to comply with an order to pay a monetary sum despite a bona fide attempt.

The relative difficulty of complying with an order is relevant to whether specific performance should be ordered because 'the only means available to the court to enforce its order [for specific performance] is the quasi-criminal procedure of punishment for contempt'.[33] Significantly, a party may be in contempt despite not having intended to disobey a court order.[34] Although there is some authority suggesting that a party who accidentally does not comply with an order will not be liable for contempt,[35] it appears this only means that an involuntary act resulting in non-compliance will not constitute contempt. It follows that where a court orders a party to perform a contractual duty, even if this party has made a genuine

[33] *Co-operative Insurance Society Ltd v Argyll Stores (Holdings) Ltd* [1998] AC 1, 12 (Lord Hoffmann).

[34] *Stancomb v Trowbridge UDC* [1910] 2 Ch 190, 194 (Warrington J); *Knight v Clifton* [1971] Ch 700, 721 (Sachs LJ); *Director General of Fair Trading v Pioneer Concrete (UK) Ltd* [1995] 1 AC 456, 479-481 (Lord Nolan); *Masri v Consolidated Contractors Intl Co SAL* [2011] EWHC 1024 (Comm), [155] (Christopher Clarke J).

[35] *VDU Installations Ltd v Integrated Computer Systems and Cybernetics Ltd* [1989] 1 FSR 378, 394 (Knox J).

attempt to comply, they may still be in contempt if the order is breached.[36] Where an order is breached despite a genuine attempt to comply, a finding of contempt usually seems disproportionate. To avoid the possibility of such a response, courts are reluctant to order the specific performance of an obligation if there is a real possibility that the order may be breached despite a bona fide attempt to comply.

This justification for generally refusing to specifically enforce contractual duties to transfer rights maps onto various notable bars to specific performance. For example, an order for specific performance will generally be refused if there is a reasonable likelihood that the order will result in 'constant court supervision'.[37] There is some ambiguity regarding precisely what this means,[38] but the general idea is that specific performance will not be ordered if there is a real possibility that the order will result in multiple applications concerning whether the order has been complied with.[39] The constant supervision bar has sometimes been rationalised on the basis that where an order for specific performance would require constant supervision, too much judicial time and effort would be taken up determining whether there has been compliance.[40] Although this policy rationale may form part of the explanation, if an order for specific performance would require constant court supervision, it is usually a strong indication that there is a real possibility the order may be breached despite a bona fide attempt to comply.

A further bar to specific performance is uncertainty.[41] This bar provides that even if an agreement is sufficiently certain to be a contract, specific performance of an obligation the agreement imposed may be denied because the obligation is too vague. So, in *Co-operative Insurance Society Ltd v Argyll Stores (Holdings) Ltd*,[42] one reason given by the House of Lords for refusing to order a tenant to perform an obligation to 'keep the demised premises open for retail trade during the usual hours of business in the locality and the display windows properly dressed in a suitable manner in keeping with a good class parade of shops' was that the obligation was too vague. Lord Hoffmann said:

> The fact that the terms of a contractual obligation are sufficiently definite to escape being void for uncertainty, or to found a claim for damages … does not necessarily mean that they will be sufficiently precise to be capable of being specifically performed … Precision is of course a question of degree and the courts have shown themselves willing to cope with a certain degree of imprecision in cases of orders requiring the achievement

[36] If a party has made a bona fide attempt to comply with the order, this will be treated as a mitigating factor: see, eg, *In re Mileage Conference Group of the Tyre Manufacturers' Conference Ltd's Agreement* [1966] 1 WLR 1137, 1162 (Megaw J).

[37] *Ryan v Mutual Tontine Westminster Chambers Association* [1893] 1 Ch 116.

[38] A Burrows, *Remedies for Torts, Breach of Contract, and Equitable Wrongs*, 4th edn (Oxford, Oxford University Press, 2019) 415.

[39] *Co-operative Insurance Society Ltd v Argyll Stores (Holdings)* (n 33) 12 (Lord Hoffmann).

[40] ibid 13.

[41] *Joseph v National Magazine Co* [1959] Ch 14.

[42] *Co-operative Insurance Society Ltd v Argyll Stores (Holdings)* (n 33).

> of a result in which the plaintiffs' merits appeared strong; … it is, taken alone, merely a discretionary matter to be taken into account. It is, however, a very important one.[43]

If the content of an obligation is vague, it will usually be unclear what an order to specifically perform the obligation requires, meaning it is more likely that the order will be breached despite a genuine attempt to comply. A similar point was made by Lord Hoffmann when his Lordship observed: '[i]f the terms of the court's order, reflecting the terms of the obligation, cannot be precisely drawn, the possibility of … oppression caused by the defendant having to do things under threat of proceedings for contempt [is increased].'[44]

The above explanation for the reluctance to order the specific performance of a contractual duty to transfer a right is applicable to claims for restitution of a transfer of a right for a failure of condition. To clarify why, the following example is helpful:

> C and D enter into an unenforceable contract for the sale of a title to 100kg of merino wool via delivery in exchange for payment of £10,000 following delivery. C performs its obligation to deliver the wool, but D, in breach of the agreement, fails to pay the agreed sum.

As observed, here D should generally come under a restitutionary duty to transfer a title to 100kg of wool of the same kind as the wool received. It is more difficult for D to comply with an order to perform this duty than for D to perform a restitutionary duty to pay a monetary sum. Despite a genuine attempt, there is a real possibility that D may breach the order because, for example, D mistakenly transfers a title to wool of a different kind than that received; because the wool D transfers is of a lower quality than the wool it received; because the wool is damaged during delivery; or because the wool is mistakenly delivered late. By contrast, it will be unusual for D to breach an order to pay a monetary sum as restitution where it has made a bona fide attempt to comply with the order.

C. Significance

The foregoing argument implies that, by analogy with orders to specifically perform contractual duties to transfer rights, where D comes under a restitutionary duty to transfer a right following a failure of condition, D should not be ordered to specifically perform this duty unless D's duty is to transfer a unique right to C. On the other hand, where D is under a restitutionary duty to transfer a non-unique right, C should not be entitled to an order compelling D to perform this duty. Rather, in this circumstance, C should be confined to a restitutionary monetary award in lieu

[43] ibid 14. See also *Morris v Redland Bricks Ltd* [1970] AC 652, 666 (Lord Upjohn).
[44] *Co-operative Insurance Society Ltd v Argyll Stores (Holdings)* (n 33) 14–15.

of an order requiring D to specifically perform its restitutionary duty to transfer a right.

V. Failure of Condition and Trusts

This section argues that where D comes under a restitutionary duty to transfer a specific right to C following a failure of condition, which a court will specifically enforce, a trust should arise. It is assumed that the trust that arises here is a constructive as opposed to a resulting trust.[45] However, if the trust that arises is a resulting trust, this would have no real bearing on the analysis.

A. Trusts and Why They Arise

To explain when a trust should be recognised following a failure of condition, it is necessary to begin by explaining what a trust is and why constructive trusts arise. Two claims are made in this regard. The first is that a trust is an indefeasible duty not to use a specific patrimonial right for one's own benefit other than to the extent authorised by an instrument governing the trust.[46] The other claim is that one circumstance where D will generally come under such a duty is where D owes a duty to transfer a specific right to C that has fallen due, and which is specifically enforceable.

i. The Alleged Fiction of the Constructive Trust

Professor Swadling has argued that a trust never arises in the absence of a declaration of trust.[47] On this view, express trusts are the only trusts. An express trust, Swadling claims, is a 'trust arising because of a declaration, whether proved by evidence or presumption'.[48] For Swadling, constructive trusts are not trusts because

[45] There is a powerful argument that resulting trusts are a redundant category: see Swadling, 'Property' (n 7) 215–16. The concept of a resulting trust is also misleading because there is nothing that results back to the beneficiary of a resulting trust: W Swadling, 'Explaining Resulting Trusts' (2008) 124 *LQR* 72, 90–91. The formation of a trust involves the creation as opposed to transfer of equitable rights. This is because, where, for example, a party holds a title to a thing 'absolutely', this party does not have both a legal and an equitable title to the thing: *DKLR Holding Co (No 2) Pty Ltd v Commissioner of Stamp Duties* [1980] 1 NSWLR 510, 518–19 (Hope JA); *Westdeutsche Landesbank Girozentrale v Islington LBC* [1996] AC 669, 706 (Lord Browne-Wilkinson).

[46] The words 'unless authorised by the terms of the trust' are intended to acknowledge the possibility that a trustee may (among other things) be a beneficiary of the trust.

[47] W Swadling, 'Orthodoxy' in W Swadling (ed), *The Quistclose Trust* (Oxford, Hart Publishing, 2004); W Swadling, 'The Vendor-Purchaser Constructive Trust' in S Degeling and J Edelman (eds), *Equity in Commercial Law* (Sydney, Lawbook Co, 2005); Swadling, 'Explaining Resulting Trusts' (n 45); W Swadling, 'The Fiction of the Constructive Trust' (2011) 64 *CLP* 399; W Swadling, 'Unjust Enrichment: Value, Rights and Trusts' (n 29).

[48] Swadling, 'Property' (n 7) 215.

constructive trustees do not hold 'rights for another or for a purpose', which Swadling regards as essential to the existence of a trust.[49] Rather, a constructive trust is an order to pay a monetary sum or transfer a right.[50] In Swadling's words:

> The question then is whether orders to pay money or transfer particular rights are properly described as trusts or whether all that is in play is an unhelpful analogy. To answer that question, we need an accurate definition of the trust. This turns out to be an extraordinarily difficult thing to find. Moreover, many definitions simply reflect the orthodoxy that the 'constructive trust' is a genuine trust. The question, however, is whether it shares sufficient features of the express trust, which undoubtedly is a trust, to deserve the same name. At its most basic, the phrase 'express trust' might be said to capture the idea of one person holding rights for another or for a purpose. This essential element, it is submitted, is missing from 'constructive trusts'.[51]

If a necessary condition for the existence of a trust is that a party has been entrusted with a right, as the language of trusteeship implies,[52] Swadling's claim that constructive trusts are not trusts is undoubtedly correct because constructive trustees are not entrusted with anything. But the phrase 'constructive trust' does not imply that constructive trustees are persons who have been entrusted with a right. The law generally uses the word 'constructive' to mean deemed.[53] For example, where someone has constructive knowledge of a fact, they are deemed to know this fact. When X is deemed to be Y, factually, X is not necessarily Y: someone who has constructive knowledge of a fact does not necessarily know the fact. But where X is deemed to be Y, X is treated as Y for at least certain purposes. It follows that if the language of constructive trust is taken seriously, a constructive trustee is someone who is deemed to have been entrusted with a right.

The idea that a constructive trustee is someone deemed to be a trustee is, however, rejected by Swadling, who makes the stronger claim that constructive trusts are orders to pay a monetary sum or transfer a right. This argument has a poor fit with the positive law. There are important legal incidents that constructive trusts share with express trusts.[54] So, it has been held that, as is the case where there is an express trust, a right held on constructive trust is unavailable for realisation and distribution to creditors in a constructive trustee's bankruptcy. In *FHR European Ventures LLP v Cedar Capital Partners LLC*,[55] for example, the Supreme Court held that where a bribe is received by an agent in breach of fiduciary duty, the agent will hold the bribe on constructive trust for its principal, which the court

[49] Swadling, 'The Fiction of the Constructive Trust' (n 47) 407.
[50] ibid 400, 405–07.
[51] ibid 407.
[52] *Williams v Central Bank of Nigeria* [2014] AC 1189, [30] (Lord Sumption).
[53] R Megarry, 'Historical Development', in *Special Lectures of the Law Society of Upper Canada 1990 – Fiduciary Duties* (Law Society of Upper Canada, 1991) 5.
[54] In addition to the cases discussed, see *Re Sharpe (a bankrupt)* [1980] 1 WLR 219; *Chase Manhattan Bank NA v Israel-British Bank (London) Ltd* [1981] Ch 105.
[55] *FHR European Ventures LLP v Cedar Capital Partners LLC* [2015] AC 250.

regarded as having the consequence that the bribe will be unavailable for realisation and distribution among the agent's creditors in bankruptcy.

Another case where a right held on constructive trust was treated as unavailable for realisation and distribution among a bankrupt constructive trustee's creditors is *Mountney v Treharne.*[56] A property adjustment order was made by way of ancillary relief in matrimonial proceedings. The order required the husband to transfer his rights in relation to the matrimonial home to his former wife. After the order had been made, but before the husband had transferred his rights, he was bankrupted on his own petition. The Court of Appeal held that the adjustment order conferred an equitable interest on the wife, analogous to the interest under a vendor-purchaser constructive trust, which was binding on the husband's trustee in bankruptcy.

There are also cases where it has been held that a constructive trustee is liable to account for and disgorge profits made using the right that it holds on constructive trust. In *Novoship (UK) Ltd v Mikhaylyuk*,[57] Longmore LJ said: '[t]he nature of the liability, as it seems to us, is that the knowing recipient or dishonest assistant has, in principle, the responsibility of an express trustee. That responsibility would include, in an appropriate case, a liability to account for profits.' And in *Fiona Trust & Holding Corporation v Privalov*,[58] Andrew Smith J said that '[t]he remedies for knowing receipt include an account of profits'. If a constructive trust is merely an order to pay a monetary sum or transfer a right, it is very difficult to explain why a constructive trustee should be liable to account for and disgorge profits.

It has also been held that liability may be imposed on a party who dishonestly assists in a breach of constructive trust, which again suggests that constructive trusts are not merely orders to pay a monetary sum or transfer a right. The leading case is *Stevens v Hotel Portfolio II UK Ltd (in liq).*[59] The claimant company, Hotel Portfolio II UK Ltd ('HPII'), owned a portfolio of London hotels. HPII sold the hotels to a company called Cambulo Comercio e Serviços Sociedade Unipessoal LDA, which was controlled by Mr Stevens, but who was acting as a nominee for Mr Ruhan, a director of HPII. Mr Ruhan failed to disclose his interest in the transaction, breaching his fiduciary duties. Following the development of two of the hotels, Cambulo Madeira resold them for a profit, with Mr Ruhan receiving a £95 million dividend. Relevantly, it was held that: (1) Mr Ruhan held this dividend on constructive trust; (2) Mr Ruhan breached his duties as constructive trustee by using the dividend to pay down loans connected to speculative projects in Qatar; and (3) Mr Stevens dishonestly assisted Mr Ruhan in this breach of constructive trust.

[56] *Mountney v Treharne* [2003] Ch 135. See also *Re Walker* [1970] ALR 300.

[57] *Novoship (UK) Ltd v Mikhaylyuk* [2015] QB 499, [82].

[58] *Fiona Trust & Holding Corporation v Privalov* [2010] EWHC 3199 (Comm), [62].

[59] *Stevens v Hotel Portfolio II UK Ltd (in liq)* [2025] 3 WLR 293. Another example is *Wambo Coal Pty v Ariff* [2007] NSWSC 589, where it was held that a mistaken payment by C was held on constructive trust by D, which was regarded as having the further consequence that a third party was liable to C under the so-called first limb in *Barnes v Addy* (1874) LR 9 Ch App 244.

ii. A Duty Not to Use a Specific Patrimonial Right for One's Own Benefit

Contrary to Swadling's view, a constructive trust is a trust in the sense that constructive trustees owe the same core duty as express trustees. This is an indefeasible duty not to use a specific patrimonial right (or set of rights) for one's own benefit other than to the extent authorised by the instrument governing the trust.[60] There are several aspects to this interpretation of a trustee's core duty that require elaboration. First, the subject matter of a trust (ie, what is held on trust) is a right as opposed to a thing.[61] This is demonstrated by the fact that shares, bank accounts, intellectual property rights, receivables and equitable rights, none of which are things (because they do not occupy a location in space-time), but are rights, may be held on trust.[62] As explained below, the idea of a right being 'held' on trust is metaphorical. What this really means is that the trustee has a particular duty in relation to how it exercises the powers it has in relation to a specific right or the privileges that the right confers.[63]

Secondly, only patrimonial rights can be held on trust. A patrimonial right is a right that is generally capable of being transferred, such as a title to goods or a patent. Not all rights are capable of transfer. For example, our rights not to be defamed or falsely imprisoned cannot be transferred.

Thirdly, the duty a trustee owes in relation to a specific right is a duty not to use the right for its own benefit (other than to the extent authorised). More exactly, the trustee is under a duty not to exercise the powers that it has in relation to the right and the privileges the right confers for its own benefit. For example, if T holds a title to a bicycle on trust for B, T will be under a duty not to exercise its power to transfer the title to the bicycle for its own benefit. T will also be under a duty not to exercise the privileges it has in respect of the bicycle for its own benefit. T will therefore be under a duty not to ride the bicycle around East Oxford for its own benefit.

The claim that the core duty of a trustee is a duty not to use a specific right for its own benefit unless authorised by the terms of the trust is supported by statements in the authorities. In *Ayerst v C & K (Construction) Ltd*,[64] Lord Diplock said that a right held on trust is held by the trustee 'not for his own benefit but for the benefit of the cestui que trust or beneficiaries'. In *Space Investments Ltd v Canadian*

[60] For a similar interpretation, see McFarlane, *The Structure of Property Law* (n 7) 551–52; R Stevens, *The Laws of Restitution* (Oxford, Oxford University Press, 2023) 222–23.

[61] See, eg, R Chambers, *An Introduction to Property Law in Australia*, 2nd edn (Australia, Thomson Reuters, 2008) [13.90]; L Smith, 'Trust and Patrimony' (2009) 28 *Estates, Trusts and Pensions Journal* 332, 379, 381, 391–92; McFarlane and Stevens, 'The Nature of Equitable Property' (n 8) 2–6; J Edelman, 'Two Fundamental Questions for the Law of Trusts' (2013) 129 *LQR* 66, 66, 72–76.

[62] This claim is also supported by the possibility of a sub-trust.

[63] *Space Investments Ltd v Canadian Imperial Bank of Commerce Trust Co (Bahamas) Ltd* [1986] 1 WLR 1072, 1073–74 (Lord Templeman). A similar claim appears to be present in J Penner, 'The (True) Nature of a Beneficiary's Equitable Proprietary Interest Under a Trust' (2014) 27 *Canadian Journal of Law and Jurisprudence* 473.

[64] *Ayerst v C & K (Construction) Ltd* [1976] AC 167, 177.

Imperial Bank of Commerce Trust Co (Bahamas) Ltd,[65] Lord Templeman similarly stated:

> a trustee has no power to use trust money for his own benefit unless the trust instrument expressly authorises him so to do. A bank trustee, like any other trustee, may only apply trust money in the manner authorised by the trust instrument, or by law, for the sole benefit of the beneficiaries and to the exclusion of any benefit to the bank trustee unless the trust instrument otherwise provides.

In *DKLR Holding Co (No 2) Pty Ltd v Commissioner of Stamp Duties*,[66] Hope JA said:

> Where the trustee is the owner of the legal fee simple, the right of the beneficiary, although annexed to the land, is a right to compel the legal owner to hold and use the rights which the law gives him in accordance with the obligations which equity has imposed on him. The trustee, in such a case, has at law all the rights of the absolute owner in fee simple, but he is not free to use those rights for his own benefit in the way he could if no trust existed. Equitable obligations require him to use them in some particular way for the benefit of other persons.[67]

Fourthly, trustees are under a duty in relation to a *specific* right or set of rights. If T has a title to 20 cows and declares a trust over its title to five of those cows, the trust will fail if it is not, objectively considered, possible to identify which five titles were intended to be held on trust.[68] It would, however, appear to be possible to hold a proportion of a specific right on trust, as evidenced by the fact that a trust will not necessarily fail if T declares that £100 standing to the credit of a specific bank account with a credit balance of £500, or 20 shares out of 100 that it holds in a public company,[69] are to be held on trust.

Finally, a trustee is under an *indefeasible* duty not to use a specific right for its own benefit for as long as it has the right. A duty not to use a right for one's own benefit is indefeasible if the duty is not conditional upon the performance of another obligation. Where a party's duty not to use a specific right for its own benefit is defeasible, there is a fixed charge and not a trust.[70]

In situations where a constructive trust arises, it is also plausible to regard the constructive trustee as owing an indefeasible duty not to use a specific right for its own benefit. Consider:

(1) C and D enter into a contract for the sale of a title to *Venus de Milo*. It is agreed that title to the sculpture is to be transferred via delivery following payment of the price in advance. C duly pays the price.

[65] *Space Investments Ltd v Canadian Imperial Bank of Commerce Trust Co (Bahamas) Ltd* (n 63) 1073–74.

[66] *DKLR Holding Co (No 2) Pty Ltd v Commissioner of Stamp Duties* (n 45).

[67] ibid [16].

[68] *Re London Wine Co (Shippers) Ltd* [1986] PCC 121.

[69] *Hunter v Moss* [1994] 1 WLR 452.

[70] *In re Cosslett (Contractors) Ltd* [1998] Ch 495, 510 (Millet LJ); R Stevens, 'Contractual Aspects of Debt Financing' in D Prentice and A Reisberg (eds), *Corporate Finance Law in the UK and EU* (Oxford, Oxford University Press, 2011) 216.

(2) D is ordered to transfer a fee simple title to land to C, his former wife, before the end of next week.

(3) D, who is P's agent, receives a title to a yacht from B as a bribe.

(4) C transfers a title to a Pollock to D. The contract is later rescinded ab initio for D's fraudulent misrepresentation when D still has the title.

(5) C mistakenly transfers a title to a unique vase to D. D knows that the transfer was made due to a mistake. There is no juristic reason for the transfer.

(6) C and D enter into a contract for the sale of a fee simple title to land. The date for completion is 9 August. On 10 August, the title has not been transferred by D despite C having paid the deposit and being ready, willing, and able to complete the sale.

In each of these scenarios, D will generally hold the relevant right on constructive trust. In each scenario, if one asks what the duty is that D owes in relation to the relevant right, the intuitive answer is a duty not to use the right for its own benefit. Why? A complete answer cannot be provided here and requires a theory of constructive trusts. But one plausible (general) answer is that, as between C and D, C is presently more deserving of a specific right that D holds than D.

The claim that D is under an indefeasible duty not to use a specific right for its own benefit in circumstances where a constructive trust arises also receives support from certain aspects of the positive law. For example, under a contract for the sale of a fee simple title to land, the vendor will generally hold the title on constructive trust from when its duty to transfer the title has fallen due.[71] After the vendor has become a constructive trustee, the vendor will be liable to the purchaser to account for and disgorge any rents or profits received.[72] This is consistent with a vendor, who is a constructive trustee, being under a duty not to use the title for its own benefit since if the vendor could retain rents or profits, the vendor would be benefiting from the title.

As observed above, the authorities also suggest that a knowing recipient of a right transferred or conferred in breach of trust is obliged to disgorge profits made using the right that it holds on constructive trust.[73] Similarly, if a fiduciary makes a profit using a right that it holds on constructive trust, the fiduciary will, subject to an allowance, be obliged to disgorge the profit.[74]

One explanation for why a constructive trustee is obliged to disgorge profits, consistent with the interpretation of constructive trusts put forward, is that a constructive trustee is under a duty not to use the right it holds on trust for its own benefit. If the constructive trustee has made a profit from the use of the right, the next best thing to the trustee not having breached its duty not to use the right for its own benefit is to disgorge the profit. Another explanation, also consistent

[71] *Wall v Bright* (1820) 1 Jac & W 494, 503; 37 ER 456, 459 (Sir Thomas Plumer MR); *Rose v Watson* (1864) 10 HLC 672, 683 (Lord Cranworth).

[72] *Brooke v Champernowne* (1837) 4 Cl & Fin 589; 7 ER 224; *Cudden v Tite* (1858) 1 Giff 395; 65 ER 971.

[73] See the authorities cited at nn 54–59 above.

[74] *Attorney General for Hong Kong v Reid* [1994] 1 AC 324, 331 (Lord Templeman).

with the present argument, is that a constructive trustee's obligation to disgorge profits is part of the constructive trustee's primary duty not to use the right for its own benefit.[75] On this interpretation, it is not a breach of duty for a constructive trustee to use the right it holds on constructive trust to make a profit, provided the profit is disgorged.[76] An order requiring the trustee to disgorge profits therefore involves the enforcement of the trustee's primary duty not to use the right for its own benefit.

iii. A Specifically Enforceable Duty to Transfer a Specific Right Creates a Trust

Where a party's duty to transfer a specific right has fallen due and is specifically enforceable, but the right has not yet been transferred, a trust will arise. In other words, a specifically enforceable duty to transfer a specific right that has fallen due will usually impose a further duty not to use the right for one's own benefit until the transfer has been made, which is a trust. A notable illustration of this principle, observed above, is that under a contract for the sale of a fee simple title to land, a vendor will generally hold the title on trust for the purchaser from when the duty to transfer the title has fallen due. Another example, also mentioned above, is that where a court orders a party to transfer a specific right, a trust will arise. A still further example is cases involving contracts for the sale of a beneficiary's equitable right under a trust.[77]

It is sometimes suggested that the reason a trust may arise where a party is under a duty to transfer a specific right is that the duty is specifically enforceable.[78] But it is mysterious how a right[79] that C has against the court to an order for specific performance can affect the duties that D owes in relation to a right before an order for specific performance has been made.[80] Put differently, it is unclear why C's right against the court to an order for specific performance should impose a duty on D not to use a specific right for its own benefit.

It should, however, be accepted that a trust will not arise where D's duty to transfer a specific right is not specifically enforceable. If D's duty to transfer a right could create a trust despite the duty not being specifically enforceable, C could circumvent the unenforceability of D's duty by collapsing the trust under the rule

[75] This justification has been provided for requiring fiduciaries to disgorge profits: L Smith, 'Fiduciary Relationships: Ensuring the Loyal Exercise of Judgment on Behalf of Another' (2014) 130 *LQR* 608, 625–32. See also P Millett, 'Bribes and Secret Commissions Again' [2012] 71 *CLJ* 583, 591–92. It is not being suggested that constructive trustees are fiduciaries.

[76] This is consistent with *Evans v European Bank Ltd* (2004) 61 NSWLR 75, where it was held (at [162]) that in the circumstances of the case a constructive trustee was under a duty to invest 'monies' it held on constructive trust.

[77] *Neville v Wilson* [1997] Ch 144.

[78] *Jerome v Kelly* [2004] 1 WLR 25, [29]–[32] (Robert Walker LJ).

[79] If it is correct to regard orders for specific performance as discretionary in some sense, then a party would have a right that the court considers exercising its discretion to order specific performance.

[80] See also McFarlane, *The Structure of Property Law* (n 7) 235–37.

in *Saunders v Vautier*.[81] In other words, the law would be saying that although it is unprepared to specifically enforce D's duty, it is still going to give C the power to collapse the trust thereby enabling C to obtain the transfer of the right, which is incoherent. To be clear, it is not being suggested that the availability of an order for specific performance of a duty to transfer a specific right creates a trust. The claim is that due to the rule in *Saunders v Vautier*, the unavailability of an order for specific performance of a duty to transfer a right provides a reason against recognising a trust.

B. When a Trust Arises Following a Failure of Condition

i. Trusts and Transfers of Rights on a Condition that Fails

It was suggested above that where C and D agreed that D's entitlement against C to a transfer of a specific right remained subject to a condition that has now failed, D should generally come under a restitutionary duty to re-transfer the right it received back to C. Thus, if C transfers a title to Picasso's *La Vie* to D on a condition that has now failed, D should generally come under a restitutionary duty to re-transfer the title to the painting it received. Further, given that Picasso's *La Vie* is unique, this duty will prima facie be specifically enforceable. Where D comes under a specifically enforceable contractual duty to transfer a specific right to C, D will generally hold the right on trust. There is no rational basis for treating the legal incidents of a restitutionary duty to transfer a specific right differently from a contractual duty to transfer a specific right. If a specifically enforceable contractual duty to transfer a specific right creates a trust, a specifically enforceable restitutionary duty to transfer a specific right also should.

Where D's entitlement against C to the transfer of a right of a certain kind (ie, a non-specific right) remained subject to a condition that has now failed, it was argued above that D should only come under a restitutionary duty to transfer a right to C of the same kind to the right it received. In other words, D will not owe a restitutionary duty to transfer a specific right to C. In this circumstance, there is no justification for treating D as under a duty not to use a specific right for its own benefit, meaning there will not be a trust. This is the position taken in respect of contractual duties to transfer non-specific rights. Treating a contractual duty to transfer a non-specific right as not creating a trust, but a restitutionary duty to transfer a non-specific right as potentially creating a trust, treats alike cases differently. Further, for reasons elaborated above, a restitutionary duty to transfer a non-specific right should not be specifically enforceable, which, as observed, provides a decisive reason against there being a trust.

[81] *Saunders v Vautier* (1841) 4 Beav 115; 41 ER 482.

ii. Where no Right is Transferred

a. Payments via a Bank Transfer

Imagine that C makes a payment of £1,000 to D via bank transfer on a condition that subsequently fails. In this scenario, D will generally come under a restitutionary duty to pay £1,000 to C. But should a trust arise? If there is a trust here, what is held on trust is not the payment made. A payment is not a right but a juristic event. Further, where a payment is made via bank transfer, no right is transferred from the payor to the payee. Given that rights are held on trust, there cannot be a trust of a payment. If a trust arises following a payment via bank transfer, what is held on trust is a proportion of,[82] or the whole of,[83] the new right the payee acquired against its bank due to the payment.

In *Bailey v Angove's Pty Ltd*,[84] Lord Sumption said that 'money paid on a consideration which has wholly failed' only creates 'personal obligations'. If what Lord Sumption meant by this is that a duty to make restitution of a payment does not create a trust, as the context would suggest, this seems correct. In the above example, following the failure of condition in respect of the £1,000 payment, D came under a restitutionary duty to pay £1,000 to C. This is not a specifically enforceable duty to transfer a specific right or any right at all. Nor is it a duty to make a payment to C from a specific bank account: D can fulfil its restitutionary duty by paying £1,000 from any account or in cash. If a contractual payment obligation or a secondary payment obligation arising due to a breach of duty does not create a trust, neither should a restitutionary payment obligation.

Unfortunately, some cases suggest that where D comes under a restitutionary duty to make a payment to C, a trust may arise. In *Chase Manhattan Bank NA v Israel-British Bank (London) Ltd*,[85] it was held that the bank account to which a mistaken payment was made was held on trust from the time of receipt. In the Australian case of *Wambo Coal Pty v Ariff*,[86] White J, relying on Lord Browne-Wilkinson's speech in *Westdeutsche Landesbank Girozentrale v Islington LBC*,[87] held that a trust may arise following a mistaken payment from when the 'payee has such knowledge of the mistake as to affect his conscience'.[88] The authorities also suggest that where C makes a payment to D in the performance of a contractual obligation that is subsequently rescinded ab initio, there may be a trust.[89] Finally, on one prominent view,[90] a knowing recipient of a payment made in breach of

[82] As where the account was in credit before the payment.
[83] As where the account was not in credit before the payment.
[84] *Bailey v Angove's Pty Ltd* [2016] 1 WLR 3179, [30].
[85] *Chase Manhattan Bank NA v Israel-British Bank (London) Ltd* (n 54).
[86] *Wambo Coal Pty v Ariff* (n 59).
[87] *Westdeutsche Landesbank Girozentrale v Islington LBC* (n 45).
[88] ibid [44].
[89] *El Ajou v Dollar Land Holdings plc* [1993] 3 All ER 717, 734 (Millett J); *Shalson v Russo* [2005] Ch 281, [121]–[127] (Rimer J).
[90] See, eg, C Mitchell and S Watterson, 'Remedies for Knowing Receipt' in C Mitchell (ed), *Constructive and Resulting Trusts* (Oxford, Hart Publishing, 2010) ch 4; R Chambers, 'The End of Knowing Receipt' (2016) 2 *CJCCL* 1; A Georgiou, 'Knowing Receipt: Continuing Trusts and Conscionability' (2022) 86 *MLR* 276.

trust, whose primary duty is to make restitution of the payment to the proper trustee,[91] holds the bank account (or a proportion of the bank account) to which the payment was made on trust.

It is mysterious why D should come under a duty not to use a bank account for its own benefit following a mistaken payment; a payment made under a contract that has been rescinded ab initio; or a payment that it knowingly received in breach of trust. There is no other area of the law where a (primary or secondary) payment obligation creates a trust.

In his academic work, Lord Burrows has argued that a trust should potentially arise where there is a mistaken payment but not where a payment has been made on a condition that has now failed. The distinction drawn by Burrows between these cases is that, in the mistaken payment context, C generally does not take the risk of D's bankruptcy, whereas, in the failure of condition context, C generally does take the risk of D's bankruptcy.[92] According to Burrows, the reason this risk is generally taken in failure of condition cases is that C will have had the opportunity to bargain for security.

The difficulty with Burrows' argument is that it does not explain why D should potentially come under a duty not to use a specific right for its own benefit following a mistaken payment. In other words, the conclusion does not follow from the premises. What does C taking the risk of D's bankruptcy have to do with D? Why does C not taking this risk mean that D should come under a duty not to use a specific right for its own benefit?[93] The converse can be said regarding failure of condition: why does C taking the risk of D's bankruptcy mean that D should not come under a duty not to use a specific right for its own benefit? The conclusion that should potentially follow from Burrows' argument is not that D should be a trustee but rather that certain 'unjust enrichment' creditors should have the same priority as secured creditors under the bankruptcy legislation. It is not an argument for D having (or not having) a duty of a certain form.

b. Possible Cases where a Trust has Arisen following a Failure of Condition in respect of a Payment

There are cases where it might appear that a trust has arisen following a failure of condition in respect of a payment. An example is certain cases involving 'automatic resulting trusts', which it has sometimes been suggested are examples of 'proprietary' restitution being awarded for a failure of condition.[94] Cases that have been referred to[95] as illustrations are *Re Abbott*[96] and *Re Gillingham Bus Disaster*

[91] *Williams v Central Bank of Nigeria* (n 52) [31] (Lord Sumption). See further R Gregson and T Pilkington, 'What's the Wrong in Knowing Receipt?' (2024) 87 *MLR* 1.

[92] A Burrows, 'Proprietary Restitution: Unmasking Unjust Enrichment' (2001) 117 *LQR* 412, 424–28.

[93] See also Stevens, *The Laws of Restitution* (n 60) 258.

[94] A Burrows, 'Conditional Intention as an Unjust Factor' in E Bant, K Barker and S Degeling (eds), *Research Handbook on Unjust Enrichment and Restitution* (UK, Edward Elgar Publishing, 2020) 350–51.

[95] P Birks, *Unjust Enrichment*, 2nd edn (Oxford, Oxford University Press, 2005) 196–97; Burrows, 'Conditional Intention as an Unjust Factor' (n 94) 351, fn 34.

[96] *Re Abbott* [1900] 2 Ch 326.

Fund.[97] In the former, a charitable trust fund had been subscribed to care for two disabled women. When both women had died, the fund had not been exhausted, and provision had not been made for the surplus. It was held that the surplus was held on resulting trust for the donors. In the latter case, a fund was raised after Royal Marine cadets were killed and injured in an accident. There was a surplus, and the surplus provision was void. It was again held that the surplus was held on resulting trust for the donors.

Where C makes a payment to D and declares an intention that the sum paid is to be held on trust, but the intended trust fails to materialise, or was initially valid but subsequently ceases to exist, D will generally hold the bank account to which the payment was made on trust.[98] For an automatic resulting trust to arise, D does not need to have agreed that its entitlement to the payment was conditional upon the bank account to which the payment was paid being held on the trust the payor intended. This is evident from the fact that the payee does not, objectively considered, need to know of the payor's intention for such a trust to arise.[99] An automatic resulting trust therefore cannot plausibly be regarded as a response to the failure of an *agreed* condition.

It is also worth observing that in many of the automatic resulting trust cases, courts have not made an order for restitution but have merely declared that a resulting trust has arisen.[100] A possible explanation for why the beneficiary has been able to recover a monetary sum from the resulting trustee is, at least in some cases, therefore that the beneficiary can collapse the trust. If this is the correct analysis, it is difficult to regard these resulting trusts as 'effecting or realising' a 'proprietary' restitutionary right.

Outside of the automatic resulting trust context, examples of cases involving trusts that have arisen in response to a failure of condition in respect of a payment that are occasionally provided[101] are *Barclays Bank Ltd v Quistclose Investments Ltd*[102] and *Muschinski v Dodds.*[103] In the former, Rolls Razor Ltd needed £209,719 to pay a dividend it had declared. The sum Rolls Razor required was loaned by Quistclose Ltd 'for the purpose of [Rolls Razor] paying the final dividend due on July 24 next'. The payment was made by Quistclose Ltd via cheque. Rolls Razor instructed its bankers, Barclays Bank Ltd, to deposit the cheque into a new separate account. It was agreed that the positive balance standing in the account was

[97] *Re Gillingham Bus Disaster Fund* [1959] Ch 62.

[98] *Vandervell v IRC* [1967] 2 AC 291, 313–14 (Lord Upjohn); *Re Vandervell's Trusts (No 2)* [1974] Ch 269, 294 (Megarry J).

[99] *Siggers v Evans* (1855) 5 E & B 367; 119 ER 518; *Childers v Childers* (1857) 1 De G & J 482; 44 ER 810; *Mallott v Wilson* [1903] 2 Ch 494. See further R Chambers, *Resulting Trusts* (Oxford, Oxford University Press, 1997) 203–09.

[100] *Re Abbott* (n 96); *Re Gillingham Bus Disaster Fund* (n 97).

[101] Burrows, 'Conditional Intention as an Unjust Factor' (n 94) 351, fn 34. It was previously common to cite *Neste Oy v Lloyd's Bank* [1983] 2 Lloyd's Rep 658, which was overruled in *Bailey v Angove's Pty Ltd* (n 84).

[102] *Barclays Bank Ltd v Quistclose Investments Ltd* [1970] AC 567.

[103] *Muschinski v Dodds* (1985) 62 ALR 429.

only to be used to pay the dividend. Before the dividend had been paid, Rolls Razor went into insolvent liquidation, which meant that the dividend could not be paid. Barclays sought to exercise its power of insolvency set-off, which Quistclose successfully challenged on the basis that the credit balance standing to the separate account was held on trust for its benefit.

Lord Wilberforce reasoned that when Barclays carried out Rolls Razor's instruction to deposit the cheque to the separate account, in circumstances where there was an agreement between Rolls Razor and Quistclose that the loan was only to be used to pay the dividend, a trust arose for the benefit of the shareholders entitled to the dividend. Call this the first trust. Lord Wilberforce thought that when Rolls Razor went into insolvent liquidation, the agreed purpose for which Quistclose's payment was made to Rolls Razor failed and so too did the first trust. Following this, Lord Wilberforce held that a second trust arose, of which Quistclose was the beneficiary. One interpretation of Lord Wilberforce's reasoning is that Rolls Razor's entitlement to the payment made by Quistclose was agreed to remain conditional upon the separate account being used to pay the dividend and that this failure of condition caused the second trust to arise.

Lord Wilberforce's two-trust analysis was rejected in *Twinsectra v Yardley*,[104] which establishes that there is only one trust in cases exemplified by *Quistclose*.[105] More specifically, *Twinsectra* holds that the proper analysis of *Quistclose* is that from the time the loan was paid to the separate account, as opposed to when the agreed purpose for the payment made to the separate account failed, Rolls Razor held the separate account on trust for Quistclose[106] but had a liberty to use the credit balance for a certain purpose.[107] Following the failure of that purpose, the liberty was terminated, but the trust was not. The *Quistclose* trust is therefore not a response to a failure of condition.[108]

In *Muschinski v Dodds*,[109] Ms Muschinski and Mr Dodds, who were in a de facto relationship, decided to purchase a fee simple title to land. On the land, they intended to erect a prefabricated house and restore a cottage for use as an arts and crafts centre. The couple agreed that Muschinski would pay the purchase price and Dodds would pay the construction and improvement costs from funds he expected to receive from his divorce and bank loans. The land was registered to Muschinski and Dodds as tenants in common. Importantly, Muschinski did not intend for Dodds to hold his half interest on trust for her. There was therefore no 'purchase-money resulting trust'. Although some improvements were made, the couple was unable to develop the land as planned, and their relationship ended. By that time, Muschinski had contributed $25,259.45 to the purchase and improvement of the

[104] *Twinsectra v Yardley* [2002] 2 AC 164.

[105] ibid [13] (Lord Hoffmann), [68]–[103] (Lord Millett). See also P Millett, 'The *Quistclose* Trust: Who can Enforce It?' (1985) 101 *LQR* 269.

[106] *Twinsectra v Yardley* (n 104) [13] (Lord Hoffmann), [81] (Lord Millett).

[107] ibid [68] (Lord Millett).

[108] ibid [74] (Lord Millett). cf *Bellis v Challinor* [2015] EWCA Civ 59, [55]–[59] (Briggs LJ).

[109] *Muschinski v Dodds* (n 103).

land and Dodds $2,549.77. Muschinski later sought a declaration that she was the 'beneficial owner' of the whole of the land.

Deane J, with whom Mason J agreed, held that Muschinski and Dodds held 'their respective legal interests as tenants-in-common upon trust (after payment of any joint debt incurred in the improvement of the property) to repay to each of her or his respective contribution and as to the residue for them both in equal shares'.[110] The suggested basis for this trust was that Muschinski's intention for Dodds to be 'beneficially entitled' to his half legal share was conditional upon the contemplated development taking place for their joint benefit and Dodds substantially contributing to the cost. Gibbs CJ held that Muschinski was 'entitled to contribution from the respondent to the extent to which she paid more than one-half of the purchase moneys' and an equitable charge over Dodds' half interest securing this sum.[111] Brennan J, with whom Dawson J agreed, held that there was no constructive trust or charge.[112]

The trust that Deane and Mason JJ would have recognised arose in circumstances where Dodds was not required to make restitution to Muschinski. There was never a payment from Muschinski to Dodds, a service performed by Muschinski for Dodds, or a transfer of a right from Muschinski to Dodds that the court ordered the reversal or restoration of. The case cannot therefore be regarded as an example of proprietary restitution being awarded on Deane and Mason JJ's preferred analysis, as the trust did not arise in circumstances where Muschinski was ordered to make restitution. In other words, the trust was not a 'proprietary' remedy that 'effected or realised' a restitutionary right the court had recognised.

VI. Conclusion

This chapter began by considering when D should come under a restitutionary duty to transfer a right to C following a failure of condition. The following principal claims were defended. First, where D's entitlement against C to the transfer of a specific right remained subject to a condition that has now failed, D should generally come under a restitutionary duty to re-transfer the specific right it received back to C. Secondly, where D's entitlement against C to the transfer of a right of a certain kind remained subject to a condition that has now failed, D should generally come under a restitutionary duty to transfer a right of the same kind as the right it received to C. Finally, where D's entitlement against C to a performance that did not involve the transfer of a right was subject to a now failed condition, D should not come under a restitutionary duty to transfer a right to C.

Having considered when D should come under a restitutionary duty to transfer a right to C following a failure of condition, the chapter examined when this

[110] ibid 458.
[111] ibid 438.
[112] ibid 445.

duty should be specifically enforced. It was argued that the considerations that justify refusing to order D to specifically perform a contractual duty to transfer a right to C apply to restitutionary duties to transfer a right. On this view, a court should only order D to specifically perform a restitutionary duty to transfer a right if the right D has come under a duty to transfer is unique.

Finally, the chapter examined when a trust should arise following a failure of condition. It was argued that where D comes under a specifically enforceable restitutionary duty to transfer a specific right to C, a trust should arise. Where, however, D comes under a restitutionary duty following a failure of condition to transfer a right merely of a certain kind to C, or a restitutionary duty to pay a sum of money to C, it was argued that there should not be a trust.

8

Conclusion

I. Unjust Enrichment Theory

This book forms part of a broader debate regarding unjust enrichment theory. As explained in chapter 1, according to unjust enrichment theory, the reason the law awards restitution in a significant number of cases resembles the reason that it allows the recovery of a mistaken payment of a non-existent debt. In the perceived core case of a mistaken payment of a non-existent debt, it is claimed that C, the mistaken payor, is entitled to restitution because D, the payee, was enriched at C's expense in circumstances where C's intention to enrich D was defective.

To date, unjust enrichment theory has featured most prominently in cases involving mistaken payments[1] and subrogation.[2] It is hard to resist the conclusion that the theory has caused difficulty in these areas.[3] In mistaken payment cases, problems have arisen largely because unjust enrichment theory misidentifies the subject matter of the claim.[4] It has never been true that restitutionary awards reverse D's enrichment at C's expense.[5] Rather, these awards reverse a payment made by C to D, a performance of services by C for D, or a transfer of a right from C to D, none of which necessarily enriches D at C's expense.[6] In the subrogation context, difficulties have arisen principally because subrogation has nothing to do with unjust enrichment[7] or, for that matter, restitution.[8]

[1] See, eg, *Deutsche Morgan Grenfell v Inland Revenue Commissioners* [2008] AC 561; *Sempra Metals Ltd v Inland Revenue Commissioners* [2008] 1 AC 561; *Samsoondar v Capital Insurance Company Ltd* [2021] 2 All ER 1105.

[2] See, eg, *Banque Financière de la Cité v Parc (Battersea) Ltd* [1999] 1 AC 221; *Menelaou v Bank of Cyprus* [2016] AC 176; *International Energy Group Ltd v Zurich Insurance plc* [2016] AC 509. These are not the only cases where unjust enrichment theory has prominently featured: see *Lipkin Gorman v Karpnale Ltd* [1991] 2 AC 548.

[3] For a similar view, see R Stevens, 'The Unjust Enrichment Disaster' (2018) 134 *LQR* 574, 591–601.

[4] R Stevens, *The Laws of Restitution* (Oxford, Oxford University Press, 2023) chs 3 and 4.

[5] ibid. See also chapter 4 of this book.

[6] For a case where a payment did not enrich the defendant, see *Ford v Perpetual Trustees Victoria Ltd* (2009) 257 ALR 658.

[7] R Gregson, 'Is Subrogation a Remedy for Unjust Enrichment?' (2020) 136 *LQR* 481. See also AM Jackman, 'Recalibrating the Restitutionary Compass: Recovery for the Non-Officious and Non-Gratuitous Bearing of Another's Legal Burden' in T Pilkington and D Winterton (eds), *Australian Restitution Law in the 21st Century* (NSW, Federation Press, forthcoming).

[8] Stevens, *The Laws of Restitution* (n 4) 153–54, 252–56. cf C Mitchell, P Mitchell and S Watterson, *Goff & Jones on Unjust Enrichment*, 10th edn (UK, Sweet & Maxwell, 2022) 1014–23, [39-05]–[39-24].

In addition to misidentifying the subject matter of the claim, there are several further respects in which unjust enrichment theory is fatally flawed. First, and fundamentally, it has never been convincingly explained why a defect in C's intention justifies ordering D to make restitution.[9] Something in C's mind is not a good reason for ordering D to make restitution.

Secondly, if the concepts that unjust enrichment theory uses are taken seriously, the theory produces anomalous results. Suppose that C has a title to one of two rare stamps. C mistakenly destroys its stamp, doubling the value of D's stamp.[10] In this example, D has been enriched at C's expense due to C's mistake and yet C should clearly not have a claim for restitution. It might be argued that enrichment and at the expense of have a specialised legal meaning that is not satisfied in this example. But this response concedes that unjust enrichment is not truly concerned with enrichments at the expense of another.

Thirdly, unjust enrichment theory cannot satisfactorily explain why restitution is awarded in certain cases. Imagine that C pays a £10,000 insurance premium to D on 6 April 2020. On 2 June 2023, legislation is passed providing that insurance contracts of the kind C and D entered into are void, dating back to 1 January 2018. The cases suggest that, subject to defences, C is entitled to restitution of the £10,000 payment.[11] Unjust enrichment theorists usually regard the ground for awarding restitution here as mistake.[12] But C was never mistaken.[13] When the payment was made, the £10,000 was due. Although Parliament can retrospectively deem a payment obligation to be void, it cannot rewrite history.[14] In response, it is sometimes suggested that in the above example restitution is awarded in response to a 'deemed mistake'.[15] This is, however, to endorse a fiction, meaning that the mistake is not truly what justifies the claim.

Fourthly, until recently, there was no case where it has formed part of the ratio that before restitution may be awarded for a failure of condition, duress, or undue influence, D must have been enriched at C's expense, and there are cases where restitution has been awarded despite D not having been enriched at C's expense.[16] There is also limited support for duress and undue influence as freestanding grounds for restitution.[17]

Fifthly, and relatedly, there are cases where restitution may be awarded where a recognised 'unjust factor' does not form part of the claim. An example

[9] F Wilmot-Smith, 'Should the Payee Pay?' (2017) 37 *OJLS* 844; Stevens, 'The Unjust Enrichment Disaster' (n 3) 578–82.

[10] D Friedmann, 'Restitution of Benefits Obtained through the Appropriation of Property or the Commission of a Wrong' (1980) 80 *CLR* 504, 532, fn 144; Stevens, 'The Unjust Enrichment Disaster' (n 3) 578.

[11] *Kleinwort Benson Ltd v Lincoln City Council* [1999] 1 AC 349.

[12] *Samsoondar v Capital Insurance Company Ltd* (n 1). cf Mitchell, Mitchell and Watterson, *Goff & Jones* (n 8) [1-25], fn 46.

[13] See also R Stevens, 'Restitution and Time' (2021) 137 *LQR* 368.

[14] *Kleinwort Benson Ltd v Lincoln City Council* (n 11) 362 (Lord Browne-Wilkinson).

[15] *Deutsche Morgan Grenfell v Inland Revenue Commissioners* (n 1) [23] (Lord Hoffmann).

[16] *Planché v Colburn* (1831) 8 Bing 14; 131 ER 305.

[17] For a more convincing explanation of the role of duress in the law of restitution, see J du Plessis, 'Duress and Compulsion' in C Mitchell and W Swadling (eds), *The Restatement Third: Restitution and Unjust Enrichment* (Oxford, Hart Publishing, 2013) ch 4. See also Stevens, *The Laws of Restitution* (n 4) 72–78.

is cases involving a performance of a contract entered into due to a fraudulent misrepresentation, which has been rescinded ab initio. There is no authority for the proposition that, in this scenario, C must prove that its performance of the rescinded contract was undertaken due to D's misrepresentation before C may be entitled to restitution. This suggests that it is the absence of a juristic reason for the performance following rescission that justifies restitution and not C's mistake induced by D's misrepresentation. The same is true regarding other vitiating factors.[18] So, if there is a performance by C of a contract that has been rescinded ab initio for duress, there is no authority for the proposition that for C to be entitled to restitution, C must prove that its performance was undertaken due to duress.

Sixthly, unjust enrichment theory has failed to convincingly explain why the existence of a juristic reason for a performance will, in some circumstances, prevent restitution from being awarded, but in others, it will not. As discussed in chapter 6, in the mistake context, the existence of a juristic reason for a performance will generally prevent restitution from being awarded.[19] However, in cases involving a failure of condition, the existence of a juristic reason for a performance generally does not prevent restitution from being awarded.[20] If the justification for awarding restitution within the law of unjust enrichment is the same (or substantially the same) regardless of the 'unjust factor', this difference cannot be justified.

Finally, to produce results that conform with our intuitions, unjust enrichment theory has had to impose further requirements, in addition to a defect in C's consent, that must be satisfied before C may have a claim for restitution and carve out multiple exceptions. To take mistake as an example, only certain kinds of mistakes count, as evidenced by the fact that mispredictions do not justify restitution.[21] A mistake will also not entitle C to restitution unless D has been enriched at its expense. A mistake will also generally not justify restitution if there is a juristic reason for the enrichment conferred.[22] And new defences, such as change of position and 'ministerial receipt', have had to be recognised. When so many exceptions have to be built in and requirements added to make the theory produce satisfactory results, it strongly suggests that something has gone wrong with the theory.

II. Restitution for a Failure of Condition

Sceptics of unjust enrichment theory have often sought to shoehorn the restitutionary claims falling into the perceived category of unjust enrichment into other areas, such as the law of property or contract.[23] These attempts have proved

[18] See also Stevens, *The Laws of Restitution* (n 4) 102–03.

[19] cf *Deutsche Morgan Grenfell v Inland Revenue Commissioners* (n 1).

[20] *Fibrosa Spolka Akcyjna v Fairbairn Lawson Combe Barbour Ltd* [1943] AC 32.

[21] *Dextra Bank v Bank of Jamaica* [2002] 1 All ER 193.

[22] *Kleinwort Benson Ltd v Sandwell Borough Council* (n 11) 407–08 (Lord Hope); *Fairfield Sentry Ltd (in liq) v Migani* [2014] 1 CLC 611, [18] (Lord Sumption); *DD Growth Premium 2X Fund v RMF Market Neutral Strategies (Master) Ltd* [2018] Bus LR 1595, [62] (Lord Sumption).

[23] SJ Stoljar, *The Law of Quasi-Contract* (Sydney, Law Book Co, 1964); S Hedley, 'Unjust Enrichment as the Basis of Restitution – An Overworked Concept' (1985) 5 *Legal Studies* 56; SJ Stoljar, *The Law*

unsuccessful principally due to their reliance upon strained interpretations of property and contract. If English law is to rid itself of unjust enrichment, plausible explanations of the grounds upon which restitution may be awarded that do not invoke unjust enrichment need to be identified. One objective of this book has been to put forward such a justification for restitutionary awards for a failure of condition.

The book has argued that the best explanation of restitutionary awards for a failure of condition is that these awards give effect to but do not enforce an agreement. More specifically, where C and D agreed that D's entitlement against C to a payment made by C to D, a performance of a service by C for D, or a transfer of a right from C to D remained subject to a condition that has now failed, restitution is justified to ensure that D is not entitled against C to the payment made, the performance of services, or the transfer of right in circumstances where it was agreed that D was not so entitled.

As explained in chapter 3, the agreement in which the condition is found does not need to be a contract (ie, an agreement creating one or more enforceable obligations between the parties to the agreement). Restitutionary awards for a failure of condition are therefore an example of legal significance being attributed to an agreement that is not necessarily a contract and in a manner that does not involve the enforcement of the agreement.

One of the principal advantages of the agreement theory is that it can explain why the failure of a condition that C subjectively intended is neither necessary nor prima facie sufficient to entitle C to restitution from D. Rather, as discussed in chapter 3, the authorities have generally suggested that the condition must, on an objective analysis, have been 'jointly understood', which is indistinguishable from, or at least extremely similar to, the condition having to be agreed. Further, by linking the justification for restitutionary awards for a failure of condition to an agreement as opposed to C's qualified intention, the agreement theory places these awards on a firm normative foundation.

The book has shown that the agreement theory of failure of condition has significant implications, the most notable of which are worth re-stating. In chapter 3, it was argued that in a claim for restitution for a failure of condition, it should not be necessary for the contract performed to have been terminated; that counter-restitution should often not be required; and that change of position should not be a defence. It was also demonstrated that failure of condition is the ground for restitution in a narrower range of cases than is conventionally believed. Notably, where a payment is made under a void contract, no juristic reason and not failure of condition should generally be treated as the ground for restitution, which is

of Quasi-Contract, 2nd edn (Sydney, Law Book Co, 1989); J Dietrich, *Restitution: A New Perspective* (NSW, Federation Press, 1998); P Jaffey, *The Nature and Scope of Restitution: Vitiated Transfers, Imputed Contracts and Disgorgements* (Oxford, Hart Publishing, 2000); S Hedley, *Restitution: Its Division and Ordering* (London, Sweet & Maxwell, 2001); C Webb, *Reason and Restitution: A Theory of Unjust Enrichment* (Oxford, Oxford University Press, 2016).

significant as it is plausible to regard change of position as a defence to restitutionary claims premised upon no juristic reason.

In chapter 4, it was argued that there is no justification for D having to be enriched at C's expense before restitution for a failure of condition may be awarded. On this view, cases such as *Planché v Colburn*,[24] where restitution was awarded despite D not having been enriched at C's expense, are correctly decided. It was further argued that if an enrichment is not the subject matter of the claim, the conclusion of the majority in *Benedetti v Sawiris*,[25] that 'subjective devaluation' should be possible, is unsupportable. A further, more theoretical, implication of D not having to be enriched is that restitutionary awards for a failure of condition do not form part of a law of unjust enrichment.

In chapter 5, it was demonstrated that it should not be necessary for there to have been a total failure of consideration before restitution for a failure of condition may be awarded, a consequence of which is that cases such as *Whincup v Hughes*[26] and *Giedo van der Garde BV v Force India Formula One Team Ltd*[27] would be decided differently.

In chapter 6, it was argued that what may justify restitution of a contractual performance for a failure of condition is the content of the contract performed itself. On this view, restitutionary awards for a failure of condition are not 'subsidiary' or 'complementary' to the law of contract. A further implication of this interpretation of the relationship between contract and restitution for a failure of condition is that whether D's entitlement against C to a contractual performance rendered was subject to a condition is a question of contractual construction.

Finally, in chapter 7, it was argued that where C and D agreed that D's entitlement against C to the transfer of a right remained subject to a condition that has now failed, D should generally come under a restitutionary duty, which a court should, in some cases, specifically enforce, to transfer a right to C. It was further argued that if D has come under a specifically enforceable restitutionary duty to transfer a specific right to C following a failure of condition, D should be treated as holding the right on trust.

[24] *Planché v Colburn* (n 16).

[25] *Benedetti v Sawiris* [2014] AC 938.

[26] *Whincup v Hughes* (1871) LR 6 CP 78.

[27] *Giedo van der Garde BV v Force India Formula One Team Ltd* [2010] EWHC 2373 (QB).

BIBLIOGRAPHY

Addison C and Cave L, *Addison on Contracts*, 7th edn (London, Stevens & Sons, 1875)
American Law Institute, *Restatement of the Law Second: Contracts 2d* (1981)
Atiyah P, *An Introduction to the Law of Contract*, 5th edn (Oxford, Clarendon Press, 1995)
Baloch T, *Unjust Enrichment and Contract* (Oxford, Hart Publishing, 2009)
Bant E, *The Change of Position Defence* (Oxford, Hart Publishing, 2009)
Bant E and Bryan M, 'Specific Restitution without Trusts' (2012) 6 J Eq 181
Barker K, 'Restitution of Passenger Fare: The Mikhail Lermontov' [1993] LMCLQ 291
Barton J, 'Contract and Quantum Meruit: The Antecedents of Cutter v Powell' (1987) 8 JoLH 48
Beale H (ed), *Chitty on Contracts*, 36th edn (London, Sweet & Maxwell, 2025)
Birks P, *An Introduction to the Law of Restitution*, rev edn (Oxford, Oxford University Press, 1989)
——'In Defence of Free Acceptance' in A Burrows (ed), *Essays on the Law of Restitution* (Oxford, Clarendon Press, 1991)
——*Restitution – The Future* (Sydney, Federation Press, 1992)
——'No Consideration: Restitution after Void Contracts' (1993) 23 UWALR 195
——'The Concept of a Civil Wrong' in D Owen (ed), *Philosophical Foundations of Tort Law* (Oxford, Oxford University Press, 1997)
——'Rights, Wrongs, and Remedies' (2000) 20 OJLS 1
——*Unjust Enrichment*, 2nd edn (Oxford, Oxford University Press, 2005)
Black O, *Agreements: A Philosophical and Legal Study* (Cambridge, Cambridge University Press, 2012)
Bridge M and Cox R, *Law of Bank Payments*, 5th edn (London, Sweet & Maxwell, 2017)
Burrows A, 'Free Acceptance in the Law of Restitution' (1988) 104 LQR 567
——'Swaps and the Friction between Common Law and Equity' [1995] 3 RLR 15
——'Proprietary Restitution: Unmasking Unjust Enrichment' (2001) 117 LQR 412
——'Absence of Basis: The New Birksian Scheme' in A Burrows and A Rodger (eds), *Mapping the Law: Essays in Memory of Peter Birks* (Oxford, Oxford University Press, 2006)
——*The Law of Restitution*, 3rd edn (Oxford, Oxford University Press, 2011)
——*A Restatement of the English Law of Unjust Enrichment* (Oxford, Oxford University Press, 2012)
——'In Defence of Unjust Enrichment' (2019) 78 CLJ 521
——*Remedies for Torts, Breach of Contract, and Equitable Wrongs* (Oxford, Oxford University Press, 2019)
——'Conditional Intention as an Unjust Factor' in E Bant, K Barker and S Degeling (eds), *Research Handbook on Unjust Enrichment and Restitution* (UK, Edward Elgar Publishing, 2020)
Chambers R, *Resulting Trusts* (Oxford, Oxford University Press, 1997)
——*An Introduction to Property Law in Australia*, 2nd edn (Australia, Thomson Reuters, 2008)
——'The End of Knowing Receipt' (2016) 2 CJCCL 1
——'Proprietary Restitution and Change of Position' in A Dyson, J Goudkamp and F Wilmot-Smith (eds), *Defences in Unjust Enrichment* (Oxford, Hart Publishing, 2016)
Chitty J and Chitty T, *A Practical Treatise on the Law of Contracts*, 3rd edn (London, Saunders and Benning, 1841)
Chitty J and Russell T, *A Practical Treatise on the Law of Contracts*, 5th edn (London, S Sweet, 1853)
Davies P, Worthington S and Hare C, *Gower: Principles of Modern Company Law*, 11th edn (London, Sweet & Maxwell, 2021)
Dietrich J, *Restitution: A New Perspective* (NSW, Federation Press, 1998)
du Plessis J, 'Duress and Compulsion' in C Mitchell and W Swadling (eds), *The Restatement Third: Restitution and Unjust Enrichment* (Oxford, Hart Publishing, 2013)

Dworkin R, *Law's Empire* (Massachusetts, Harvard University Press, 1986)
Edelman J, 'The New Doctrine of Partial Failure of Consideration' (1996) 15 Australian Bar Review 229
——'The Meaning of Loss and Enrichment' in R Chambers, C Mitchell and J Penner, *Philosophical Foundations of the Law of Unjust Enrichment* (Oxford, Oxford University Press, 2009)
——'Liability in Unjust Enrichment Where a Contract Fails to Materialise' in A Burrows and E Peel (eds), *Contract Formation and Parties* (Oxford, Oxford University Press, 2010)
——'Change of Position: A Defence of Unjust Disenrichment' [2012] 92 BULR 1009
——'Restitution of (Property) Rights' in E Bant and M Bryan (eds), *Principles of Proprietary Remedies* (NSW, Lawbook Co, 2013)
——'Two Fundamental Questions for the Law of Trusts' (2013) 129 LQR 66
——'The Laws of Restitution by Robert Stevens' (2024) 140 LQR 321
Edelman J and Bant E, *Unjust Enrichment*, 2nd edn (Sydney, Hart Publishing, 2016)
Endicott T, 'Objectivity, Subjectivity and Incomplete Agreements' in J Horder (ed), *Oxford Essays in Jurisprudence*: Fourth series (Oxford, Oxford University Press, 2000)
English J, *Discharge of Contractual Obligations* (Oxford, Oxford University Press, 2025)
Evans W, *An Essay on the Action for Money Had and Received* (1998) 6 RLR 1
Feldman S, 'Rescission, Restitution, and the Principle of Fair Redress: A Response to Professors Brooks and Stremitzer' (2013) 47 VULR 399
Fried C, *Contract as Promise: A Theory of Contractual Obligation* (Cambridge, Mass, Harvard University Press, 1981)
Friedmann D, 'Restitution of Benefits Obtained through the Appropriation of Property or the Commission of a Wrong' (1980) 80 CLR 504
Gallanis T (ed), *The Oxford Edition of Blackstone's Commentaries on the Laws of England: Book III* (Oxford, Oxford University Press, 2016)
Gardner J, *From Personal Life to Private Law* (Oxford, Oxford University Press, 2018)
Georgiou A, 'Mistaken Payments, Quasi-Contracts, and the "Justice" of Unjust Enrichment' (2022) 42 OJLS 606
——'Knowing Receipt: Continuing Trusts and Conscionability' (2022) 86 MLR 276
Goff R, 'Reform of the Law of Restitution' (1961) 24 *Michigan Law Review* 85
Goodwin J, 'Failure of Basis in the Contractual Context' (2013) 21 RLR 24
Grantham R, 'Change of Position-Based Defences' in E Bant, K Barker and S Degeling (eds), *Research Handbook on Unjust Enrichment and Restitution* (UK, Edward Elgar Publishing, 2020)
Gregson R, 'Is Subrogation a Remedy for Unjust Enrichment?' (2020) 136 LQR 481
——*Subrogation and Marshalling* (Oxford, Hart Publishing, 2024)
——'The Limits of Implication' (2025) 141 LQR 413
Gregson R and Pilkington T, 'What's the Wrong in Knowing Receipt?' (2024) 87 MLR 1
Guest A (ed), *Chitty on Contracts*, 25th edn (London, Sweet & Maxwell, 1983)
Häcker B, *Consequences of Impaired Consent Transfers* (Oxford, Hart Publishing, 2009)
Harrison G, *The Law of Tender* (London, Stevens & Sons, 1908)
Havelock R, 'A Taxonomic Approach to Quantum Meruit' (2016) 132 LQR 470
Hedley S, 'Unjust Enrichment as the Basis of Restitution – An Overworked Concept' (1985) 5 LS 56
——*Restitution: Its Division and Ordering* (London, Sweet & Maxwell, 2001)
Hellwege P, 'Unwinding Mutual Contracts: *Restitutio in Integrum* v the Defence of Change of Position' in D Johnston and R Zimmermann (eds), *Unjustified Enrichment: Key Issues in Comparative Perspective* (Cambridge, Cambridge University Press, 2002)
Ibbetson D, *A Historical Introduction to the Law of Obligations* (Oxford, Oxford University Press, 2001)
Jackman AM, 'Recalibrating the Restitutionary Compass: Recovery for the Non-Officious and Non-Gratuitous Bearing of Another's Legal Burden' in T Pilkington and D Winterton (eds), *Australian Restitution Law in the 21st Century* (NSW, Federation Press, forthcoming)
Jackman IM, *The Varieties of Restitution*, 2nd edn (NSW, Federation Press, 2017)
Jaffey P, *The Nature and Scope of Restitution: Vitiated Transfers, Imputed Contracts and Disgorgement* (Oxford, Hart Publishing, 2000)

Krishnaprasad KV, *Unjust Enrichment and Countervailing Obligations* (Oxford, Hart Publishing, 2025)
Leggatt G, 'Making Sense of Contract: The Rational Choice Theory' (2015) 131 LQR 454
Lodder A, *Enrichment in the Law of Unjust Enrichment and Restitution* (Oxford, Hart Publishing, 2012)
Lurie S, Towards a Unified Theory of Breach' (2003) 19 JCL 250
Maher F, 'A New Conception of Failure of Basis' [2004] 12 RLR 96
Mann F, *The Legal Aspect of Money*, 5th edn (Oxford, Oxford University Press, 1992)
McFarlane B, *The Structure of Property Law* (Oxford, Hart Publishing, 2008)
——'Proprietary Estoppel and Failed Contractual Negotiations' [2005] C&PL 501
McFarlane B and Stevens R, 'In Defence of *Sumpter v Hedges*' (2002) 118 LQR 567.
——'The Nature of Equitable Property' (2010) 4 J Eq 1
——'What's Special About Equity?: Rights about Rights' in D Klimchuk, I Samet and H Smith (eds), *Philosophical Foundations of the Law of Equity* (Oxford, Oxford University Press, 2020)
McInnes M, 'Enrichment' in E Bant, K Barker and S Degeling (eds), *Research Handbook on Unjust Enrichment and Restitution* (UK, Edward Elgar Publishing, 2020)
——'The Measure of Restitution' (2002) 52 UTLJ 163
McKendrick E, 'Frustration, Restitution and Loss Apportionment' in A Burrows (ed), *Essays on the Law of Restitution* (Oxford, Clarendon Press, 1991)
Megarry R, 'Historical Development' in *Special Lectures of the Law Society of Upper Canada 1990 – Fiduciary Duties* (Law Society of Upper Canada, 1991)
Micheler E, 'Farewell to Quasi-negotiability? Legal Title and Transfer of Shares in a Paperless World' [2002] JBL 358
Millett P, 'The *Quistclose* Trust: Who can Enforce It?' (1985) 101 LQR 269
——'Restitution and Constructive Trusts' in W Cornish, R Nolan, J O'Sullivan and G Virgo (eds), *Restitution: Past, Present and Future* (Oxford, Hart Publishing, 1998)
——'Bribes and Secret Commissions Again' [2012] 71 CLJ 583
Mitchell C and Mitchell C, '*Planché v Colburn* (1831)' in C Mitchell and P Mitchell (eds), *Landmark Cases in the Law of Restitution* (Oxford, Hart Publishing, 2006)
Mitchell C and Watterson S, 'Remedies for Knowing Receipt' in C Mitchell (ed), *Constructive and Resulting Trusts* (Oxford, Hart Publishing, 2010)
Mitchell C, Mitchell P and Watterson S, *Goff & Jones on Unjust Enrichment*, 10th edn (UK, Sweet & Maxwell, 2022)
Mitchell P, 'Artificiality in Failure of Consideration' (2010) 29 UQLJ 191
O'Sullivan D, Elliott S and Zakrzewski R, *The Law of Rescission*, 2nd edn (Oxford, Oxford University Press, 2014)
Peel E, *Treitel on The Law of Contract*, 15th edn (London, Sweet & Maxwell, 2020)
——*Frustration and Force Majeure*, 4th edn (London, Sweet & Maxwell, 2022)
Penner J, 'The (True) Nature of a Beneficiary's Equitable Proprietary Interest Under a Trust' (2014) 27 CJoLJ 473
Perillo JM, 'Misreading Oliver Wendell Holmes on Efficient Breach and Tortious Interference' (2000) 68 *Fordham Law Review* 1085.
Pilkington T and Winterton D, *Australian Restitution in the 21st Century* (NSW, Federation Press, forthcoming)
Pilkington T and Winterton D, 'Void Contracts, Counter-Restitution, and Change of Position' (2022) 138 LQR 21
Putnam H, 'Meaning and Reference' (1973) 70 JoP 699
Simpson AWB, *A History of the Common Law of Contract* (Oxford, Clarendon Press, 1975)
Smith L, 'The Mystery of "Juristic Reasons"' (2000) 12 SCLR (2d) 211
——'Understanding Specific Performance' in N Cohen and E McKendrick (eds), *Comparative Remedies for Breach of Contract* (Oxford, Hart Publishing, 2005)
——'Trust and Patrimony' (2009) 28 ETPJ 332
——'Fiduciary Relationships: Ensuring the Loyal Exercise of Judgment on Behalf of Another' (2014) 130 LQR 608

Smith S, *Rights, Wrongs, and Injustices: The Structure of Remedial Law* (Oxford, Oxford University Press, 2019)
Stevens R, 'Objectivity, Mistake and the Parol Evidence Rule' in A Burrows and E Peel (eds), *Contract Terms* (Oxford, Oxford University Press, 2007)
——*Torts and Rights* (Oxford, Oxford University Press, 2008)
——'Contractual Aspects of Debt Financing' in D Prentice and A Reisberg (eds), *Corporate Finance Law in the UK and EU* (Oxford, Oxford University Press, 2011)
——'When and Why Does Unjustified Enrichment Justify the Recognition of Proprietary Rights?' (2011) 92 BULR 919
——'Rights Restricting Remedies' in A Robertson and M Tilbury (eds), *Divergences in Private Law* (Oxford, Hart Publishing, 2016)
——'The Unjust Enrichment Disaster' (2018) 134 LQR 574
——'What is an Agreement?' (2020) 136 LQR 599
——'Restitution and Time' (2021) 137 LQR 368
——*The Laws of Restitution* (Oxford, Oxford University Press, 2023)
——'Repeal the Law Reform (Frustrated Contracts) Act 1943' in E Peel and R Probert (eds), *Shaping the Law of Obligations* (Oxford, Oxford University Press, 2023).
——'Before We Begin: Defining Contract' (draft manuscript)
Stoljar SJ, *The Law of Quasi-Contract* (Sydney, Law Book Co, 1964)
——*The Law of Quasi-Contract*, 2nd edn (Sydney, Law Book Co, 1989)
Swadling W, 'Orthodoxy' in W Swadling (ed), *The Quistclose Trust* (Oxford, Hart Publishing, 2004)
——'The Vendor-Purchaser Constructive Trust' in S Degeling and J Edelman (eds), *Equity in Commercial Law* (Sydney, Lawbook Co, 2005)
——'Policy Arguments for Proprietary Restitution' (2008) 28 LS 506
——'Ignorance and Unjust Enrichment: The Problem of Title' (2008) 28 OJLS 629
——'Explaining Resulting Trusts' (2008) 124 LQR 72
——'The Fiction of the Constructive Trust' (2011) 64 CLP 399
——'Property' in A Burrows (ed), *English Private Law*, 3rd edn (Oxford, Oxford University Press, 2013)
——'The Nature of Knowing Receipt' in P Davies and J Penner (eds), *Equity, Trusts and Commerce* (Oxford, Hart Publishing, 2017)
——'Unjust Enrichment: Value, Rights, and Trusts' (2021) 137 LQR 56
Tang HW, 'An Unjust Enrichment Claim for the Mistaken Improver of Land' [2011] 75 CPL 8
Treitel G, *The Law of Contract*, 8th edn (London, Sweet & Maxwell, 1991)
Virgo G, *The Principles of the Law of Restitution*, 4th edn (Oxford, Oxford University Press, 2024)
Webb C, *Reason and Restitution* (Oxford, Oxford University Press, 2016)
Weinrib E, 'The Normative Structure of Unjust Enrichment' in R Grantham and C Rickett (eds), *Structure and Justification in Private Law: Essays for Peter Birks* (Oxford, Hart Publishing, 2008)
——'Correctively Unjust Enrichment' in R Chambers, C Mitchell and J Penner (eds), *Philosophical Foundations of the Law of Unjust Enrichment* (Oxford, Oxford University Press, 2009)
——*The Idea of Private Law*, 2nd edn (Oxford, Oxford University Press, 2012)
——'The Corrective Justice of Liability for Unjust Enrichment' in E Bant, K Barker and S Degeling (eds), *Research Handbook on Unjust Enrichment and Restitution* (UK, Edward Elgar Publishing, 2020)
Wigmore J, 'Responsibility for Tortious Acts: Its History' in Association of American Law Schools (ed), *Select Essays in Anglo-American Legal History*, vol 3 (Boston, Little, Brown, and Company, 1909)
Williston S, 'Rescission for Breach of Warranty' (1903) 16 HLR 465
Wilmot-Smith F, 'Replacing Risk-Taking Reason' (2011) 127 LQR 610
——*Failure of Condition* (Oxford DPhil thesis, 2013)
——'Reconsidering "Total" Failure' (2013) 72 CLJ 414
——'Should the Payee Pay?' (2017) 37 OJLS 844
——'Termination after Breach' (2018) 134 LQR 307
——'Term Limits: What is a Term?' (2019) 39 OJLS 705

——'Contract and Unjust Enrichment in the High Court of Australia' (2020) 136 LQR 196
——'Extra-Contractual Claims' in R Wilmot-Smith and P Darling (eds), *Wilmot-Smith on Construction Contracts*, 4th edn (Oxford, Oxford University Press, 2021)
Winterton D, *Money Awards in Contract Law* (Oxford, Hart Publishing, 2015)
Winterton D and Pilkington T, '*Mann v Paterson Constructions Pty Ltd*: The Intersection of Debt, Damages and Quantum Meruit' (2021) 44 MULR 679
Zimmermann R and du Plessis J, 'Basic Features of the German Law of Unjustified Enrichment' [1994] 2 RLR 14

INDEX

www.ingramcontent.com/pod-product-compliance
Ingram Content Group UK Ltd.
Pitfield, Milton Keynes, MK11 3LW, UK
UKHW021829081026
476415UK00003B/126

9 781509 989911